Heidegger and Aristotle

SUNY series in Contemporary
Continental Philosophy

Dennis J. Schmidt, editor

Heidegger and Aristotle

The Twofoldness of Being

Walter A. Brogan

STATE UNIVERSITY OF NEW YORK PRESS

Published by
State University of New York Press, Albany

© 2005 State University of New York

Printed in the United States of America

For information, address State University of New York Press,
194 Washington Avenue, Suite 305, Albany, NY 12210–2384

Production by Kelli Williams
Marketing by Michael Campochiaro

Library of Congress Cataloging-in-Publication Data

Brogan, Walter, 1945–
    Heidegger and Aristotle: the twofoldness of being / Walter A. Brogan.
        p.   cm. — (SUNY series in contemporary continental philosophy)
    Includes bibliographical references and index.
    ISBN 0-7914-6491-1 (hardcover: alk. paper) ——
    ISBN 0-7914-6492-x (pbk.: alk. paper)
    1. Heidegger, Martin, 1899–1976. 2. Aristotle. 3. Ontology—History.
    I. Title. II. Series.
    B3279.H49B743 2005
    193—dc22   2004024570

10 9 8 7 6 5 4 3 2 1

For my mother, Lillian Berry Brogan

CONTENTS

ACKNOWLEDGMENTS

Heidegger says that the cause of something is that which is responsible for its coming into being. In this regard, I am indebted to many besides those I will name here, whose gift to me cannot be repaid. I am especially grateful for their patience and encouragement. Sandy Brown has allowed me to see that there are no limitations to the possibilities of being and being together. My son Daniel first taught me to appreciate birth and nature in the hills around Rielingshausen. He and my son Steven are a constant reminder of the wonder of life. My philosophical life began with the provocation of my brother Harold, and I owe to him not only a lifelong feast of philosophical conversation, but an awareness of what it means to live life fully and be a great human being. All of my brothers and sisters have been incredibly supportive.

I am grateful to John Sallis for his formative intellectual inspiration and guidance, but especially for what he has taught me about the connection between philosophy and friendship. The graduate students I have taught over the years at Villanova have been an indispensable resource for me. In very specific ways, I am grateful to Elaine Brogan, James Risser, Jerry Sallis, Dennis Schmidt, Peter Warnek, and my colleagues at Villanova for all they have contributed to my work.

PREFACE

This book offers a study of the central texts in which Heidegger presents his phenomenological reading of Aristotle's philosophy. Heidegger's readings span the corpus of Aristotle's philosophy, with particular emphasis on the *Physics, Metaphysics, Ethics,* and *Rhetoric.* I claim in the book that Heidegger has a sustained thematic focus and insight that govern his overall reading of Aristotle—namely, that Aristotle, while attempting to remain faithful to the Parmenidean dictum regarding the oneness and unity of being, nevertheless thinks being as twofold. It is this philosophical discovery that permits him, within the framework of the Greek understanding of being, to account for the centricity of motion in the meaning of being, what I call Aristotle's kinetic ontology.

On the basis of a detailed reading of sections of the *Physics* and *Metaphysics,* I try to defend Heidegger's controversial claim that metaphysics for Aristotle is as much physics as physics is metaphysics. This is accomplished in chapters two and three, devoted to his reading of *Physics* B1. These chapters show how Heidegger attempts to draw out the affinity of Aristotle's treatment of *phusis* to the original Greek sense of *phusis* as a word for being in general. Given that Aristotle's account of nature involves a treatment of motion and change, Heidegger's reading shows, against many of the traditional accounts of Aristotle, that becoming and therefore privation belong to the very meaning of *ousia,* Aristotle's word for being.

In chapter four, on Heidegger's reading of Aristotle's *Metaphysics* Θ1–3, I try to show similarly that *dunamis,* force, is central to Aristotle's manifold sense of being. Heidegger's reading of *dunamis* and *energeia* calls into question many of the traditional accounts of Aristotle's *Metaphysics* that reduce Aristotle's sense of being to the categorial sense of substance alone.

In chapter five, I turn to a consideration of Heidegger's controversial readings of Aristotle's practical philosophy, with special emphasis on ethics and rhetoric. I claim that, in Heidegger's reading, Aristotle's treatment of ethics is not primarily focused on normative questions, but is concerned with what one might call an ontology of human being. It becomes clear through a study of these early Heidegger courses on Aristotle's ethics and rhetoric how great an influence Aristotle is on the genesis of Heidegger's own original analysis of human existence in his major work, *Being and Time*. Heidegger couches these readings of Aristotle in the context of the overcoming of a certain kind of dualistic Platonism, to which he argues Aristotle is responding. These discussions hearken back to the first chapter of the book, where I try to show that Heidegger not only reads Aristotle as a phenomenological thinker, but also derives his own unique sense of phenomenology from his dialogue with Aristotle.

The book oscillates between commentary and thematic focus. One of my primary objectives is to offer a careful and detailed analysis of several of the most important of Heidegger's works on Aristotle. One of the strategies I employ is to subject Heidegger's interpretation of specific Aristotelian concepts, as they arise in the context of his translations of Aristotle passages, to a broader test in terms of other passages and texts. For this reason, for example, I frequently cite passages from the *Metaphysics* in an attempt to assess the validity of Heidegger's revolutionary reading of the *Physics*. What becomes evident from this approach is that Heidegger's readings of sections of Aristotle's work, such as *Physics* B1 and *Metaphysics* Θ1–3, are carefully chosen by Heidegger to implicate Aristotle's philosophy as a whole. Because one of my primary objectives is to offer an exegesis of Heidegger, I do not frequently point out how radical a challenge his work on Aristotle presents to most traditional accounts. Anyone knowledgeable of the history of Aristotle interpretation will readily recognize this challenge. To some extent, the confrontation occurs at the level of translation, and I had the temptation to provide a standard translation as a contrast to Heidegger's. This would no doubt have had some value for readers of this text, and I would encourage careful consultation of the Greek as well as available alternative translations. In the end I decided against doing this because it in effect canonizes or castigates the standard translations, and neither of these positions is desirable. One of Heidegger's great contributions is to return the reader constantly to a philosophical concern with the Greek words themselves, and to free the interpretation of Aristotle from its bondage to a translated vocabulary derived from the Latin. A word like "substance," from the Latin word "*substantia*," is already an interpretation as well as a translation of the Greek word "*ousia*." Heidegger's reading of Aristotle does not take for granted this Latinization.

As is true of Aristotle, Heidegger is a thinker who understands the importance of method in philosophy. One of the primary parts of chapter one of this text is devoted to methodological considerations. Heidegger makes his own method of approaching Aristotle explicit in his 1922 essay, "Phenomenological Interpretations of Aristotle: Indications of the Hermeneutic Situation," intended as an Introduction to a book on Aristotle that never appeared. It becomes clear that what most of all provoked Heidegger's interest in Aristotle's philosophy during his early years was his realization that Aristotle employs a phenomenological approach to philosophy. It is arguably the case that Heidegger's transformation of Husserlian phenomenology into his own, and especially his interest in the history of being and the importance of a "destruction" of that history as a way of raising the question of being, has its roots in his reading of Aristotle. Heidegger finds in Aristotle a thinker who is attuned to the ontological difference, and who provides a critique of his predecessors precisely because they attempted to understand being on the basis of beings. Aristotle's resolution of the *aporia* of Greek philosophy, and especially his capacity to address the elusive problem of movement on an ontological level, lies in his appreciation of this distinction. On the other hand, in Heidegger's view, Aristotle's methodological approach also takes for granted and leaves unquestioned the basic meaning of being for the Greeks, namely, constant presencing. Aristotle thinks within the ontological difference, but does not think the difference as such. Heidegger's own original philosophical task is generated out of the limits of Aristotle's thinking, which is one way of articulating the close relationship of Heidegger to Aristotle, even in his own work.

Beyond these methodological and exegetical considerations, this book has a thematic focus. I try to show that there is a basic approach in all of Heidegger's analyses, and a profound interest that governs all of his interpretations. This interest on one level will appear to you to be self-evident. It is expressed in the claim that Aristotle thinks being as twofold. The obviousness of this claim can be seen when one considers the most well-known position of Aristotle—namely, that philosophy is the study of being, and this means the study of *archē*, being as principle or origin. Aristotle insists against the view of his predecessors that the *archē* is twofold. Aristotle's discussion of contraries, his claim that beings have co-constitutive principles such as matter and form, potentiality and actuality, and so on, his analysis of the reciprocal relationship of generation and corruption, and especially his consideration of privation and nonbeing in relationship to being, all point to the centricity of this sense of a double *archē*. Despite this evidence, Heidegger insists that this twofoldness of being has been ignored or misread in the tradition that is supposed to be based on Aristotle. Frequently, interpretations of substance metaphysics in Aristotle have failed to give an account of this sense of being. Aristotle's philosophy attempts to think the twofoldness of *phusis* without denying the oneness that characterizes being. Human beings can grasp the twofoldness to the extent that their *logos* (itself a double *logos*) stands in the between that is opened up in the space of this duplicity of being and beings. Heidegger's explanation of the double stance of Aristotle's *logos* is made particularly clear in his treatment of *epagōgē,* which is traditionally translated as induction, and in his analysis of the relationship between *logos* and *eidos.* These interpretations are studied in chapters two and three. But the cognizance of the twofoldness of being that is, according to Aristotle, essential for philosophical understanding also gets interpreted by Heidegger as the horizon for the bringing together of theory and practice in service to ontology, as Heidegger interprets it in his treatment of *sophia* and *phronēsis* (see chapter five).

This book is intended primarily for scholars and students of Heidegger and Aristotle. I hope that it serves those who wish to gain further access to Heidegger's thought and to the relationship of his thought to his work on Aristotle. But I have not emphasized the usual approach to this material, which focuses on it for the sake of demonstrating that the genesis of Heidegger's thought, especially in *Being and Time,* can be found in his study of Aristotle. Indeed in chapter five, I have tried to show this, especially in connection with a reading of Aristotle's *Ethics* and an analysis of the section on death in *Being and Time,* where I claim that being-toward-death is the condition for community and friendship in Aristotle's sense. But for the most part, my hope is that the book serves to show the cogency of Heidegger's interpretation of Aristotle for its own sake, and that it assists a growing community of ancient Greek scholars who are engaged in phenomenological approaches to the reading and understanding of Aristotle. If Heidegger's revolutionary interpretations of Aristotle become more widely known and appreciated in the community of scholars of ancient philosophy as a result of this book, the primary intention of my work will have been fulfilled.

Chapter One

MARTIN HEIDEGGER'S RELATIONSHIP TO ARISTOTLE

Heidegger's Phenomenological Reading of Aristotle

Martin Heidegger is a key figure in twentieth-century philosophy. His work on Aristotle, a strong focus in the early stages of his career, plays an important role in the genesis of his thought and has a formative influence on his unique understanding of phenomenology. In some regards, one could rightfully claim that it was his reading of Aristotle that made it possible for him to redefine for himself the task of phenomenology, a philosophical direction and method first articulated by his teacher, Edmund Husserl. In fact he says as much in his essay, "My Way to Phenomenology."[1] More important for the purposes of this book, Heidegger's interpretation of Aristotle had a significant impact on Aristotle scholarship in Germany in the early part of the twentieth century, and the controversial and revolutionary implications of his interpretations of Aristotle, and ancient Greek philosophy in general, continue to help shape the resurgence of interest in ancient Greek philosophy among continental philosophers today. Even in America, where the study of Greek philosophy is dominated by the Anglo-American methodological approach, Heidegger's interpretations of Aristotle have indirectly impacted scholars through the work of Leo Strauss and others. Indeed, Strauss was a student of Heidegger's in Freiburg at the time of the Aristotle breakfast club, as Heidegger's early morning Aristotle classes were dubbed. These seminars and lectures were attended not only by Strauss but also by Hans-Georg Gadamer and Hannah Arendt, and many other well-known students of Heidegger.

Heidegger had already taught several courses on Aristotle in Freiburg before going to Marburg, and several of his students went on to become well-known Aristotle scholars in their own right. There is ample testimony from these students of Heidegger about the philosophically formative effect of these seminars. Often, according to their own accounts, their work was presented under the direct influence and guidance of Heidegger's early lecture courses. Thus, Helène Weiss, in her work on Aristotle, says: "I have freely made use of the results of Heidegger's Aristotle interpretation which he delivered in lectures and seminars."[2] The Aristotle works of Walter Bröcker, Ernst Tugendhat, Karl Ülmer, and Fridolin Wiplinger, among others, are all equally indebted to Heidegger's revolutionary interpretation of Aristotle.[3]

In this book, I hope to recreate at least a little of the excitement among ancient Greek scholars that was generated in Germany by Heidegger's early phenomenological readings of the Greeks. In the last few years, several of the Aristotle courses have become available due to the publication of the *Collected Works* of Heidegger. These Aristotle courses were given over a span of many years, and I should begin by acknowledging that I will not primarily be tracing a developmental thesis, as others have done with regard to Heidegger's reading of Aristotle, and its influence on his major work, *Sein und Zeit*.[4]

Many Heidegger commentators[5] consider Aristotle's work to be one of the most influential forces in the development of Heidegger's own philosophical approach. Heidegger himself attested to this in his essay "My Way to Phenomenology":

The clearer it became to me that the increasing familiarity with phenomenological seeing was fruitful for the interpretation of Aristotle's writing, the less I could separate myself from Aristotle and other Greek thinkers. Of course I could not immediately see what decisive consequences my renewed preoccupation with Aristotle was to have.[6]

Though not the primary focus, one of the purposes of this book will be to demonstrate and assess the impact of Aristotle on the development of Heidegger's thought.[7] Heidegger's major work, *Sein und Zeit,* was published in 1928. Prior to this, he taught in Freiburg and Marburg, and many of his courses were on Aristotle. In 1922, he offered a course entitled *Phänomenologische Interpretationen zu Aristoteles: Ontologie und Logik*.[8] In 1924, he gave a course called "*Grundbegriffe der aristotelischen Philosophie*," one that appeared in 2002 as Volume 18 of Heidegger's *Gesamtausgabe*.[9] This course, which focuses in large part on Aristotle's *Nichomachean Ethics* and *Rhetoric*, was followed by a course now published as *Platon: Sophistes* that contains a lengthy analysis of Aristotle's *Nichomachean Ethics* Book VI. Over the same period, he offered other seminars on Aristotle's *Ethics, De Anima,* and *Metaphysics*.[10]

This confrontation with Aristotle continued into the twenties and thirties with courses on Aristotle's *Rhetoric, Metaphysics,* and *Physics,* as well as extended analyses of Aristotle's treatment of logic and truth.

Since so much of Heidegger's work in the early twenties was focused on Aristotle, it stands to reason that Aristotle is a hidden interlocutor in Heidegger's first major published work, *Sein und Zeit.* But the explicit attributions and references to Aristotle in this work are few and far between, outside of section 81 where he offers his well-known, but brief "destruction" of Aristotle's treatment of time in *Physics* IV.[11] Much speculation has been written regarding the unpublished and incomplete final division of *Sein und Zeit,* which promised an extensive, critical reading of Aristotle. Much of this speculation assumed that Heidegger would have demonstrated in that unpublished portion of the text the oblivion of being that occurs through Aristotle's work and subsequently in the history of Western philosophy.[12] And indeed, this may well have been a dimension of his ultimate aim. However, it is now clear from the increasing availability of his early Aristotle courses that Heidegger's reading of Aristotle is far from critical in that sense. What he for the most part offers instead is a revolutionary interpretation of Aristotle that aims to show his "greatness," not because he gave birth to metaphysics, which is not untrue, but because he preserves, even in the face of his teacher Plato, an echo of originary Greek thinking. Heidegger tries to draw out of the inherited texts of Aristotle the resonances of this more radical way of thinking, if only in the end to be able more genuinely to trace the ambivalence and undecidability at the heart of Aristotle's thought. Recently, with the publication of Heidegger's *Collected Works,* these early, formative courses are beginning to be published. Several of them have been translated into English. The result of the increased availability of these materials has been a significant surge of interest in the question of the role of Aristotle in the genesis of Heidegger's unique understanding of phenomenological philosophy.[13]

Heidegger scholars such as Theodore Kisiel and Thomas Sheehan in the United States are certainly correct in the pivotal role they assign to Heidegger's interpretations of Aristotle in the development of Heidegger's thought prior to *Sein und Zeit.*[14] Indeed, Heidegger acknowledges in *Sein und Zeit* his indebtedness to ancient Greek philosophy as the impetus for his own original work: "But the question touched upon here is hardly an arbitrary one. It sustained the avid research of Plato and Aristotle, but from then on ceased to be heard *as a thematic question of actual investigation.*"[15] One recent Italian author, Franco Volpi, went so far as to title one of his essays: "*Being and Time,* a translation of Aristotle's *Nicomachean*

Ethics?"[16] In chapter five, I attempt to offer an account of *Sein und Zeit* that, in agreement with Volpi, sees this work as having been made possible in part by Heidegger's discovery that Aristotle's practical thinking is ontological and offers an account of human community that does not fall prey to the limitations of normative or biological treatises on human behavior. Part of my task in this book, then, will be to examine these lecture courses on Aristotle and the link they provide to a fuller understanding of Heidegger's own thought.

The major thrust of this book, however, will not so much be concerned with a better understanding of Heidegger through his reading of Aristotle. Rather, the focus will be on what we can learn about Aristotle from Heidegger. We will discover, in examining many of the most central of Heidegger's works and essays on Aristotle, that the prevalent, long-standing belief that Heidegger reads Aristotle as *the* metaphysician *par excellence* is erroneous. Those who assume that Heidegger's philosophy involves an overcoming of the forgetting of being that starts with Aristotle's distortion of early Greek thinking will be surprised by what they read in this book. As suggested earlier, this false impression of the confrontation between Heidegger and Aristotle stems in large part from the announced final division of *Sein und Zeit,* which never appeared and was supposed to have contained a detailed destruction of Aristotle's account of time. But Heidegger's well-known essay on Plato's teaching on truth, so critical of Plato, no doubt also led many to assume that if Heidegger sees Plato in this way, as having transformed truth into correctness and representation, then so much the worse for his student Aristotle.[17] But, instead of a critique of Aristotle as the first metaphysician, Heidegger offers a persuasive and revolutionary rethinking of Aristotle's work, which he argues is more original and radical than that of his teacher Plato. Heidegger goes as far as to claim: "Aristotle never had in his possession what later came to be understood by the word or the concept 'metaphysics.' Nor did he ever seek anything like the 'metaphysics' that has for ages been attributed to him."[18] Indeed, Heidegger directly associates his own understanding of phenomenology with Aristotle's philosophy. In *The History of the Concept of Time,* he writes: "Phenomenology radicalized in its ownmost possibility is nothing but the questioning of Plato and Aristotle brought back to life: *the repetition, the retaking of the beginning of our scientific philosophy."*[19]

Many of Heidegger's most important essays and volumes on Aristotle are, in actuality, extended translations of key passages from the texts of Aristotle. These interpretative "philosophical" translations and commentaries open up a new way of reading Aristotle that challenges many long held philosophical views that are embedded in more standard, though often less "faithful," translation decisions. Indeed, much of the very vocabulary and central concepts of philosophy, for example, substance and accident, essence, potentiality and actuality, matter and form, and so on, are inherited from a Latinized version of Aristotle. Thus, Heidegger's new "translations" of these terms and concepts often challenge presuppositions about Aristotle rooted in "metaphysical" interpretations of his terminology. Through these translation/commentaries on key passages in the central texts of Aristotle, Heidegger opens up a way of understanding the entire corpus of Aristotle's work that demands a radical rethinking of our traditional assumptions about this "father" of Western thought. These texts also help to dispel the unjustified impression conveyed by critics of Heidegger that he disregards philological and scholarly care in his "speculative" interpretation of Greek philosophy. Even though Heidegger's phenomenological reading of key passages from Aristotle may force us to reexamine our basic understanding of Greek philosophy (and therefore of the Western tradition), nevertheless these interpretations remain thorough and careful renderings of Aristotle's thought that derive their force from the texts themselves. They also teach us how to read texts in a philosophically penetrating way. In a course on Book Θ1–3 of Aristotle's *Metaphysics,* Heidegger says of this kind of reading of Aristotle: "It is necessary to surpass Aristotle—not in a forward direction, in the sense of a progression, but rather backwards in the direction of a more original unveiling of what is comprehended by him."[20]

The dialogue between Aristotle and Heidegger spans across the horizon of Western culture and is itself a richly philosophical endeavor; one that, in a manner of speaking, transcends the privileged, isolated domain of either thinker alone. In the next section, I will address a series of issues regarding hermeneutics in general, and related questions of history and tradition, that call into question the space within which we are attempting to do philosophy here, the space between ourselves on the one hand, and Aristotle and Heidegger on the other, namely, the space of commentary.

What It Means to Read Aristotle as a Phenomenologist

In 1922, Heidegger wrote a lengthy Introduction to a book on Aristotle he was planning for publication.[21] This Aristotle book itself never appeared, eventually supplanted by *Sein und Zeit,* which was presented for publication in 1927. Prior to this Introduction to a book on Aristotle, Heidegger published only one work, his 1915 habilitation on Duns Scotus. Yet he had become a famed teacher. It was on the strength of his Duns Scotus work, as well as his teaching reputation, that Paul Natorp invited him to apply for a position in Marburg. To obtain this position, Heidegger put together in three weeks this Introduction in order to outline his plans for the book, and explain the historically situated, hermeneutic framework of his research on Aristotle. Of course, it was a distillation of the work he had done in weaving together phenomenology and Aristotle over the course of several preceding years.

In the plan for the Aristotle book that he sent to Natorp, Heidegger begins by presenting some remarks on the hermeneutic situation involved in any contemporary reading of Aristotle. As in his Introduction to *Sein und Zeit,* he speaks in this essay of the need for any ontologically fundamental approach to begin with a destruction of the history of philosophy. Heidegger understands this deconstructive reading not only as an overcoming of the bias and prejudices that arise from an unclarified relationship to the past, but as a movement between destruction and retrieval. Hermeneutics not only dismantles the tradition, it also retrieves an authentic philosophical dimension of that tradition that tends to get covered over in the uncritical way in which the tradition is handed down. This double movement of destruction and retrieval is not to be understood as two separate stages of philosophical investigation, where one moves from the first task to the second, but rather as a belonging together and reciprocity between these two tasks such that this double movement is itself Heidegger's way of returning to Aristotle. Ironically, it becomes evident that Aristotle also practices this way of philosophizing, as can be seen in Book I of the *Physics* and *Metaphysics,* where Aristotle begins by situating his own philosophical questions in relationship to his predecessors. For Aristotle, this task is not merely a preliminary investigation, but a philosophical way of recovering and discovering the questions that motivate his own project.

The overall objective of Heidegger's preliminary discussion of hermeneutics is to show that originary philosophy today requires a return to Aristotle. That is, by turning to Aristotle we can free philosophical inquiry for the possibility of genuine questioning that constitutes it as philosophy. Thus, Heidegger quotes Hegel favorably, in his essay "Hegel and the Greeks," when Hegel says: "If one were to take philosophy seriously, nothing would be worthier than to hold lectures on Aristotle."[22] It is not for the sake of Aristotle, or because Aristotle is somehow privileged in his access to being, that Heidegger and Hegel say this, but rather because of their hermeneutic appraisal of the contemporary philosophical situation.

Why is philosophy always a double movement of destruction and recovery? Because, Heidegger contends, philosophy, as ontology, is fundamentally historical. The genuine pursuit of the question of being, the task of philosophy, is the same as the pursuit of the historical meaning of being. To recover the meaning of being requires a gathering back of that which is the ongoing source of tradition. The meaning that this historical approach to the question of being uncovers, as we know also from *Sein und Zeit,* turns out to be time. Already in 1922, Heidegger has in mind that the return to Aristotle will permit a more radical investigation of the question of time.[23]

Ontological research, according to Heidegger, is basically historical in character. The situation of understanding is hermeneutical, that is, always already found in an interpretation, historically embedded. Any philosophical, systematic articulation of the categories of being must therefore remain historical. Heidegger is attempting to reach beyond the division of system and history:

If the basic question of philosophical research, the question of the being of entities, compels us to enter into an original arena of research which precedes the traditional partition of philosophical work into historiological and systematic knowledge, then the prologomena to the investigation of entities in their being are to be won only by way of history. This amounts to saying that the manner of research is neither historiological nor systematic, but instead phenomenological.[24]

In explicating the facticity of understanding—in his 1922 essay he calls this the hermeneutic situation—Heidegger uncovers the major difficulty that must be considered in all attempts at philosophical inquiry. Any reading of Aristotle that professes to let what Aristotle says be seen from itself must first of all make explicit and let be called into question its own situation, and the horizon in which it operates. The possibility of truly being addressed by an ancient text on its own terms requires that we free ourselves from our familiar and customary horizon. The task of interpretation then becomes a genuine questioning in which we open ourselves to the possibility of new paths and perspectives. Because of this tendency in history to cover over the originary questioning that discloses being, the task of phenomenology becomes what Heidegger calls the "destruction" of the tradition. The destruction of the tradition has the positive aim of destructuring the sedimented deposit of knowledge in order to set free the creative roots and vital sources that are preserved in this history.

Philosophy is defined by Heidegger as the attempt to open up again the domain of originary thinking, and the release of this radical questioning. In contrast, Heidegger suggests that Western metaphysics, while governed by such originary, radical questioning, often holds these questions in a repository. In *The End of Philosophy*, he says that metaphysics "can never bring the history of being itself, that is, the origin, to the light of its essence."[25] The tradition is viewed as a deposit of doctrines that develop and progressively work out the meaning of being. Aristotle and Greek philosophy are thereby taken to be primitive expressions of truths that have since been incorporated or superseded by a higher development and systemization that surpass it.

It is clear from Heidegger's writings that he considers a de-structuring of Aristotle's works to be essential if philosophy and thinking are to be set free for their proper task. But simply returning to Aristotle is not so simple. If it is true that every historical epoch of philosophy owes its impetus to the Greeks, it is also true that our interpretation of the Greeks has derived from assumptions rooted in later history (Scholasticism, for example). And this confusion is not accidental. It reflects an essential characteristic of interpretation itself (fallenness). But we should not cast Heidegger's hermeneutic project of reading Aristotle in terms of an attempt to view Aristotle as a non-metaphysician. Such a project would be naive. Heidegger says: "The greater a revolution is to be, the more profoundly must it plunge *into* its history."[26] The return to the origin of the tradition is not a return to a past that is now over. Heidegger says: "Repetition as we understand it is anything but an improved continuation with the old methods of what has been up to now."[27] The historical life of a tradition depends on a constantly new release and interpretation of the overabundance that cannot be confined to any one saying. Language is founded on this unsayable origin, and the disclosure of this originary *logos* is essentially a creative and poetic response to being.

The way in which one gives expression to an understanding of being is not arbitrary. It is not our own planning or direction that makes possible a genuine conversation in which we bring what is yet unthought in the history of being into the open. Rather, it is our opening ourselves to listen with an ear that is sensitively attuned for the unthought and unexpressed possibilities hidden in the tradition. The creative word that expresses this hidden source of a text does not merely describe what is present, but calls it forth by returning it into the unconcealment of its being. A human being can uncover the hidden possibilities for thought only insofar as he first listens to the meaning of being that addresses and claims him through the text. "Destruction means: to open our ears, to make ourselves free for what addresses us in the tradition as the being of beings. By listening to this address, we attain the correspondence (*Entsprechung*)."28 Only if we are attuned and ready to let it say something to us will the "phenomenon" itself guide our interpretation. Only then will phenomenology be possible. Only then will our questioning be an ontological pursuit. The overcoming of tradition is not an abandonment or surpassing of what has come before. It is rather something like a thinking that delivers over the past to its possibility. Heidegger says: "That which is original occurs in advance of all that comes. Although hidden, it thus comes toward historic man as pure coming. It never perishes, it is never something past."29

Heidegger reads Aristotle's philosophy as the end and fulfillment of Greek thought. He says: "The great begins great, maintains itself in existence only through the free recurrence of greatness, and if it is great also comes to an end in greatness. So it is with the philosophy of the Greeks. It came to its end with Aristotle in greatness."30 Because Aristotle's thinking is the end of Greek philosophy, it also brings this philosophy to its inherent limitations. The end of Greek thought is not an end that stops or reifies the movement of this thought, but one that lets it be brought forth into presence and unconcealment. But here lurks the danger that requires us to read Aristotle with a certain degree of ambivalence. At the end of Greek philosophy, Aristotle's thinking stands forth in this end and can be taken therefore as something available and at-hand. As such it is simply a body of doctrines that are handed down to us. Taken in this way, philosophical thinking stops and history begins.

In the decline of ancient Greek civilization, the presupposed understanding of being was being threatened, and needed to be preserved. That is, it needed to be grounded and justified so that it could be secured against the decline. Aristotelian philosophy arose out of this need and the experience of this threat, this *Bekümmerung* as Heidegger names it in his 1922 essay on Aristotle. Thus, it is within Aristotle's very project that metaphysics is initiated. Heidegger says:

We shall master Greek philosophy as the beginning of Western philosophy only if we at the same time understand this beginning in its originating end. For the ensuing period it was only this end that turned into the 'beginning,' so much so that it at the same time concealed the original beginning.31

Thus, it is within Aristotle's philosophy that we also find the origin of the forgottenness of being that determines the history of metaphysics, an oblivion that Heidegger's philosophy aims to overcome. But it would be very misleading to conclude that Heidegger's interpretation of Aristotle focuses primarily on this aspect of Aristotle's philosophy. Many commentators on Heidegger's philosophy assume that Heidegger understands Aristotle in metaphysical terms, and they argue that he places his own thinking in opposition to Aristotle. Thus, Werner Marx writes: "we regard ourselves as justified in terming the thinking from Plato and Aristotle to Hegel simply as 'the tradition' and viewing, on the other hand, Heidegger's thinking as the attempt toward a 'turning-away' from this tradition."[32] But in fact, as we will see, Heidegger's preoccupation in his readings of Aristotle is quite the reverse of this assumption. He is much more concerned to free Aristotle from Romanized and Christian interpretations and to retrieve the radical, originary, and nonmetaphysical dimension of Aristotle's philosophy.

The Lost Manuscript: An Introduction to Heidegger's Interpretation of Aristotle

As more and more of Heidegger's work on Aristotle became available, and it became more and more evident that Aristotle was an influence and constant source of insight along the path of Heidegger's own philosophical thinking, one could only regret that Heidegger's short but seminal 1922 piece on Aristotle, referred to as the Aristotle-Introduction, had been lost during the war. The rediscovery of the complete version of this essay, the one that had been sent by Heidegger to Marburg and Göttingen in support of his nomination for a position at these institutions, helps to further our understanding of the important link between Heidegger's early work on Aristotle and the development of his own method of phenomenology.

This 1922 essay, titled "Phenomenological Interpretations with Respect to Aristotle (Indications of the Hermeneutic Situation)," begins with an explanation of philosophy as hermeneutic phenomenology, and addresses the implications of this for a genuinely philosophical interpretation of the history of philosophy and of philosophy itself as historical. Hans-Georg Gadamer addresses this deconstructive and hermeneutic aspect of Heidegger's reading of Aristotle in his prefatory remarks to the publication of the 1922 essay in the Dilthey Jahrbuch.[33] In fact, Heidegger's treatment in this essay of factical life and the philosophical practice of destruction is remarkably Gadamerian. It confirms, perhaps more so than any other available text, that Gadamer's understanding of the hermeneutic destruction of texts, and his notion of a fusion of horizons, has its roots in Heidegger's project of fundamental ontology. Gadamer reports that he labored over virtually every line of this text and found it full of ingenious insights that have not become superfluous through the recent publication of Heidegger's early courses.

As the primary text on the basis of which Gadamer went to study with Heidegger and over which he pondered in his own very influential understanding of hermeneutics, the discovery of this text might also be said to be the resurfacing of the link that connects Gadamer to Heidegger, a link that goes through Aristotle. For this to be entirely and even more dramatically true, one would have to accept Gadamer's insistence that what is going on in this discussion of factical life and Aristotle is an enormous struggle by Heidegger to release himself from and come to terms with his (and Western history's) entanglement in Christian theological concepts and consciousness. Gadamer insists that this critique of the Christianized reading of Aristotle—through Scholastic eyes—was the reason for the revolutionary impact of Heidegger's Aristotle interpretation. Thus Gadamer entitled his own prefatory remarks on this essay: "*Heideggers theologische Jugendschrift.*" According to Gadamer, this is the horizon within which Heidegger is questioning during this period.

Indeed, textual evidence abounds to lend credence to Professor Gadamer's claim. Heidegger says that "destruction" is concerned with *how* we stand in relationship to the tradition:

Destruction is rather the authentic way in which the *present* must be encountered in its own basic movements, and encountered in such a way that thereby the *ständige Frage,* the persistent questioning, breaks out of history to the extent that it (the present) is concerned with the appropriation and interpretation of the possibility of a radical and fundamental experience.[34]

According to Gadamer, Heidegger defines his own standpoint, out of which his own philosophical question arose, as stemming from Lutheran theology and late scholastics such as Duns Scotus. That is, it was his attempt to philosophically appropriate these figures that led him back to Aristotle's philosophy as the ultimate horizon and primary source of the philosophical and theological position that dominated this later historical period. Indeed, Heidegger makes the claim that the works of Kant, Hegel, Fichte, Schelling, and so on are rooted in uncritically appropriated Lutheran theological presuppositions.[35] Luther himself, in turn, is said to have retrieved Pauline and Augustinian sources and developed his thinking as a confrontation with Scholasticism. Ultimately, Scholasticism depended on a distorted transmission of Greek concepts into Latin.

It would be misleading, however, to conclude from Gadamer's provocative title—"Heidegger's Theological Early Writings"—that this text is in any way a theological essay. This is a title that Gadamer takes up, at least in part, to parody Dilthey's decision to give the same title to the discovery of the early works of Hegel. But in this essay, Heidegger only briefly refers to his earlier theological concerns and makes the explicit point that Scholastic as well as Lutheran reformed theology need to be brought to their source in Aristotle and that this overturning of theology through philosophy is central to the movement of destruction in the text. Indeed, we will see that one of the striking characteristics of Heidegger's ontological reading of Aristotle's *Metaphysics* is its incompatibility with the theologically oriented readings of Thomistic philosophy. In dismantling what he calls onto-theology, Heidegger clearly sees Aristotle on the side of ontology. In fact, there is a telling footnote in his 1922 Aristotle essay in which Heidegger insists on the fundamentally atheistic perspective of all genuine philosophizing and hints that it was because the history of philosophy remained guided by a theological bias that it was unable to fully and genuinely philosophize.[36] He queries whether the idea of a philosophy of religion is not itself contradictory, even though his own courses had more than once bore this title.

Phenomenology, Heidegger demonstrates, is not just a hermeneutically naive appeal to the things themselves, as if it were a matter of recapturing or approximating some lost original position. It is the self-address of factical life. Heidegger's pervasive claim in this essay is that philosophy *is* life, that is, the self-articulation from out of itself of life.[37] This is why Heidegger says that genuine philosophy is fundamentally atheistic.[38] To the extent that theology takes its cue from outside factical life, it can never do philosophy. All philosophical research, and Aristotle is seen as paradigmatic, remains attuned to the life situation out of which and for the sake of which it is inquiring. The first sections of this essay have to do with this situatedness, this overwhelming facticity, that defines the being of life.

What Heidegger emphasizes in his "destruction" of the history of philosophy in the second part of this essay is not the ability to point out the various trends and interdependencies that can be traced through the history of philosophy. The more important task of destruction is to bring into focus and set apart the central ontological and logical structures at the decisive turning points of history. This is accomplished through an originary return to their sources. Though the source is never an "in itself" that is captured, so that Aristotle's philosophy could no more capture this origin than could that of his followers, Heidegger considers the turning of Aristotle's thinking to be especially crucial.[39] This is certainly, at least in part, because of Aristotle's peculiarly phenomenological bent. The fact that Heidegger looked to Aristotle for help in clarifying the many ways of being and knowing that found the possibility of hermeneutic phenomenology complicates the traditional explanation of Heidegger's destruction as a critical movement back through the history of philosophy in order to overcome it. In the case of Aristotle at least, Heidegger discovers that the very future of philosophical thinking has already been prepared for but covered over by the scholasticism of the tradition.

One of the clearest indications of the legitimacy of efforts that have been undertaken to show the link between the genesis of *Being and Time* and Heidegger's work on Aristotle is found in this manuscript where Heidegger announces that the question he is asking as he approaches Aristotle's texts is the question of the being of human being.[40] He makes clear that his projected reading of Aristotle is to be a *Daseinsanalytik,* a questioning about the being who experiences and interprets being. His aim in reading Aristotle is to uncover *"der Sinn von Dasein,"* the various "categories" that constitute the way of being that in some manner always already is in relationship to being. It is indeed fascinating and informative that so many of the sections of *Being and Time* were already so cogently and compactly presented here in outline form. Already in place in 1922 was much of the philosophical vocabulary of *Being and Time,* words like *Sorge, Besorgen, Umwelt, Umgang, Umsicht, Bedeutsamkeit,* and so on. This is the text in which Heidegger begins to speak of the notion of *Verfallen,*[41] not as an objective event that happens to one but as an "intentional how," a way of being directed toward life that constitutes an element of facticity and is the basic character of the movement of caring. What are not so clearly fixed in these pages are the strategy and divisions of *Being and Time.* Themes like death, the averageness of *das Man,* individual existence as possibility, truth as unconcealing wrestling from concealment (a notion of truth, as we will see, that Heidegger attributes to Aristotle), the tendency of life to drift away from itself in fallenness—these themes are not so clearly divided in these pages as they are in *Being and Time.* In some regards, in reading this essay, one gets a better sense of the interdependence of each of the parts of *Being and Time.*

One of my purposes in using Heidegger's 1922 outline for his Aristotle book as the framework for my own initial remarks is to show that the plan for his interpretation of the *Physics* and *Metaphysics,* though the actual courses and texts do not appear until the thirties, is already in place in the early twenties. There is a certain identifiable strategy that Heidegger employs in his reading of Aristotle, and a certain basic insight into Aristotle that governs all of his interpretations. This insight, as I previously stated, is simply that Aristotle thinks being as twofold. The capacity to reveal the twofold is the defining characteristic of human being, according to Aristotle. Thus, Heidegger says, in this 1922 essay, that the guiding question of his Aristotle interpretation will be: what is the sort of object and character of being that Aristotle had in mind in interpreting and experiencing human life? Is human life interpreted on its own terms or within the framework of a broader understanding of being that Aristotle brings to bear on his interpretation of human being?[42] Heidegger's claim is that the primordial sense of being for Aristotle—the field of beings and sense of being that govern his general understanding and interpretation of beings—is production.[43] For the most part, beings are interpreted in their being as available for use in our dealings (*Vorhandensein*). Thus, according to Heidegger's analysis, the idea that Aristotle employed a theoretical, impartial, and objective model of understanding the being of beings is false. Beings are understood in terms of how they appear (their look to us or *eidos*) and in terms of their being addressed and claimed in a *logos* oriented to and by its surroundings. Heidegger insists that Aristotle's word for being—*ousia*—still resonates with its original sense of availability for use, in the sense of possessions or belongings.[44] Heidegger insists further that Aristotle's ontological structures arise from this preliminary way of grasping beings in general. The question is whether human being is also analyzed on the basis of this general conception of being in terms of production.

In saying that production governs the Aristotelian conception of being, Heidegger is not arguing that Aristotle understood all beings including human being on the basis of a model drawn from *technē*. What is at issue, rather, is something like world, though Heidegger does not make this explicit in this essay. Beings from *technē*, produced beings in the sense that their coming to be is handled and managed by a craftsperson, natural beings, and human beings all are produced differently, but all are interpreted (through *technē* or *epistēmē* or *phronēsis*) as ways of being produced or brought forth. In fact, when it comes to making explicit the ontological structure of beings, Aristotle's field of research is not beings from *technē* at all but beings from *phusis*.[45] The primary text for an ontological investigation of produced beings is the *Physics*. Inasmuch as beings are understood in terms of their being-produced, movement must be what constitutes their being. Aristotle's *Physics* is primarily an investigation of moved-beings and of being-moved as the way of being of these natural beings. Finally, the *Nichomachean Ethics* is about the "movement" or way in which one becomes human.

A significant portion of Heidegger's treatment of *Nichomachean Ethics* VI in this Introduction to his projected book on Aristotle has to do with the meaning of *alētheia* and its relationship to *logos* and *legein*. It is seldom noted or paid attention to, but Heidegger is certainly correct that Book VI of the *Ethics*, which treats dianoetic (intellectual) excellence or virtue, is a treatise on truth. The virtuous intellect is virtuous to the extent that it holds in truth and safeguards (*Verwahrung*) the disclosure of beings. Aristotle says in the beginning of Book VI that the *ergon*, the work of both parts of the intellect (theoretical and practical), is truth. Furthermore, inasmuch as they are virtues, these parts of the soul are *hexeis*, habits or dispositions. That is, theoretical wisdom and practical wisdom function like moral virtues. They are ways of being disposed toward what is, of being extended in relationship to what is, of revealing what is. In other words, the issue is not about specific acts of the intellect that relate us to things but about a way of being for which revealing, being extended toward, and intending are characteristic. When this availability of intellectual life is operative, then the intellect is excellent; when involvement is cut off, then this way of being is defective.

As in the *Logik* course three years later,[46] Heidegger here distinguishes two modes of truth. Noetic truth necessarily comes before and makes possible the kind of truth displayed in the propositions or logical truth of language. This more original noetic revealing discloses the *archē*, that out of which beings emerge and that which is responsible for their being. This is the original *legein*, the gathering into the oneness of being. Aristotle calls this *alētheia*, this mode of revealing, philosophical thinking (*Met.* 1003 a1), a beholding of being (*theōrein*) as being, a letting beings be seen as being. Philosophical knowledge is in part a simple standing in the presencing of being. Aristotle says that no falsity or deception is possible in this noetic way of seeing, this pure *Vernehmen*. But then Heidegger makes a somewhat controversial claim.[47] He says that for Aristotle this noetic activity that is open to the truth of being is accomplished in two different ways: through *sophia* (*hinsehendes Verstehen*, inspective understanding) and through *phronēsis* (*fürsorgende Umsicht,* solicitous circumspection).[48] According to Heidegger, both *sophia* and *phronēsis* are noetic activities, ways of accomplishing our relationship to what is in a primordial manner. What then is the difference between them? Heidegger suggests that the difference between *sophia* and *phronēsis* is that different realms of beings are revealed in these intellectual dispositions. Heidegger translates *phronēsis* as *Umsicht* (circumspection). He also, at least implicitly, offers *Sorge* (care) as another translation. In this text, *Sorge* has mostly to do with one's dealings in everyday factical life, what Heidegger calls *Sorgensumsicht.* To the extent that in *Sein und Zeit Sorge* is the defining term for Dasein's ownmost being, retrieved from fallenness, it is noteworthy that he uses the term here in a distinctly practical sense and in connection with circumspection and practical dealings.

What specifically concerns Heidegger in this text is the movement of this practical disclosure wherein the fullness of the moment of being (the *kairos*)[49] can draw back into itself its past and future. *Phronēsis* is here understood as a way of having one's being, a *hexis.* Just as the analysis of death that preceded this discussion belonged to the broader context of the question of factical life, so here also Heidegger has not so clearly worked out the primacy of the future and of possibility as he later formulated it in *Sein und Zeit.* In this regard, his analysis here of Aristotle's project is still close to Husserl and his concept of phenomenology. But this is also because Aristotle has in mind being-produced and being at hand as produced as the primary meaning of being. In other words, beings are understood primarily in terms of their having already been produced and their standing there in their availability for use. That is to say, being-present is the primary *ecstasis* of time for Aristotle, and perhaps also for the early phenomenology of Husserl and Heidegger. Thus, Heidegger says "'the not-yet' and 'the already' are to be understood in their unity, that is, they are to be understood on the basis of an original givenness."[50]

But, as Heidegger shows, this way of "having" its being that belongs to human factical life is peculiar. There can be no pure, atemporal beholding of such being since the resolute moment of *praxis* is always already caught up in the coming to be of factical life. Therefore, *phronēsis,* though a kind of revealing and a noetic activity, always shows itself as *eine Doppelung der Hinsicht,* "a doubling of the regard."[51] Human life is situated in this double regard of *phronēsis* as a way of revealing and seeing being. Heidegger says this double view of Dasein, this duplicitous, twofold character of Dasein's being in Aristotle's treatment of it, has been decisive for the history of our understanding of factical life. The failure to think this twofold in its character as a doubling movement led to a splitting of the analysis into two different movements—something like apophantic circumspection and something like intuitive contemplation. In other words, a dualistic interpretation of human life replaced Aristotle's understanding of human life as held in a double regard. That is not to say that the seeds of this misunderstanding are not already found in Aristotle to some extent, in his insistence that *sophia* is a higher way of revealing than even the disclosing that emerges out of the doubling regard of *phronēsis*.

Let us look then at Aristotle's treatment of *sophia*, wisdom. In contrast to his rather approving attitude with regard to Aristotle's understanding of *phronēsis*, Heidegger's treatment of that other noetic activity, *sophia*, is ambiguous. He clearly attempts to show that *sophia* has to do with divine movement, not the movement of living being. The mistake that has pervaded the tradition, namely, interpreting all being on the basis of what is revealed in *sophia* has its roots in a certain theological bias, as Heidegger laid out in an earlier part of this text. But it also can be traced to a certain ambiguity on the part of Aristotle. To a certain extent, Aristotle's concern about the eternal and necessary movement of divine being causes him to define living being in terms of what it is not, that is, in terms of its not being necessary and eternal. This covers over, to some extent, the more original and positive access to the peculiar kind of movement and being that is involved in the case of living beings. Among the many Heideggerian notions that come into play in his 1922 Aristotle essay is the notion of authenticity. Hermeneutic philosophy is inauthentic when it imposes structures from outside on what is being investigated, rather than following the movement from out of itself, and making this movement of facticity explicit in its origin.

But, more important, Heidegger also finds that the dominant concern with the movement of production—with *technē* and *poiēsis*—and the use of produced beings as exemplary beings in Greek ontology has its roots in this same failure to properly distinguish *sophia* and *phronēsis*. For, *sophia* is also the appropriate basis for the way of revealing that is involved in *technē*. In other words, art is governed by a kind of understanding of *sophia*. *Sophia* is a privative way of revealing that requires a looking away from the beings as they are revealed in circumspective dealings and replacing it instead with a way of dealing with beings that involves a kind of bare care-less looking. When beings from *technē* become the exemplary beings for the analysis of living being, then the double regard and the double movement that we discussed earlier, the movement of those beings whose *archē* belongs to their being and does not come from outside, gets over-looked. The being of a being is seen as outside of the being itself.

What *sophia,* in the sense Aristotle speaks of it when he means philo-sophical thinking, uncovers in its pure beholding is the *archē* of beings, the origin. Philosophy takes for granted the concern for beings and raises that concern to the level of questioning why. This question points in the direc-tion of what lets the being be revealed. The treatise where he makes this *archē*-questioning explicit is the *Physics.* The *archē* as the movement that constitutes the being of beings is the subject matter of this treatise. The starting point for *archē*-research, that is, for an ontological investigation of beings, is the fact that beings move. To deny motion is to preclude oneself from the question. The Eleatics did precisely this. Their insistence was that being has to be understood, as Parmenides dictated, as one and not many. But motion implies a manifold. Thus, they concluded, motion cannot be. Aristotle instead will attempt to think multiplicity at the heart of unity.

Heidegger does use the words Dasein and *Existenz* in this essay in refer-ence to his interpretation of Aristotle, but for the most part he speaks of factical life. Facticity is the fundamental way of being that constitutes human life for Aristotle, in Heidegger's understanding. In fact Heidegger uses the word care (*Sorge*) to characterize this movement of facticity. Exis-tence is interpreted here as a possibility *of* factical life that can be retrieved only indirectly by making facticity questionable. To do this—to make fac-tical life questionable—is the task of philosophy. Heidegger calls this ques-tioning movement of retrieve the decisive seizing of existence as a possibil-ity of factical life. But this existential return is also a recovery from the movement of fallenness that Heidegger calls an *Abfall,* a descent from it-self, and a *Zerfallen,* a movement of dispersion and disintegration. But the primary category of life (Dasein) is facticity rather than existence. It is the movement of fallenness and not existence that opens up world and that Heidegger here explains through the care structure. Thus, in 1922, under the influence of Aristotle, Heidegger still remained preoccupied with phen-omenological concerns over facticity.

Existence, as a countermovement to care and the movement of fallen-ness, has a temporality other than that of being in time. It occurs in the kairological moment and is not called care but the *Bekümmerung,* the worry or affliction of being. Through the Greek notion of the *kairos,* Hei-degger has here already begun to distinguish temporality from the chrono-logical sense of time associated with being in time. In a very revealing foot-note, Heidegger suggests that the notion of care needs to be thought more radically, and even points to the possibility of thinking of care in terms of ecstatic temporality through a retrieval of the Greek middle-voice form.[53] Heidegger suggests that we should think care (*Sorge*), here associated with *Umsicht* (*phronēsis*) or circumspection, as comparable to the way the middle voice operates in ancient Greek, as a movement and countermovement, as a recoil of being; in which case, he says, *Bekümmerung* would be *die Sorge der Existenz*, the care that belongs to existence.[54] This probably marks the place of a major shift in Heidegger's thinking that prepared the way for *Sein und Zeit*. The back-and-forth double play between fallenness and existence that is signaled by Heidegger's invocation of the Greek middle voice also indicates a suggestion by Heidegger on how to read the relationship between facticity and existence, even in his later work. As care reveals being in the world, so the existential moment opens Dasein to the whole of being. But, the existential *Gegen* opens Dasein to a not-being that belongs to its very way of being. Heidegger suggests that Aristotle recognized this in his notion of *sterēsis*, a notion of nonbeing and refusal that Aristotle says (against the Eleatics) belongs to being itself. Referring to chapter 7 of the *Physics*, Heidegger says that the basic category of *sterēsis* dominates Aristotle's ontology. *Sterēsis* means lack, privation. It can also mean loss or deprivation of something, as in the example of blindness, which is a loss of sight in one who by nature sees. *Sterēsis* can also mean confiscation, the violent appropriation of something for oneself that belongs to another (*Met.* 1022 b33). Finally, Aristotle often calls that which is held as other in an opposition of contraries a privation. Heidegger will point out in his later essay on *Physics* B1 that Aristotle understands this deprivation as itself a kind of *eidos*.[55] Thus, *sterēsis* is the lack that belongs intrinsically to being. According to Heidegger, with the notion of *sterēsis* Aristotle reaches the pinnacle of his thinking about being. Heidegger even remarks that Hegel's notion of negation needs to be returned to its dependency on Aristotle's more primordial conception of the not.[56]

In the context of Heidegger's discussion of privation and ontological lack, it becomes clearer why Heidegger introduces a discussion of death and the finality of factical life in this 1922 essay on Aristotle. Factical life is such that its death is always somehow there for it, something that always stands in sight for it as an obstinate and uncircumventable prospect of life. What Heidegger discovers here, then, is a kind of double movement, a movement and a countermovement, a dual movement of descent and recall that unfolds the span within which human life is. This doubling, middle-voiced *kinēsis* is the authentic mode of being of life.

One of the most powerful aspects of this essay is Heidegger's cogent characterization of the nature of philosophy. One could argue that the entire essay is about this. Philosophical research is the taking up and carrying out of the movement of interpretation that belongs to factical life itself. Philosophy is radical, concernful questioning because it positions itself decisively at the movement wherein the threatening and troubled character of life—*die Bekümmerung der Existenz*—unfolds, and holds itself steadfastly out toward the questionability of life. Thus, Heidegger describes philosophy as letting the difficulty, the *aporia*, of life gain articulation by engaging in an original, unreduplicatable, and unrepresentable moment of repetition. For Aristotle, the focus of this aporetic, philosophical thinking is, of course, the *archē*. The philosopher wonders about the origin of what is. The *aporia*, the stumbling block that the philosopher needs to think and address, is this: the origin must be one and yet, as Aristotle shows, the origin is manifold. The philosopher is called upon to think the unitary multiplicity of being, in particular, the twofoldness of being, the double *archē*. This task of thinking is approached in different ways by Aristotle, but the twofoldness of being is Aristotle's fundamental insight.

Chapter Two

THE DOUBLING OF *PHUSIS:* ARISTOTLE'S VIEW OF NATURE

Given the number of courses and texts that Heidegger devotes to Aristotle in the decade after his 1922 Introduction to the never actually written book on Aristotle, it may seem surprising that I have decided to turn first to his 1939 text, devoted to a commentary on Aristotle's *Physics* B1, before discussing these other works. But, for Heidegger, the fundamental horizon of Aristotle's philosophical questioning is the problem of movement, and it is in the *Physics* that Aristotle most explicitly addresses this issue. In the following chapters, we will see that Heidegger reads the *Metaphysics* in such a way as to highlight the centrality of the concepts of *dunamis* and *energeia* as ontological notions that take up the problem of movement at the very heart of Aristotle's notion of *ousia* and his understanding of being. And even in his treatment of Aristotle's notion of *psuchē* and his reading of Aristotle's *Rhetoric* in his 1924 course, *Grundbegriffe der aristotelischen Philosophie,* the problem of *Bewegung* plays a central role in his analysis. By turning first to his reading of the meaning of *phusis* in Aristotle's philosophy, we can set the stage for the more comprehensive claim that the task that motivates Aristotle's philosophical project in general is the study of the being of *kinēsis.*

Heidegger returns to Aristotle in the 1930's, teaching, for example, a course on Aristotle's *Metaphysics* Θ1–3 in 1931, and the 1937–1938 course on logic and Aristotle's notion of truth called *Grundfragen der Philosophie: Ausgewählte Probleme der Logik.*[1] Although the 1939 essay, "Vom Wesen und Begriff der *Phusis:* Aristoteles' *Physik* B1,"[2] is clearly indebted to his work on Aristotle in the 1920s, it is nevertheless not merely coincidental that he wrote this essay on Aristotle's understanding of nature during this period, which is so much influenced by Hölderlin, for whom nature is in many ways the source of the poetic overturning of metaphysics.

Heidegger claims not only that Aristotle's *Physics* is the *never-adequately studied, foundational book of Western philosophy* (WBP 312), but also that in *Physics* B1 Aristotle gives "the interpretation of *phusis* that sustains and guides all succeeding interpretations of the essence of 'nature'" (WBP 313). Both of these are rather overarching claims and the implications of their possible legitimacy are rather enormous. Combined with his additional claim that "metaphysics" is just as much "physics" as physics is "metaphysics"(WBP 312), we can conclude that for Heidegger the perspective within which the *Metaphysics* should be read is the question of nature. Indeed, to the extent that the *aporia* about nature concerns the problem of movement, Aristotle says as much repeatedly.

In a reference to Hölderlin's hymn, "As when on feast day," Heidegger comments that in this poem nature again becomes a word for being (WBP 310). We are accustomed to speaking of being in general, and then of nature as a realm of beings alongside other beings that are. But Heidegger's philosophy attempts to retrieve a sense of the meaning of nature that is not reducible to what might be considered a regional ontology. From the outset, any discussion of Heidegger's treatment of the notion of *phusis* in Aristotle must keep this project clearly in mind. And it is equally important to understand that it is not merely a matter of retrieving an archaic meaning of *phusis* that stands for being in general. This would only amount to word substitution, even though it would be an important clarification in its own right. Rather, what is implied in Heidegger's project is a destruction of the distinction between general ontology and regional ontology that Heidegger considers to be a later, non-Greek development in philosophy, even if its roots can be traced back to Aristotle. What Heidegger is discovering in Aristotle's ontology is the remains of a pre-metaphysical, primordially Greek, phenomenological sense of being.

Thus, in his treatment of Aristotle's notion of *phusis,* Heidegger speaks of the essence of *phusis,* but he is very careful not to speak of the being of *phusis,* a misleading phrase that finds its way into Thomas Sheehan's original English translation of Heidegger's 1939 *Physics* B1 essay, but fortunately is corrected in the version that appears in *Pathmarks.* The original translation of the word *Wesen* in the title as being gave the impression that Heidegger's essay was about the being of *phusis,* as if *phusis* referred to a realm of entities about which we are asking the question of being. But Heidegger's main point is that *phusis* originally is the word for being, and that this meaning still resonates in Aristotle's philosophy of nature. Thus, in Heidegger's view, it would be mistaken to assume that the *Physics* is about nature and the *Metaphysics* about being, even if including the being of nature. It might, in a sense, be possible to speak, in Heideggerian terms, of the being of nature, but then the "of" would have to be understood as genitive rather than objective. That is, one would have to mean the belonging together of being and nature. To speak of the being of nature in the latter, objective sense would be to fall prey to a notion of nature as constituting a region of beings alongside other regions of beings such as those constituted through *technē*. Indeed, Aristotle does often use the term in this sense. But the ambiguity of the notion of *phusis* in Arisotle, which resonates both as a word for being in general and as a word for a particular region of beings, is the exact problematic Heidegger wishes to address in the 1939 essay. Therefore, rather than the being of nature, Heidegger speaks of the essence of nature. One might well translate "*Wesen der Phusis*" as "the nature of nature." Remembering the oft-argued Heideggerian claim that for the ancient Greeks essence meant presencing, perhaps we could say that the topic of Heidegger's essay on the meaning of *phusis* in Aristotle is: how does nature come to presence? What is the presencing of nature?

I want to take a different tactic in the next two chapters, commenting on this text of Heidegger's in a somewhat splintered way. Rather than a holistic approach, I am going to try to proceed here in a more piecemeal fashion, akin to the strategy Werner Marx used some years ago in introducing some of the key elements of a Heideggerian reading of Aristotle's ontology, emphasizing basic terminology and summarizing Heidegger's basic way of understanding these Aristotelian terms.[3] This will mean that the forest will be presupposed as we look at the trees. But of course Heidegger never writes outside of a vision of the whole that guides his study. So, it will for the most part remain implicit that the guiding insight of the whole of Heidegger's essay is that, for Aristotle, *phusis* is the name for the twofoldness of being and, furthermore, *phusis* is the name Aristotle gives for the double movement that belongs to this way of being. This will become clearer when we approach Heidegger's discussion of *genesis* and *sterēsis* toward the end of the next chapter.

The Meaning of Phusis

In the introductory passages of this essay, Heidegger points to an etymological connection between *genesis,* as one of the Greek words for the meaning of *phusis,* and the Roman word *natura* (from *nasci*), which means to be born, to arise from.[4] Nature signifies "that which lets something originate from itself (*aus sich entstammen läßt*)" (WBP 309). But this connection to coming to be is no longer heard in the modern word "nature," and nature has come to be understood as a fixed realm that is contrasted with other realms of beings. Thus, nature is understood by contrasting natural beings with beings that belong to a realm above nature, the supernatural. Or else, nature is contrasted to art, or history, or spirit, and so on. In each case, nature seems to be the predominant term in the twofold differentiation, the term from which the other realm is delineated as opposite to it. But, these dichotomies are, in fact, governed by a wider conception of being within which these regions of beings are contrasted. Whenever we address the question of nature, we are also implicitly raising the question of beings as a whole. Finally, the question of the human being's relationship to nature is at least implicitly relevant in uncovering these relational pairs that determine, by way of contrast, the meaning of nature. For it is the human being who is capable of defining what is on the basis of these delimiting oppositions. So there is an entire web of interconnected and often confused issues that demand our attention.

The dichotomies that Heidegger lists—nature and grace, nature and art, nature and history, nature and spirit—show that in the history of Western thought, "nature" has been understood as an area of beings whose specific character can be determined by differentiating them from other beings. Thus, in contrast to nature, grace is that which is above nature, and the artwork is that which is not natural but made. Or if nature is understood as material, then spirit is nonmaterial. In each case, there is an opposition, a twofold, each side of which is understood in terms of the other. Neither nature nor its contrary can be understood outside of this opposition. The question of what holds this opposition together remains unasked. Further, one needs to ask what nature must be in itself in order for it to be able to stand in a relation to that which opposes it. Each opposition is stated in terms of a *not*, such that what is held to be different from nature remains determined by it. In all of these dichotomies, Heidegger says, "'Nature' is not only an opposing term but essentially takes precedence" (WBP 310). At the basis of the contrast between two realms of beings lies an understanding of *phusis* as the being of beings. Heidegger recognizes in Aristotle's way of laying out the philosophical understanding of *phusis* an attentiveness to this originary sense of *phusis* as the dichotomous meaning of being in general. When this double sense of *phusis* remains unquestioned, the separation of being and beings becomes prominent, resulting in the splintering of philosophy into regional ontologies.

Heidegger's basic point is to insist that, in Aristotle's philosophy, the "nature" of beings as a whole is always implicitly addressed when we concern ourselves with an understanding of nature. A hint of this is still contained in our other use of the word nature, when we speak of, for example, the nature of the human being. Heidegger's aim in his reading of Aristotle is to show the inseparability of the question of being and the question of nature. For Aristotle, the turn to metaphysics is not a question of leaving behind the subject matter of the *Physics* in order to explore the sense of another realm of being. Rather, Heidegger says, the study of being in the sense of beings as a whole is called meta-physics, the science that goes *after* natural beings, namely, the science of *phusis*, the knowledge of nature. For similar reasons, Heidegger makes the rather provocative claim that the "differentiation of 'nature and spirit' is a completely non-Greek dichotomy" (WBP 313). That is, the Greeks did not think of science as an activity of spirit that examined a certain group of available objects. This way of conceiving of the separation of subject and object is no longer attuned to the phenomenological sense of being Heidegger recovers in his study of Aristotle.

Finally, Heidegger alludes in the beginning of this essay to our own age and to his interpretation of technology and the global planning of modern times and says that today the world is shifting out of joint (WBP 312). The nexus of the relationality of human being and nature is being replaced by a notion of world order. In technology, the human being's orientation toward beings brings to fulfillment the withdrawal of being.[5] For Heidegger, the issue of world is fundamental to an understanding of nature. Heidegger attributes the birth of technology to a reductive transformation of the Aristotelian sense of nature, causality, and motion. Heidegger's claim that the world is out of joint implies that the interconnectedness and relationality at the heart of what is, and the understanding of which is necessary in order to ask about nature, is endangered in our time and replaced by planning. One of Heidegger's strategies for coping with this danger is to raise anew the question of the relationship between *phusis* and *technē* in Aristotle's philosophy.

Heidegger's Ontological Interpretation of Movement in
Aristotle's Philosophy

Heidegger begins his discussion of *Physics* B1 with a quote from *Physics* A2, 185a 12ff: "But from the outset it should be (a settled issue) for us that those beings that are by *phusis,* whether all of them or some of them [those not in rest], are moving beings (i.e., determined by movedness)" (WBP 313). Indeed, Aristotle maintains that the problem of movement was the stumbling block in the attempt of his predecessors to think about being. In this quote, Aristotle seems to be saying that he will simply take it for granted that *the* philosophical question is the question of *kinēsis.* But the opposite is the case. Unlike his predecessors, whom Aristotle accuses of having lazily neglected the question of movement,[6] Aristotle promises to devote the most strenuous philosophical effort to place the question of movement at the center of his thought, and to view it as the most fundamental question when addressing the question of being. Heidegger says that Aristotle was the first to raise the issue of movement to a philosophical level.

Heidegger cautions us about a basic confusion at the heart of this issue. It is not the particular motion from place to place that is under investigation, but rather how such beings that have the power to move of themselves are. For these beings to be, movement must belong to their very way of being. The fact that these beings at any given time may be at rest does not mitigate the fact that movement must characterize their way of being. The opposition of motion and rest has its origin in this movedness or being-moved. Rest is not the negation of being-moved. Rather it is the concentrated and fulfilled expression of this way of being. In the history of metaphysics, there is a tendency to exclude motion from being and to understand motion as nonbeing. Thus, the eternal and permanent are held to be more being than the changing and finite. In such a framework, the question of movement, the being of *kinēsis,* being in the sense of movement, gets bypassed.

The fundamental question of *kinēsis* is not a question about the behavior of beings. To use Heideggerian terms, the *Physics* is not an ontic inquiry, but an ontological inquiry. In Book A of the *Physics,* Aristotle says that had his predecessors seen this *phusis,* they would not have turned away from coming to be and change, and their ignorance would have been dispelled.[7] Moreover, he says, this *phusis,* this being-moved, does not violate the fundamental premise about being—namely, that being either is or is not. Actually, *Physics* A 8 is quite pronounced on this issue. It is about how the law of non-contradiction, that being and nonbeing cannot both be at the same time, does not preclude the reality of natural beings that come to be and whose being is co-constituted by privation (191 b26–192 a27). The *aporia,* he says, that befuddled his predecessors regarding the existence of changing beings is solved by his discovery of the notion of potentiality. *Dunamis* becomes for Aristotle the *archē*, the governing principle and source, of natural beings, the being of beings that move.

The Phenomenology of Seeing and the Recognition of Movement as the Being of Beings

At *Physics* A2, 185 a12ff, Aristotle announces as a presupposition of the investigation that natural beings are constituted by movement. He says this is immediately evident through *epagōgē* (induction). In *Prior Analytics* 67 a22ff, Aristotle says: "it never happens that a person knows the individual (the particular) in advance; rather he receives knowledge of the individual by induction (*epagōgē*—leading it forth) and, as it were, through recognition." *Epagōgē* means the ability to hold together the seeing (*nous*) of the whole and the seeing (*aisthēsis*) of the individual that is constituted by this whole. It is because human being is the site of this correlation that we can see beings in their being and understand the being of beings. In the *Posterior Analytics* 100 a16, Aristotle says: "what is perceived is the individual, but the perception is in relation to the whole." Further, he says at 100 b4, "it is clear that we must know that which is first by *epagōgē*. For even perception (*aisthēsis*) lays claim to (*empoiei*) the whole (*katholou*) in this way."

Knowledge of the whole is not arrived at by abstracting one common characteristic from a series of individuals. It is the individual that manifests in its being its common ground with other beings. The individual man Callias, Aristotle says, appears, but he shows himself as a man and thus we "see" the whole. The individual, when it stands in its being, always already shows itself in relation to other beings when it shows itself as it is. The knowledge that Aristotle seeks here in the *Physics* can only be reached within the framework of a "phenomenology" of beings that asks the question what beings must be such that they can at all show themselves as they are; and a phenomenology that asks who the human being is such that we can "see" and "recognize" beings in their being. *Epagōgē* means to point to this capacity to understand beings as a whole.

In *Sein und Zeit,* Heidegger seeks to clarify the meaning of phenomenology in his own thought, a meaning clearly implied in his discussion of Aristotle's notion of *epagōgē*, through a consideration of the Greek origin of this word. He secures the meaning of phenomenology as "to let what shows itself be seen from itself, as it shows itself from itself"[8] by letting the word "phenomenology" disclose from itself what it means. Phenomenology contains the two words "phenomenon" and "*logos.*" It is by returning to the Greek meaning of these words that we can gain access to their original significance.

Heidegger points out that the Greek word *phainomenon* means what shows itself, the self-showing, the manifest.[9] The verb *phainesthai* is a form of *phaino* that means to bring into the light of day. The phenomena (often identified with *ta onta,* the Greek word for beings) are that which can be brought to light. The Greeks grappled with the problem of preserving a genuine and original vision of what becomes manifest. They recognized that beings can also appear to be what they are not, and, therefore, the word *phainomenon* can also mean what looks like or seems. Heidegger points out that seeming to be is intrinsically dependent on the possibility of self-showing. Only what can show itself is capable of semblance. This semblance is a derivative form of self-showing, as we will see in Heidegger's discussion of Aristotle's sense of truth.[10] But even in semblance, a self-showing that shows itself as something other than it is, there lies the possibility of a genuine and original access to the phenomenon.

Both Heidegger and Aristotle were engaged in the project of winning back a discovery of beings that were already hidden and distorted in the way they showed themselves. Both thinkers recognized that only by giving an account of this privative character of beings, as an intrinsic way in which they can be, could a genuine access to the phenomenon itself be recovered. "What already shows itself in appearance prior to and always accompanying what we commonly understand as phenomena, though unthematically, can be brought thematically to self showing."[11] Phenomenology places the self-showing of these beings on a more radical footing. Phenomenology is the way, the method, in which the being of these beings can be approached and brought to light. The self-showing of beings is the starting point of all phenomenological investigation. But because being reveals itself in beings that are always already interpreted in some way, there must be a movement from our ordinary experience of beings to the phenomenological. This in turn grounds and makes accessible in its being the being that shows itself. Aristotle takes the ordinary experience of natural beings as moved beings and asks what their being must be if they show themselves in this way.

By returning to the Greek roots of the word "phenomenology," Heidegger shows that there is an inner connection between what is meant by the

Greek notion of *phainomenon* and the meaning of *logos. Phainomenon* means the self-showing, what is manifest. *Logos* lets something be seen from itself. Hence, phenomenology means: "To let what shows itself be seen from itself, just as it shows itself from itself."[12] Heidegger's analysis of the Greek roots of the term and his understanding of phenomenology in terms of the Greek understanding of being places phenomenology on a new path. Husserl's call to return "to the things themselves" urged an analysis of the transcendental ground that makes possible the disclosure of beings. For Husserl, this was the transcendental consciousness, and the task was to unfold the intentional structure of consciousness that constitutes the what and the how of that which it experiences. For Heidegger, the task of phenomenology is rather to make explicit, to bring to language and to formulate, what already shows itself, not in the human subject, but in itself. As Aristotle says: "the cause of the present difficulty (the seeing of *alētheia*) is not in the matter but in ourselves. For, as the eyes of bats are to the blaze of day, so is the *nous* in our soul to that which through *phusis* is most manifest of all" (*Met.* 993 b8ff).

Aristotle's method of thinking is phenomenological; through *epagōgē,* he achieves a preliminary understanding of the being of beings. However, he has yet to interpret, to lay bare and exhibit, the ground of this understanding. That is what Aristotle accomplished, according to Heidegger, in his *Physics:* "The first coherent and thoughtful discussion, on the basis of its way of questioning, about the essence of *phusis,* comes down to us from the time of the fulfillment of Greek philosophy; it stems from Aristotle" (WBP 312). By going through *epagōgē* toward beings one encounters in experience in such a way that one brings them into relation with the *archē* that governs them, one recognizes that natural beings are *kinoumena* whose way of being is to be moved. This characteristic of being-moved is the presupposition on which all investigation of science is founded. Aristotle says: "Scientific knowledge through demonstration is impossible unless one already knows the first, immediate starting points."[13] *Aisthēsis* presupposes the vision of the whole, of the *archē* that governs beings and makes seeing possible. "It is *nous* that apprehends the *archē.*"[14]

In the *Physics,* Aristotle sets out to make explicit this preunderstanding of beings as a whole established through the movement of *epagōgē.* Through *epagōgē,* he achieves a preliminary understanding of the being of beings; in the course of the *Physics,* this understanding is articulated. *Epagōgē* is neither the seeing of beings as a whole, nor the perception of a particular being. *Epagōgē* is the way of knowing that moves between the twofold way in which human beings are related to what is. *Epagōgē* gathers this twofold way of knowing into one. Thus, *epagōgē* is not the study of individual beings in order to abstract the universal from them. As Joseph Owens states: "The notion of abstracting a 'universal' or 'essence' from singulars does not occur in Aristotle."[15] In *epagōgē*, we do not look toward a part of the being, but toward the being as such, as a whole. Therefore, we see it as it necessarily is and as it necessarily reveals itself in our repeated encounters with it.

In Heidegger's view, Aristotle's appeal to *epagōgē* is proof that his philosophical method is phenomenological. His task is to take beings in the way they show themselves and let them be seen in their being. So Heidegger says in *My Way of Phenomenology*:

What occurs for the phenomenology of the acts of consciousness as the self-manifestation of phenomena is thought more originally by Aristotle and in all Greek thinking and existence as *alētheia*, as the unconcealedness of what is present, its being-revealed, its showing itself. That which phenomenological investigations rediscovered as the supporting attitude of thought proves to be the fundamental trait of Greek thinking, if not of philosophy as such.[16]

When Aristotle begins by asserting that *kinēsis* is the way of being of natural beings, his beginning is not arbitrary. Aristotle's method of thinking is phenomenological. He recognizes the proper role of *logos* in the study of phenomena. His task is to take beings in the way they show themselves and let them be in their being. This initial formulation of his project in the *Physics* receives greater articulation and deeper significance as he lets the matter unfold in the course of his investigation. The preliminary starting point of Aristotle's investigation of *phusis* is the recognition through *epagōgē* that natural beings are constituted in their being through *kinēsis*. Movement is the way of being of natural beings. Movement is the "phenomenon" that opens up in the course of this study a unique access to an ontological understanding of nature.

The Meaning of Cause in Natural Beings: Heidegger's Rejection of Agent Causality

In the very first sentence from *Physics* B1, Aristotle states: "Of beings (as a whole), some are from *phusis*, whereas others are by other 'causes.'" Aristotle establishes in *Physics* A that the study of *phusis* is the study of the *archē* of natural beings. Our task in the *Physics*, he says, is to further delineate the nature of this *archē*. Here we are given a first indication of what is meant by *archē* and thus by *phusis. Phusis* is an *aition.* This word is typically translated as cause. But Heidegger warns us that it is not meant in our sense of causality, although this is what is typically assumed of Aristotle. Causality here is not about the way one thing affects or "effects" another. This kind of causality, the producing of an effect, is only a derivative sense of being a cause. It presupposes that there are beings whose being is such that they can be related to each other as cause and effect and can change in these reciprocal ways. Aristotle is concerned about the *archē* or original source of this relationality. The particular motion that a being happens to undergo is not what is being referred to here by cause. Cause is a more fundamental *kinēsis* that belongs to the way of being of beings that move. Heidegger suggests that cause here means: "what is responsible for the fact that the being is *that* being that it is."

Inasmuch as Aristotle is known to speak of a manifold of causes: *hulē, eidos, telos,* and *technē,* how we understand causality will determine how we come to interpret these other key notions in Aristotle's philosophical vocabulary. How are *hulē, eidos,* and *telos* together constitutive of and responsible for the being of natural beings? The German word for cause is more helpful than our own. *Aition* is translated by Heidegger as *Ur-sache,* the source of the thing. Heidegger also uses the German word *Vershulden* as a translation of the Greek *aitia,* a word that means responsibility, cause, as well as guilt and debt. The cause is that to which the being is indebted in its very being. It is the original guilt that Anaximander spoke of in the fragment on cosmic injustice when he said that the *apeiron,* that which is unlimited, is that from which coming to be arises and returns, "giving satisfaction to one another and making reparation for their injustice, according to the order of time."17

We can examine this notion in Aristotle further by considering his explanation of the four causes that are responsible for the bringing forth of a produced being in *technē.* Beings produced in this way are differentiated from natural beings by Aristotle because they do not come forth on their own. Even though this differentiation is essential for our discussion, Aristotle frequently uses the more accessible realm of *technē* to gain insight into the meaning of *phusis.* In the example of the silver chalice or bronze statue "that out of which a being comes to be and endures is named a cause, for example, the bronze of the statue or the silver of the chalice" (*Physics* 194 b24). Without the *hulē,* bronze or silver, the statue or chalice would not be what it is. Therefore they owe their being to their "matter." But the matter is not solely responsible. Only when the matter appears and is shaped in its *eidos,* its aspect, is it a statue or chalice. In asking, for example, why these bricks and stones are a house, "the question is why the matter is some definite thing" (*Met.* 1041 b4–8). The house is not simply a composite of bricks and stones, "no more than a syllable is merely its elements" *(Met.* 1041 b12ff).* "In the case of all things which have several parts and in which the totality is not, as it were, a mere heap, but the whole is something besides the parts, there is a cause" (*Met.* 1045 a7–10). It is this unity of its being that accounts for its being something and this unity is never just a collection of parts. This is why Aristotle could not uncover the mode of the being of beings as being-moved simply by gathering data about the movement of beings, but had rather to understand and interpret the ground of this movement. The chalice is not merely a heap of silver, but owes its being to its being-placed in this appearance (*eidos*) of a chalice.

The third and most significant cause is *telos,* the end in which a being is fulfilled. Aristotle gives the example of walking: "Why is he walking about? We say: 'to be 'healthy' and, having said that, we think we have assigned the cause" (*Physics* 194 b33–35). In speaking of the "matter," the bricks and stones of a wall, Aristotle says: "though the wall does not come to be without these, it does not owe its being to these, except as its material cause; it comes to be for the sake of sheltering and guarding [the *telos*]" (*Physics* 200 a6–11). The *telos* is not the end or stopping of something, but rather, as that which gives it its place, it allows it to be what it is, to fulfill its being. Aristotle places particular importance on this cause. He says:

It is plain that this kind of cause is operative in beings which come to be and are by *phusis.* And since *phusis* means two things, *hulē* and *eidos,* of which the latter is the *telos,* and since all the rest is for the sake of the *telos,* the *telos* must be the cause in the sense of "that for the sake of which" (*Physics* 199 a29f).

The *telos* is responsible for what as matter and what as aspect co-constitute the being of a being. A saw is "for the sake of" sawing. It must therefore have a certain matter and a certain aspect that will allow it to be what it is. The *telos* is precisely this coming into its appearance (*eidos*). Thus, "both causes (matter and the aspect as end) must be stated by the physicist, but especially the end; for that is the 'cause' of the matter, not vice-versa" (*Physics* 200 a31–32).

Heidegger speaks in his essay "The Question Concerning Technology" of the technological viewpoint that reverses this Aristotelian insight that a being is determined in its being by its *telos,* even in its "matter." Thus, the modern mechanistic viewpoint sees beings as primarily material to which they must assign a "value" and use. Beings, according to Aristotle, already have, in their being, a way of being that is granted to them by their being.

But what brings together into a definite being these three ways of being responsible for? In the case of the silver chalice, a product of *technē*, it is the silversmith. It is he who, in a gathering of the three previous causes through careful consideration, brings forth into appearance the chalice. The silversmith is not a *causa efficiens,* but is rather responsible for the particular coming together into a belonging of the "matter" that is appropriate to an "aspect" for the sake of the production of the sacred vessel. The four causes, in their interrelated ways, together "let what is not yet present arrive into presencing."

Ontological Movement and the Constancy of Beings

Phusis has been understood as the "cause" of natural beings. We have seen that Aristotle understands *aitia* here as the bringing together of the being into its *eidos* and *telos*. He offers a further insight into this role of *phusis* when he characterizes beings that come to be by *phusis* as "*sunestōta*"— constant and enduring. Heidegger emphasizes the basic meaning of this word: *syn* means together and the verb *histēmi* means to cause to stand or bring to a standstill, to place. Animals and plants and so on are natural in the sense that they stand forth together in this way—that is, they owe their enduring to nature. Heidegger suggests that the Greeks understood the character of all beings in terms of their way of being constant. Beings are to the extent that they are constant and continuous, to the extent that they endure in their being. In this sense, we can extend our discussion further by understanding cause to mean that which is responsible for the standing forth together of being, for the withstanding capability of beings. *Phusis* is the singular *aition* that is responsible for gathering the causes that bring the being to stand in its being.

The task here is to think this meaning of beings as a whole in the way it characterizes beings that move. It would seem that constancy and movement are opposites. But that which comes to a stand and remains standing holds itself "there," that is, it sustains itself in its limits (its *peras*). Aristotle does not understand the way the being holds itself in its *telos* in the sense of a stopping or coming to an end. Such a notion of end would only mean that the being ceases to be. Aristotle says: "beings from *phusis* are those which by a continuous (*sunechēs*) movement arrive at their *telos*" (*Physics* 199b16). *Telos* means a holding itself together of movement, a movement that is gathered up in the arrival and contained there. *Telos* means end in the sense of what fulfills movement, the fullness of movement. That is why Aristotle calls *kinēsis* "the most fundamental characteristic of natural beings" (*Physics* 253 b9).

Aristotle tries to think the kinetic character of being in a way that does not deny the Greek sense of being as standing there and preserving itself. The being of beings is emerging into presence and standing-there; it is also preserving itself in this appearance. We must think these two together as Aristotle does when he speaks of *phusis*. But in thinking the togetherness of these opposing notions of emerging forth and preserving, we must also hold them apart. Otherwise movement is impossible. Heidegger suggests that this twofold meaning of *archē* as *Ausgang* (the origin in the sense of that out of which something emerges forth) and *Verfügung* (ordering in the sense of governing over and preserving) can be translated as originating ordering or ordering origin. The two movements are equiprimordial, though in a sense opposite.

Through our discussion of *sunestōta*, we tried to think through one of the basic reasons for the inability to grasp movement on an ontological level. The difficulty is that the Greek conception of being is tied to the notion of permanence and endurance. Such emphasis on the abiding character of what truly is would seen to preclude motion, except perhaps as an illusory or accidental quality that has nothing to do with the being of what is. Heidegger, following Aristotle, has questioned this assumption that endurance excludes movement. Being endures in the sense that its movement is continuous; beings that are come to a stand and hold themselves together. The movement is gathered up in the arrival and bound therein.

There is also a temporal dimension to this sense of being. Natural beings endure in the way they "have" their being, but also in that they remain and last in being. This temporal dimension of preserving their presence, Heidegger says, must be thought together with the other sense of enduring. Thus, Heidegger insists on an interconnection between time and movement. Both belong to the way of being of physical beings. The notion of endurance has nothing to do with simply being fixed in space; nor does it have to do with simply lasting in time, except in a derivative sense. Because of the enduring character of such beings, one can take them as independent objects that a perceiving subject happens to come across. But, Heidegger claims, "For the Greeks, the human being is never a subject, and therefore non-human beings can never have the character of object (standing against)" (WBP 316). It is not our being conscious of the being or our seeing of the being that makes it stand there, but rather, for Aristotle, a being from *phusis* brings itself to stand, gathers itself in a stand, and holds itself there in its being-together. It is this bringing itself into presence (*parousia*) that is its way of enduring. Aristotle says: "It is not because we think truly that you *are* white, that you are white, but because you are white, we who say this have the truth" (*Met.* 1051 a7). The enduring which is a mode of being of those beings that appear in their being is not due to their "objective" character, but is granted to beings in their being. The being of beings *is* the enduring presence of what is. It is this character of enduring that, rather than excluding becoming and moving, sustains it and makes it possible. Heidegger says:

The Greeks do not conceive of being present and abiding primarily in terms of mere duration. For the Greeks, a totally different trait predominates in being-present and abiding—at times specifically expressed through *para* and *apo*. To be present is to come close by (*an-wesen*), to be here in contrast and conflict with to be away (*ab-wesen*).18

Through the analysis of Aristotle's use of the word *sunestōta*, we have gained two insights: the being of beings is emerging into presence and standing together; it is also enduring in this presence, preserving itself in its appearance. We must think these two together as Aristotle does when he speaks of *phusis*. Just as we have before us the task of thinking of rest and movement as belonging together in *kinēsis*, so also must we think the enduring and emerging forth of beings in its sameness, in order to be able to show how natural beings are in their being. But once again it is important to keep in mind that this togetherness is a togetherness of opposites, and thus the two must also be thought in their separateness from each other, which is precisely how Aristotle thinks of movement. As we have said previously, this double character of *kinēsis* is the *phusis* of natural beings.

Phusis *as the Granting of Place: Change and the Place of Beings*

The path to the essential insight into the *kinēsis* that belongs to *phusis* is blocked for us by the modern tendency to regard the primary form of movement as change (*metabolē*) of position in space. This narrow view of movement makes it difficult to understand the "ontological" significance that Aristotle attaches to *metabolē*. Aristotle gives examples of motion and lists movement with respect to place, increase and decrease, and alteration as examples. Heidegger has unique insights into each of these kinds of motion, but we will focus on the meaning of locomotion. Heidegger says that this sense of motion has come to mean movement pure and simple, thereby making it impossible to read Aristotle's *Physics* properly. When beings are taken as simply there in space, then motion is understood in terms of change of position in space. But movement of location is one, among other, types of movement, "not movement pure and simple" (WBP 318). A being can stay put and still change through increase or alteration, for example. Besides that, the Greek sense of place or *topos* has been understood to refer to spatial location and thus movement has been considered only in terms of change of position in space. But the Greeks had no notion like our modern notion of "location of a mass in space." Space rather is understood as the "place" of a being. A natural being for Aristotle is never reducible to its material extension. It is always a concrete being, a *todē ti*, a "this" (*Met.* 1003 a8). Only that which is a being can take its place and leave it. Place is not an indifferent container that defines the being. Rather, the being arrives in its place and thereby its place first comes to be. Aristotle defines place as *to peras*, limit or boundary (*Physics* 212 a7) of the surrounding body. The boundary, Heidegger says, is that at which something begins its essential unfolding (*Wesen*).[19] The place is the limit of a separate, embodied being. This is why Aristotle speaks of relations such as contact, touch, and succession whenever he discusses place. Only an embodied physical being is capable of touching and reaching out toward its proper realm. It is because the being is a body, and thus is separate and yet belongs to a *koinon*, a community with other beings, in such a way that it can interact and exchange with others, that movement is possible. In other words, the fundamental cause of these movements is the way of being of those beings that can move. This way of being is bodily. The difficulty Aristotle faces, the stumbling block of Greek philosophy, is to show how beings can endure and still have movement as their way of being. A being comes forth into its place, and grants itself a place by gathering itself into appearance as a whole that endures in its being.

The understanding of the being of natural beings that is beginning to take shape in our discussion is that only a being that endures, stands, and is held in its *telos* can be. Only as a unity can a being be. And yet natural beings, which are moving beings, cannot be simply one. Aristotle has shown that the acknowledged oneness of being does not require a reduction of this being to a single element (*stoicheion*) or ground from which all else can be derived. The oneness of being is rather the unity of a belonging together. The selfsameness of being is not static. Rather, it originates from a oneness that constantly gathers the many ways of being into a unity and a whole. Aristotle is attempting to show how a natural being can be one and yet manifold in its being. Only if *metabolē,* change, holds together the manifold and lets it belong together as one can beings be.

Aristotle states frequently that "every change is *from* something *to* something" (*Physics* 225 a1). He makes clear what he means by a change from something: "that which changes withdraws from (*apoleipo*—to leave behind, to forsake, to be absent) that from which it changes; and withdrawing, if not the same thing as changing follows it (*akoleutheō*)" (*Physics* 235 b9–11). Heidegger insists that this withdrawing-emerging is what the Greeks meant by *metabolē.* Thus, a characteristic of change is that it is *no longer* that from out of which it changes. But every change is not only a change from something but also to something and toward something. In *Sein und Zeit,* Heidegger gives a helpful example of what is meant by the being-toward of *metabolē:* "The fruit ripens itself, and this ripeningcharacterizes its being as fruit . . . the not-yet is already included in its own being, by no means as an arbitrary determination, but as a constituent."[20]

No longer being and not-yet being are fundamental characteristics of change and thus of natural beings. Only by showing how the standing and enduring of natural beings presuppose relationality among beings and incorporate the from-out-of-which and being-toward of change can Aristotle achieve his task of clarifying the meaning of *phusis.*

We interpreted the notion of *metabolē* as change in the sense of a sudden turning, a transition that involves presence and absence. Aristotle says that every *metabolē* is a transition from something to something. This involves a drawing away and projecting beyond. *Metabolē* was understood as a kind of movement and therefore a kind of continuity, but a continuity that has rupture belonging to its very core. Natural beings continue to be by withdrawing from what has been and holding back from and resisting what is to be. We will get a better grasp of this when we consider, in chapter four, Heidegger's treatment of *Metaphysics* Θ1 and his discussion of the *poiein-pathein* structure.

Aristotle says that philosophy is wondering about the archē and *aitia* of beings. Philosophy begins by wondering about the *to ti ēn einai,* about the essence or, literally, about that which is already there and always already there in our encounter with beings. We now see that this thereness and constant oneness of beings is imbued with motility and temporality. The understanding of being that is beginning to take shape in our discussion is that only a being that endures, stands, and is held in its *telos* can be. Only as a unity can a being be. And yet natural beings, which are moving beings, cannot be simply one. Otherwise the most significant and fundamental movement of all, coming to be (*genesis*), would be impossible. Aristotle is attempting to show how a natural being can be one and yet manifold in its being.

The Complex Relationship of Phusis *and* Technē

In the opening remarks, Heidegger spoke of the many different interpretations of nature that have been offered in history. He pointed out that these interpretations were always offered in dichotomies on the basis of which, under the guidance of an underlying understanding of nature, beings from nature were differentiated from another way of being. He called this a decision, recalling the power of Zeus in Hesiod's account when Zeus distributed the territory belonging to each of the gods. Here the incision separates two regions of beings: natural and artificial. Both have being, but each have their being in a different way. In other words, it is not a question of two different senses of being, but of two different ways in which beings belong to being. In both cases, movement and being produced or brought forth into being characterize the way of being. But in each case the movement of production occurs in a different way. No doubt Heidegger's appeal to an *Abhebung* in Aristotle's way of approaching a philosophy of the movement of being is in contrast to Hegel's dialectical movement or *Aufhebung*. The being-together and being-as-a-whole of beings does not imply a notion of a totality of beings. Likewise, Heidegger's claim that the Greeks knew nothing of modern subjectivity no doubt is an implicit critique of Hegel's philosophy of spirit. But, then, what is the role of the one who makes this *Ent-scheidung*, this decision. For this, we turn to an analysis of *technē*.

The distinction between natural beings and produced beings serves to further articulate the way in which *kinēsis* is the being of natural beings. Produced beings also have *kinēsis* as their way of being but the *archē*, the impulse to change, does not arise of itself. Produced beings depend for their being on another—on human being. In contrast, natural beings emerge out of themselves and stand forth in their being of themselves. In the emergence of both kinds of beings, humans play a role, but the role is different. In "Building Dwelling Thinking" Heidegger traces the origin of the word *technē:* "The Greek for 'to bring forth or to produce' is *tikto.* The word *technē,* technique, belongs to the verb's root 'tec.' To the Greeks, *technē* means neither art nor handicraft, but rather a letting something appear among the things present as this or that, in this way or that way."[21] In "The Origin of the Work of Art," Heidegger argues that *technē* originally meant the same as *epistēmē;* it was a mode of knowing and *alētheia*—a revealing and disclosing of beings. *Technē* does not primarily mean the act of making. It is not the actions of the artist that are at issue but the way of disclosing and relating to beings that is the basis for these actions. Heidegger translates *technē* as *Sichauskennen,* which means "knowing one's way around," being familiar with the beings among which one lives so as to know how to let beings appear in one's world. It is the kind of knowing that one carries along in one's everyday dealings and which makes it possible for one to situate oneself in the midst of things. It is this knowledge that governs all bringing forth. Aristotle says in the *Nichomachean Ethics:*

All *technē* is concerned with the realm of coming to be, that is, with planning and deliberating on how something which is capable both of being and not being may come into being, a thing whose *archē* is in the producer and not in the thing produced (1140 a10–14).

In the *Metaphysics,* Aristotle says that the architect is not wiser because he can do things but because he holds himself in relation to *logos* (dwells in *logos*) and knows the causes (981 b6–7).

Just as there is an essential sameness of meaning in *epistēmē* and *technē* (both are guided by *nous,* see the whole, and are ways of *alētheia* governed by *logos*), so also the contrast between *phusis* and *technē* is made within an essential sameness in that both are ways of revealing, ways in which beings show themselves as they are; both have to do with beings whose way of being is *kinēsis.* It is this essential sameness that allows Aristotle, throughout his works, to so often decline to differentiate between these two ways in which beings are. His intention here, though, is to bring to light the way natural beings are revealed by freeing the horizon of this difference through his discussion of *technē.* Thus, we are not discussing here different kinds of beings, but beings that reveal themselves or are disclosed in different ways.

Technē is a gathering together of something (a *logos* in the sense of *legein*), this gathering being directed by its preview (*prohairesis*) of what it is to be brought forth. The being is revealed according to the *eidos,* which is the end (*telos*) toward which the gathering is performed. But, for *technē*, this *eidos* does not already exist in the being that itself has brought itself into its *telos*. The *eidos prohaireton* is in the mind of the architect as the one for the sake of which the product is brought forth.

But what is the *hulē*, the matter from which *technē* can bring forth its product? The one who has *technē* finds this already there in her dealings. It is there from *phusis*. Thus, *phusis* is always present in *technē*, but it does not show itself forth as itself. Beings produced by humans are not natural. And yet the not is not such as to completely deny the relation to nature that is present in such beings. And so the question emerges, what is the being of beings from *phusis* such that they can show themselves as they are not? Natural beings tend by nature toward their fulfillment. However, they do not come to be necessarily. If nothing gets in the way, they will come to be. But they are related to other beings in such a way that they can be affected by them. This *pathein* belongs to their way of being and is not extrinsic.

Technē approaches and relates to natural beings in terms of their possibility of being used in a certain way as *hulē* for its product. This helps us to understand certain things about natural beings. That such beings can be taken and perceived in ways that they are *not*, in and of themselves, means that such beings must have this "not" as a characteristic of their way of being. Also, if natural beings can be taken over and made into other beings, that is, incorporated in a way that they no longer have a being of their own but only appear accidentally in another being, then such beings must already be related to other beings in such a way that they can be radically affected by them.

Aristotle separates produced beings from natural beings because of their way of being brought forth and insofar as they belong to and are grasped in a given address. We have seen that *technē* is a kind of *logos* and we have seen that in the realm of *technē* natural beings are addressed not as they are in themselves, but in terms of how they can be appropriated in the production of something of use. We need now to take a closer look at this "categorial" way of understanding beings and its implications for our task of understanding the movement of *phusis*. Certainly any far-reaching interpretation of Aristotle, which Heidegger's surely is, will have to relate that interpretation to Aristotle's treatment of the categories. In fact, in Heidegger's work on Kant, he sees as crucial to the limitation of Kant's philosophy his unquestioning taking over of the categories from Aristotle with the assumption that the categories are based on modes of assertion and therefore founded in judgments.22 Heidegger maintains that the problem of the categories cannot be dealt with under the guidance of the distinction between subject and object, although the prominence of the categorial understanding of being has its roots in the distinction. Nietzsche calls the categories the supreme *values* and suggests that "faith in the categories of reason (goal, unity, truth) is the cause of nihilism."23 Perhaps the understanding of the human being's relation to beings in terms of subjectivity, which Heidegger says is foreign to the Greeks, can be traced back to the step philosophy takes in understanding "the many senses of being" of which Aristotle speaks solely in terms of categories, and then relating the categories to assertion and judgment. When this is done, human being is seen as the determiner of the being of beings (*logos* is reason), the one who projects a meaning and stability that ground the movement and "becoming" of beings, but is outside it. While this is in a way true of *technē* (although even here the *eidos* for Aristotle is not an idea that is "imposed" on a being), it is not at all the way Aristotle characterizes the being of natural beings; being is also spoken of as a oneness that is manifold (*Met.* 1051 a34-b1), but these are not categories for Aristotle. The way of *logos* that reveals being is a listening and a response, a letting-be that is precisely not a covering over (with a value) or manipulating. Natural beings have their *archē* in and of themselves and do not require *technē* in order to come forth in their being. Thus, the *logos* and way of knowing that address natural beings as such must be other than the *logos* of *technē*. Heidegger says that the desire to understand natural beings is "a challenge to look into the unfathomable depths of the essence of being which is denied to every *technē* because it renounces any claim to know and to ground *truth* as such" (WBP 328).

We have already seen an indication of what kind of address the categories involve when Aristotle named several different kinds of movement and rest in natural beings: increasing and decreasing, locomotion and alteration (*Physics* 192 b14). These are kinds of motion that originate and are governed by *phusis*. Aristotle clarifies later that such motions are "certainly not *phusis* but by *phusis* and according to *phusis*" (*Physics* 192 b31ff). That is, they do not constitute the being of natural beings but are governed by it. Aristotle refers to the schema of the categories at *Met.* 1026 a35 and includes quality, quantity, place, and time. All of these categories are addressed as being in relation to *ousia*.24 *Ousia* is understood as the *archē* that lets these manifold relations be embodied and held together.25 These categories can be said to be "in" the being, whereas *ousia* is never present "in" a being.26 It rather constitutes the being of the being; it is that which the being *is*. If *ousia* is the *archē* of natural beings, and the *archē* is twofold or manifold, as Aristotle shows it is in Book I of the *Physics*, then we must be careful not to confuse the "structure" of *archē* with the manifold of categories that is unified through the *archē*.

Since movement is the way in which natural beings are, the categories must also be understood in terms of movement. We find ourselves constantly tempted to express this guiding insight (achieved by Aristotle though *epagōgē*) by first speaking of natural beings and then saying that such beings move. This way of looking at movement is inadequate to understand how *phusis* as *ousia* is *kinēsis*. However, it can be appropriate to speak of beings constituted by *ousia* as moving from one place to another or as growing or withering, or as being late or early. In this case, we view natural beings as simply *there* and then understand change as something these beings undergo. We fail to question the nature of the being-there.

The understanding of beings as objects and the categories as properties that these objects have prevents us from seeing that for Aristotle these ways of being are constituted by movement. The kind of movement that characterizes each of the categories is called by Aristotle *enantia*—the movement from out of something to its opposite. "Speaking generally, rest is the contrary of motion. But the different forms of motion have their own contraries in other forms; thus destruction is the contrary of generation, diminution of increase, rest in a place of change of place" (*Cat.* 15 b1ff). Even the category of quality or alteration is said to be a movement between contraries. Thus becoming-healthy is from out of sickness. All change is from something to something and the categories are the various ways in which beings interact with each other and form themselves. It is these various ways in which beings can change that allows the craftsman in *technē* to take beings he encounters and lead them forth under his control. *Technē* presupposes a knowledge of the categorial ways beings can be determined. It presupposes a relation to the *kinēsis* of natural beings. Motion on this level is not arbitrary but determined by the interrelation of opposites that stand in relation to one another and *are* in this relation. Thus, a being can be healthy and stay healthy only by a movement that holds itself in resistance to its opposite. The "objectivity" of beings is not something contributed by a subject but is founded on the *koinon* of beings in movement.

Aristotle always speaks on two levels in his works. Thus, even in *On the Categories*, he points beyond the "ontic" discussion of categorial movement to the "ontological" foundation. Thus, quantity "in the strict sense" is not the movement between the contraries of increase and decrease, but the oneness of being. Only in that a being is one can it get bigger or smaller.[27] Likewise generation and destruction have their foundation in *ousia,* and locomotion has its foundation in rest in the sense of being-placed (in its *eidos*). In the same way, time which is here discussed ontically in terms of 'before' and 'after,' has its foundation in the *aei,* the being that is always there and thus can be "in" time. The discussion of *hen, ousia, aei,* and so on is a discussion of the ontological foundation for the *kinēsis* of and between beings. This does not mean that *kinēsis* is excluded from discussion on this level and that movement is only understood "ontically" in Aristotle. Rather the task is to understand the being of *kinēsis*—to understand *kinēsis* in itself as such. Only by showing how *hen, ousia,* and *aei* each belong to *kinēsis* can Aristotle uncover the being of *phusis.*

Aristotle was the first to think out the categories (quantity, quality, relation, etc.) as at the basis of our ordinary ways of addressing beings. Thus, the philosophical categories were discovered by Aristotle by meditating on the meaning of *ousia* in its everyday usage. In the passage from *Physics* B1 that Heidegger analyzes, the word category is in fact used in this ordinary sense of "address." In our dealings with beings, we address them as what they are—as a bed or robe, and so on. It is this naming that lets a being appear in a context of meaning and brings the being into public view as being such and such. Thus, for example, when we address a being as a door or say that a door is large, we point out something and let what we are talking about be seen in a certain way. Heidegger suggests that this meaning of category can be grasped by looking at the literal sense of the Greek word *kata-agoreuein.*

Agoreuein means to speak in public, to announce something publicly, to bring something into the open. *Kata* means something on high regard to something below; it means the view toward something. Thus *katēgorein* means to reveal and make public something by regarding it expressly as what it is.[28]

When we call something a house or a tree, we name it according to its *eidos,* its aspect. It is when we see a being in this way that we truly know it. Aristotle points out that we do not call a box wood but wooden, since it could also be made out of metal and still be a box (*Met.* 1049 a20). "The woodenness is *sumbebēkos,* it only appears along with what the bed authentically and properly is" (WBP 324). We can, of course, also address ourselves to the woodenness of the particular bed we are considering. But then we do not name what is essential to a bed. Rather we recognize that something natural has been used in the forming of the bed. Inasmuch as wood is there "in" the bed, Aristotle tells us, the bed does have a source of movement that is natural, but it has it only incidentally and not inasmuch as it is a bed. A bed that is brought forth into its *eidos* by *technē* does not have the source of its own movement (as a bed) in itself. Thus, when a being, whether natural or made, is said to be *this* being here (*todē ti*), we do not address ourselves to that from out of which it has come, but rather to the aspect. It is the *eidos* that allows it to be seen as the being that it is. This is why Aristotle says that the master craftsman is the one who knows how to see rather than the one who does things (*Met.* 981 a31ff) and why only such a person can teach how to learn a craft. Heidegger says in *What Is Called Thinking*: "All the work of the hand is rooted in thinking. Therefore thinking itself is man's simplest, and for that reason hardest, handiwork."[29]

When we call this particular being, for example, a pen, we must already silently address it *as* a thing of use. The "as" something has a structure of its own that Aristotle brought to philosophical clarity in his discussion of the categories. Thus, as a pen, this thing is *not* mere ink or plastic. It is this thing *and* not that thing. It is a separate being on its own, a *this*. It's "thisness" is determined not by what it is made out of, but by the *eidos* into which it has been formed. The coming into and away from the aspect of being a pen is the movement that determines what this item is. Likewise, when we address this item as blue, we presuppose, without calling attention to it, the category of "quality" and the movement of opposites (*enantia*) within this category. Aristotle does not derive these categorial determinations by abstracting from particular *statements* about a thing and recognizing the ways in general in which the mind judges when it makes assertions about things. "The 'categories' lie at the basis of the everyday ways in which we address being, which are developed into assertions ('judgments'); only for this reason can the categories *in turn* be discovered by using the assertion, the *logos*, as a guide" (WBP 323).

Our brief discussion of Aristotle's understanding of the categories is intended to clarify the way in which *technē* produces things. The craftsman has in mind the *eidos*, the aspect or outward appearance, of what is to be brought forth. In producing, for example, a bed, he keeps in mind this "look" and addresses what he finds around him in terms of their readiness to be used and directed toward this end. In doing so, he does not name what he encounters according to what it is in itself (e.g., a tree) but rather reveals ways in which it can be "taken," as hard and as such and such a size, and so on. He selects and appropriates from his environment what is suitable to be shaped into a bed. As a bed, the wood is no longer perceived as a being in itself. It is rather that out of which a bed is made. It belongs to the bed, but does not constitute what a bed is, as such. The tree has a way of being in itself that is essentially different from the way of being of produced things. *Phusis* is not something that a being has in addition to what it is. It is, as Heidegger says, not like a motor inside a being that pushes it forward so that it can be brought forth into its *eidos.* When *technē* handles a natural being for the sake of producing something, it produces something other than the being it found there. It is able to do so because, in advance, it has taken into consideration the categorial ways these beings are and can be. "Had not philosophy at one time expressly thought through the categories of nature which are mechanically and technically exploitable, there would be no such thing as a diesel motor."[30]

Our discussion of *technē* has served to clarify the way in which natural beings have their being. Both natural beings and produced beings have movement as their way of being. But in natural beings, this movement belongs to the being itself. Natural beings emerge from out of themselves and hold themselves in this emergence. On the other hand, produced beings originate and are governed by something outside of themselves—the *technē* of the craftsperson. The ability of human beings to produce beings has been shown to be founded on a prior and presupposed awareness of the being of natural beings. It is though this familiarity with the world in which beings emerge that humans are able to be productive. But the ability to bring beings forth though *phusis* is denied to the human being. Only the being that has this power within itself can do so. The human being's way of bringing forth beings is not natural; it is based on a learned familiarity with what is and can be; it is learned.[31] The human being can employ this knowledge by allowing beings that have this power in themselves to emerge out of themselves, but he can never induce this power. "*Technē* can only cooperate with *phusis;* it can to a certain extent promote healthiness. But it can never replace *phusis* and become itself the *archē* of health" (WBP 327). Nevertheless, *technē* is a mode of revealing, of bringing beings (of allowing beings to come) into unconcealment. It is the *archē,* the cause, of the emerging and that which governs the coming into presence of produced beings.[32] Even here though, *technē's* power is limited. To determine what he can bring forth, the human being must rely on experience—on the beings that it finds already there in the world in which he or she dwells. It is this attention to and concern with what is already there that leads humans to forget the origin of this being-there and their ability to stand in that origin. In order to understand *phusis,* this prior knowledge needs to be awakened in us. Thus, Aristotle says: "For learning proceeds for all in this way— through that which is less knowable by nature to that which is more knowable . . . our task is to start from what is more knowable to oneself and make what is knowable by nature knowable to oneself" (*Met.* 1029 b3).33 Aristotle has prepared us to look toward this horizon for our understanding of beings by showing the difference between *technē* and *phusis.* Our discussion of *technē* has shown that *technē* presupposes an awareness of the being of beings. It presupposes an understanding of *phusis.* This awareness can be taken for granted in *technē* and even not explicitly recognized since *technē* is not concerned with the being of beings but with the way such beings can be used. But when we pose the question of what natural beings are in themselves and the question of what makes *technē* possible, then we open ourselves to a new level of consideration.

The Horizon for Understanding Phusis: *The Meaning of* Ousia

Our understanding of *phusis* has thus far been circling around a gradually deepening complex of issues. *Phusis* is *archē;* it is *aitia;* it is *metabolē.* *Phusis* itself has been left untranslated by Heidegger.34 He suggests now that we might possibly be able to translate it as *Aufgang,* but even this is not much help unless we have followed the steps Aristotle has taken thus far and can read into this word the fullness and determinateness of meaning that Aristotle has given to the word *phusis.* The German word *aufgehen* from which *Aufgang* is derived has itself a certain richness of meaning. It can mean to ascend, to rise (the dough rises), to open up (the plant sprouts), to dawn (the sun dawns on the horizon), to burst forth, to be bound together, to break loose.35 The Germans speak of the *Aufgangspunkt,* the point of appearance, for instance, the point at which the sun appears on the horizon. The preposition *auf* signifies motion to a place as well as rest in a place. *Aufgang* means appearance as well as the way, the steps toward this appearance. The word *Gang,* from *gehen,* means movement, flow, passage. It can also mean the passageway itself through which something moves. Finally it can mean gear in the sense of the gears of a car, that which controls the movement and gets it going. As difficult as it is to translate *phusis* into German, it is equally difficult to find an English work to fully translate *Aufgang. Phusis* is the coming into appearance and thus the appearance itself. We will translate it as upsurgence. However, Heidegger points out that the real difficulty in translating *phusis* lies in the fact that we are involved in a hermeneutical problem. Our translation of *phusis* relies on our interpretation of the meaning of *phusis* in Aristotle. But up to this point, all of Aristotle's attempts to bring to light the meaning and structure of *phusis* have been preliminary. Heidegger calls it a "*Vorspiel.*" For we have not yet clarified the horizon in which the entire interpretation moves. In the next passage, Aristotle names this horizon *ousia.*

Phusis, therefore, is what has been said. And everything that contains within itself an emerging and governing (*archē*) which is constituted in this way 'has' *phusis.* And each of these beings *is* (has being) in the manner of beingness (*ousia*). That is to say, *phusis* is a lying-forth from out of itself (*hupokeimenon*) of this sort and is in each being which is lying-forth. However, each of these beings, as well as everything which belongs to it in and of itself *is* in accordance with *phusis.* For example, it belongs to fire to be borne upward. That is to say, this (being borne upward) is certainly not *phusis,* nor does it contain *phusis,* but rather it is from out of *phusis* and in accordance with *phusis.* Thus what *phusis* is is now determined as well as what is meant by 'from out of *phusis*' and in accordance with *phusis.* (*Physics* 192 b32–193 a2; WBP 329)

This passage introduces the central thought of Aristotle's philosophy: *ousia.* Heidegger first translates it as *Seiendheit,* beingness, and seeks to avoid the more familiar translations—"substance" and "essence." It is clear that these traditional translations, and the layers of Aristotelian interpretation that surround them, are more problematic than helpful in our attempt to understand what has been happening up to this point. *Ousia* is the way of being of natural beings that are constituted by movement. This passage suggests that there are other ways of being besides *ousia* and indeed that other beings besides natural beings may have *ousia* as their way of being. *Ousia* is the horizon in which we are to further grasp how it is that *kinēsis* constitutes natural beings. Thus, *kinēsis* is to be understood in terms of *ousia.* Since the traditional interpretation of *ousia* as substance or essence excludes movement from consideration, it misses its meaning completely.[36] We will have to try to understand what Aristotle meant here from Aristotle himself.

Heidegger points out that Aristotle was the first to decide to take the word *ousia* out of its everyday context and assign a specific philosophical meaning to it, a meaning that nevertheless has its roots in the ordinary usage of the work. Liddell and Scott point out, as does Heidegger, that the word is first used as a term for one's possessions, one's property (WBP 330).[37] Plato plays with this meaning in the *Republic* when Socrates accuses Cephalus of being defined by his external wealth and belongings.[38] In traditional ontology what a being has (its accidents and properties) is distinguished from what a being is (*ousia*). Thus, what a being has can change while what a being is remains permanent throughout these changes. This split between existence and essence is denied in the original meaning of *ousia*. "The Latin translation of *ousia* as *essentia* (since Boethius) doesn't get at the Greek *ousia;* this word is richer, it also means *existentia*."[39] *Ousia* is a participial form of *einai*—to be. Thus "beingness" is a literal translation. How are we to understand beingness in terms of one's home and belongings and thus allow Aristotle's philosophical insight into the meaning of being to emerge from this original sense? Heidegger looks to the German *An-wesen* for guidance. It too originally means property and homestead and is a form of the German word for being:[40]

In Aristotle's time, *ousia* is used both in this sense (of property) *and* in the meaning of the fundamental term of philosophy. Something is present. It stands in itself and thus manifests itself. It is. For the Greeks, "being" basically meant this being-present (*Anwesenheit*). But Greek philosophy never returned to this ground of being and to what it conceals. It remained on the surface of the presencing itself (*des Anwesenden selbst*) and sought to observe them in their available determinations.[41]

Still Heidegger maintains that even though the mystery of presencing that was concealed in the manifestation of beings was never directly addressed by the Greeks, this presencing that Aristotle names *ousia* was nevertheless experienced by them, and indeed they dwelled in this experience:

Wherever the thinking of the Greeks gives heed to the presencing of what is present, the traits (*Züge*) of presence which we mentioned find expression: unconcealedness, the rising from unconcealedness, the coming and going away, the duration, the gathering, the radiance, the rest, the hidden suddenness of possible absenting. These are the traits of presencing in whose terms the Greeks thought of what is present. But they never *gave* thought to the traits themselves, for presencing did *not* become problematical or questionable to them as the presencing of *what* is present. Why not? Because the only thing for which *they* asked, and perhaps had to ask, responded and replied, that is, answered to their questioning in these traits of presencing which we mentioned.[42]

When *ousia* becomes translated as "actuality" by the Romans, the last traces of this "drawing power" of *ousia* become hidden. The actuality of beings gains prominence as the primary way of understanding being and the problem of being gets interpreted on the basis of beings. The origin is forgotten. In attempting to understand the Greek vision of being and beings, we are attempting to go beyond the givenness and availability of beings and to look into the horizon that gives rise to the advent of beings. Aristotle names this horizon *ousia*. "And indeed the question which was raised of old and is raised now and always, and is always the subject of doubt, namely what being is, is just the question, what is *ousia*" (*Met.* 1028 b3–5). The question of what *ousia* is and how *ousia* constitutes the being of beings becomes the focus of Aristotle's *Physics* and *Metaphysics*. Aristotle is struggling to bring to light what always already lies in advance of our knowledge of beings, and that therefore cannot be derived from this knowledge. In the history of metaphysics, this way of approaching the question of being was not only overlooked, but forgotten. The granting of beings and the concealment of this granting were taken for granted.

Because something ontic is made to underlie the ontological, the expression *substantia* functions sometimes in an ontolsoftware, sometimes in an ontic meaning, but mostly in a meaning which shifts about in a hazy mixture of the two. But behind this slight difference of meaning lies hidden a failure to master the fundamental problem of being.[43]

The transition from the understanding of being as *phusis* (e.g., in Heraclitus) to the understanding of *phusis* as *ousia* in Aristotle marks the end of Greek philosophy. The struggle is itself a great struggle and thus a great and originary intellectual achievement for Aristotle. Aristotle thereby remains within the greatness of Greek philosophy. Metaphysics rests in the security of his grasp. History begins. To properly understand the meaning of *ousia* we have to return this concept to its source in the Greek struggle to give witness to being.[44] We must stand within the difference that lets beings be. This difference, though hidden, still reigns within the tradition. The traces of this granting that first opened up beings, however, have become obfuscated in the history of that tradition. Heidegger's rereading of Aristotle reopens and releases the power of Aristotle's thinking: "The crucial and decisive guiding principle of Aristotle's interpretation of *phusis* is: *phusis* has to be conceived as *ousia*, as a way and mode of presencing" (WBP 331).

Aristotle tells us in that passage how we are to understand *phusis* in terms of *ousia*: "*phusis* is a lying-forth from out of itself (*hupokeimenon*)." *Phusis* constitutes the lying-forth of beings. The beings themselves are not *phusis*. Rather they are 'from out of' *phusis* and 'in accordance with' *phusis*. Natural beings "have" *phusis* as their way of beingness.

Phusis is not itself a being but that which allows beings to be. Aristotle stresses often that this *archē* is not separate, outside of, or existing independently of beings. We have already been cautioned against conceiving of *phusis* in terms of an external or internal motor that pushes beings into being. Phusis is rather the *way* in which beings are. It is neither a being outside of and in control of being; nor is it the beings themselves. It is the presencing of beings. This presencing will be the horizon for the rest of Aristotle's discussion of *phusis*. Aristotle began with a preontological awareness (through *epagōgē*) that *kinēsis* is the way of being of natural beings. Guided by a phenomenological analysis of natural beings and our everyday understanding of beings through *technē*, we have reached the central meaning of being—*ousia*. This meaning now throws light on what has gone before. A repetition of the investigation is required to show that *ousia* is the unifying meaning of being of which our understanding of the structure of beings depends.

It is the fact that *ousia* is the meaning of being that gives rise to the many ways in which being is spoken about. These many ways of being originate out of a sameness. "So, too, there are many senses in which a thing is said to be, but all refer to one . . . if, then, this is *ousia*, it will be with regard to *ousia* that the philosopher must grasp the *archē* and *aitia*" (*Met.* 1003 b5; b18–19). We know from Book I of the *Physics* that the *archē* and *aitia* must be more than one. Indeed to account for the being of beings, Aristotle posits a twofoldedness—beings are to be understood in terms of contraries. These contraries have their unity in *ousia*—the horizon for the understanding of beings—the presencing of beings and the structure or way in which beings are present. "And nearly all thinkers agree that being and *ousia* are composed of contraries" (*Met.* 1004 b30). Aristotle's understanding of contraries cannot be mistaken as a polarization of opposites that must be taken in isolation from each other. Contraries in Aristotle's way of thinking are that which arises out of the essential resistance, the *polemos* that Heraclitus names as what gives rise to being. As Heidegger states it:

This struggle, as Heraclitus first thought it, first lets being (*das Wesende*) separate into contraries; it first lets position and standing and rank become present. Cleavages, intervals, distances, and joints open up in such separation. In the confrontation world comes to be. Conflict does not divide, much less destroy unity. It constitutes unity, it is a binding-together (*logos*). Polemos and logos are the same.[45]

Conflict constitutes unity—the unity of contraries. Thus, these dichotomies cannot be resolved in a higher order. They do arise out of a sameness, but this sameness is precisely what constitutes their difference.

In the previous passage of Aristotle's, we find a first attempt to say how this sameness (*ousia*) governs the beings to which it gives rise. *Phusis* as *ousia* is a kind of lying-forth (*vorliegen/hupokeimenon*) and "in" beings that lie-forth and are present in this way. *Ousia* is understood as that which constitutes the being-there of beings. Beings are present. Their thereness is signaled out from the wider original meaning of *ousia* as that which one owns. *Ousia* is what makes possible that humans can claim properties and possession as their own. It gives rise to the availability of beings. Heidegger translated *hupokeimenon* as *Vorliegen*, the lying-present of itself. In Latin this Greek word was translated as *subjectum,* that which lies under. Although literally correct, the Latin interpretation errs in that it has lost sight of the meaning of *ousia* as presencing. It is through *ousia* that the meaning of *hupokeimenon* is to be understood. Aristotle says that *ousia* is *to ti ēn einai,* that which is always already there (*Met.* 1007 a22); in contrast, *sumbebēkos* is that which just happens to be together with that which is and is not itself a lying-forth on its own. *Hupokeimenon* names the givenness, the thereness, of what has come forth.

Heidegger points to a participial problem in translating *hupokeimenon,* which in Greek can mean both the lying-present itself and something that lies present. A similar ambiguity exists in Greek with the participle *on,* which can mean being or a being. He reminds us that this confusion is not accidental, but points to "the unusually rich and manifold forms of the participle in the Greek language—the truly philosophical language" (WBP 331). In this ambiguity is concealed the ontological difference that was forgotten by metaphysics. It is this *difference* that governs Aristotle's meaning of *hupokeimenon* and constitutes the horizon for his understanding of the relation of being and beings. Aristotle considers the ability to stand in this difference to be what distinguishes the philosopher from the sophist—

That is why we say Anaxaoras, Thales and people like them have philosophic but not practical wisdom, when we see them ignorant of what is to their own advantage; and why we say they know things that are remarkable, admirable, difficult and divine, but useless; because it is not human goods that they seek.[46]

To stand within this difference is to be able to distinguish the divine from the human (*Met.* 983 a5ff). Aristotle says that such a stance is beyond the reach of proof. The correctness of one's vision is not subject to demonstration. It is a matter of seeing. In terms of Plato's allegory, one cannot reach knowledge of what is by examining the shadows. It is a question of being in advance turned in the right direction. If such vision is lost and the horizon of one's interpretation is forgotten, it cannot be regained by manipulating the shadows and extracting opinions on the basis of one's observations. These observations themselves depend on the perception of being (*phusis*) that one is trying to regain. In the following passage, Aristotle makes clear how important the understanding of this difference is for the philosophical study of *phusis*.

But it would be ridiculous to try to prove *that phusis is*. For this (being as *phusis*) comes to light of itself since /not that/ many beings of this kind are present among beings. A demonstration of what comes to light by itself and from out of itself— and especially a proof which proceeds by going through those things which cannot grant the appearance—this is the mark of a man who is unable to distinguish (*krinein*) that which is given by itself to all knowledge from that which is not. But that this (such an inability to differentiate) can happen is not beyond the realm of possibility. That is, a man born blind could indeed try though a series of reflections to get some knowledge of colors. In this case, such people will inevitably come up with assertions about the nominal meanings of the names for colors; however, they thereby perceive (*noein*) nothing at all of the colors themselves. (*Physics* 193 a3–9; WBP 332)

We can conclude from this passage that Aristotle would not have held much hope for the meaningful success of a kind of linguistic analysis that did not examine its own foundations. One also wonders how the attempt to derive the "categories" from *assertions* about things could have been attributed to Aristotle in the light of such remarks. We are now at a transitional point where the limits of a certain kind of *logos*—human language and demonstration—are encountered. The *Physics* is not simply an attempt to draw out all of the implications and consequences of the way in which we can speak of natural beings. Nor is it merely trying to determine how we can speak correctly about natural beings. The necessary character of human *logos* that guarantees its "correctness" is not due to the address but what is addressed. The way beings show themselves determines the character of our language. Therefore, our language cannot determine the way things show themselves. The predicament of this circle cannot be resolved by appeals to modes of logic or by defining our terms more precisely.

The security of demonstration is of no avail. The solution is simpler and more fundamental. It cannot be proven afterwards that being is because being is already in advance granted whenever we address beings in a certain way. But this granting is not simply something given that humans can simply see. Seeing is not only having a correct view but it is a *krinein*. "Differentiating between what shows itself in advance and what does not show itself of itself is a *krinein* in the genuine Greek sense, a separating of what is *higher* in rank from what is lower" (WBP 334). There is a certain irony in the attempt to prove that *phusis* is. Clearly, proof involves demonstration about beings. Thus, it attempts to reduce being to a being that can be available and analyzed. But being is not available in this way. The method of science must be abandoned here. "We want to participate in the preparation of a decision; the decision: is science the measure of knowledge, or is there a knowledge in which the ground and limit of science, and thus its genuine effectiveness, are determined."[47] The human being is the site where the relation of being and beings in their sameness and difference is decided and shown. This is not an arbitrary decision but a de-cision that is the privilege of the human being because he stands in the midst of beings and stands in relation to being.

The recognition that ultimate questions are not subject to proof surfaces again the question of the method that philosophy employs to engage at the level of enquiry that is demanded of it. All other modes of enquiry presuppose that the groundwork in which they operate has already been established for them. This way of proceeding by taking for granted this foundation is acceptable in science but not in philosophy. The whole attempt at such proof is a failure to recognize the difference between an investigation of beings and the question of being. Heidegger says this failure (*Irren*), the forgetting of this difference, governs the history of metaphysics.[48] That such a failure cannot be attributed to Aristotle distinguishes this treatise on the *Physics* from all other Physics which have emerged since then. What makes such an attempt at proof ridiculous is not the lack of results and information that such procedures can achieve—for clearly Aristotle, above all, believed in the capacity of demonstration to acquire genuine knowledge. The attempt is laughable because the misunderstanding of the scope of demonstration forgets its own limitations and attempts to know afterwards what it must already know in advance. "Some indeed demand that even this shall be demonstrated, but they do so through want of education; for not to know of what things one should demand demonstration, and of what one should not, argues want of education" (*Met.* 1006 a 5ff). Aristotle considers the failure to see the difference between these two ways of questioning, and to separate the higher from the lower, to be the main reason for the difficulties of his predecessors.[49] It was clearly his intention to win this distinction in his discussion of the difference between *phusis* and *technē*. The level on which we have to proceed to advance further in our enquiry about *phusis* is inaccessible to *technē* and demands a knowledge that *technē* presupposes, but a kind of knowledge that is essentially different from *technē*. "That which everyone must know who knows anything, he must already have when he comes to a special study. Evidently then such an *archē* is the most certain of all" (*Met.* 1005 b17ff).

When proof is set up as the only criterion for knowledge, then this kind of knowing and this level of questioning get passed by. Being then is said to be incomprehensible to humans, beyond the reach of human beings. The meaning of being becomes a matter of faith.

We encounter beings as actualities in a calculative business-like way, but also sci-entifically and by way of philosophy, with explanations and proofs. Even the as-surance that something is inexplicable belongs to these explanations and proofs. With such statements we believe that we confront the mystery.[50]

When being is conceived in such ways, then philosophy gives up its essen-tial task: "That which already stands in view is seen with the greatest diffi-culty, is very seldom grasped and almost always falsified into a mere ad-dendum, and therefore simply overlooked" (WBP 333).

Another confusion that has arisen because philosophy has allowed proof to become its methodological standard is the acceptance of such no-tions as the indefinability of being. The meaning of definition and its rela-tion to demonstration in Book Z of the *Metaphysics* needs to be studied. If definitions have to be grounded in demonstrations under the auspices of logic, and yet demonstration presupposes definition, then our only appeal is to a starting point that is itself indefinable. But for Aristotle any defini-tion of being is unfounded, not because being is indefinable, but because being and definition are the same. Limit (*peras*) and definition (*horismos*) belong to the being of beings.

At the outset, *epagōgē* was named as "the way to what is already seen but not yet understood, much less conceptualized. This is what accom-plishes the fore-sight and looking beyond which sees what we ourselves are not and could never be" (WBP 334). Aristotle has now reached the point at which the understanding of what has been witnessed in *epagōgē* becomes an issue. His task is to win this understanding of *ousia*. Understanding *dia-noia* is not merely the seeing of being, but the ability to interpret beings in the light of this view. *Dianoia* is this capacity that allows human beings to stand out in relation to beings and to know their being. Understanding is the subject matter of Book VI of Aristotle's *Nichomachean Ethics.* "In discussing the excellence of the soul, we said some are of character and others of understanding . . . in what follows we will deal with excellence in understanding."[51] In the rest of the chapter, *dianoia* is not explicitly analyzed. Rather, *nous, technē, epistēmē,* and so on are considered. This indicates that the interrelation of these various ways of knowing is constituted by *dianoia.* In the part of the soul that has this "*logos,*" Aristotle distinguishes between two paths (*tropos*) that *logos* follows. "On the one path we see beings whose *archē* is not able to be in another [we have seen this to be the characteristic of natural beings]; on the other path we see what is able to be governed by another [we have seen this to be the path of *technē*]."[52] *Dianoia* is the relationship between these two paths.

In the *Grundprobleme der Phänomenologie,* Heigegger writes:

> No understanding of being is possible which is not rooted in a comportment to beings. Understanding of being and comportment to beings do not merely fall accidentally together. Rather they unfold themselves as always already lying hidden in the existence of Dasein, as required by the ecstatic-horizonal constitution of temporality and as made possible by it in its belonging-together.[53]

In *Sein und Zeit,* Heidegger chooses the Greek word *ekstasis* to convey what he means by this capacity of man to achieve the level of reflection and method of inquiry that is required to pursue the question of being outside of the scope of proof and demonstration. At first glance, this seems inconsistent with Aristotle's use of the word. Aristotle uses the word *ekstasis* in the sense of displacement, that which does not hold itself in its place and thus changes.[54] It is thus the opposite of *stasis,* a placing of a being in its limits. The human being, *Da-sein,* must then somehow be *there* in its place in a way that is different than the *stasis* of natural beings. Dasein stands out from (*existere*) its place and reaches beyond it. Heidegger sees this as what characterizes the being-there of Dasein. In Greek, *ekstatikos* means inclined to depart from, an inclination that often borders on madness.[55] The being of Dasein is a mode of understanding (*dianoia*). Understanding is a directing itself toward and holding what it grasps, but also a moving away from the immediacy of that grasping toward the being of what is being understood. "Thus the Dasein of historical man clears the way for the opening of being in beings. He is a falling-between, the sudden event in which the boundless overpowering of the power of being emerges and arrives in a work as history."[56]

Aristotle's discussion of the attempt to prove that *phusis* is further clarifies the problem of the categories. To attempt to draw out an idea of being from our observation of the categorial ways in which beings are determined is to behave like the blind man who tries to say what colors are by analyzing how they are named. Before we can understand the meaning of these categorial determinations, we must already have silently addressed beings as to what they are. We must already have *ousia* in view. The tendency to behave like the blind man in this regard is rooted in the apparent obviousness of these matters in our everyday lives. "And our relation to being is difficult to keep in view because it seems to be made easy for us by our familiar comportment to beings, so easy in fact that it seems like it could be supplanted *by* this relation and seems like it consists in nothing other than this relation" (WBP 335). In this case, the difference between the way of *phusis* and the way of *technē* is forgotten and natural beings get interpreted on the basis of our technical relations to beings. In order to regain the proper level of inquiry for the question of *phusis,* Aristotle takes this ordinary way of relating to beings and returns it to its source. Only through a repetition of the question of *phusis* and *technē* on the basis of *ousia* as the horizon for understanding the being of beings can Aristotle's work proceed with the proper foundation. Aristotle accomplished this task in his confrontation with Antiphon, and we will take up the study of this achievement in the next chapter.

Chapter Three

THE DESTRUCTURING OF THE TRADITION

Aristotle's Confrontation with Antiphon

Aristotle says:

For those who wish to get clear of difficulties, it is advantageous to discuss the difficulties well; for the subsequent free play of thought implies the solution of the previous difficulties, and it is not possible to untie a knot which one does not know. (*Met.* 995 a26–30)

Aristotle's confrontation with Antiphon in *Physics* B1 raises the central questions that are involved in the meaning of *phusis*. It is only with an awareness of these difficulties that the breadth of Aristotle's venture becomes evident. What is at stake are the method and task of Aristotle's project. This task is twofold. On the one hand, *phusis* has to be understood ontologically, that is, in terms of *ousia*. This understanding of *phusis* is the originary grasp that permits us to see beings in their being. On the other hand, this understanding of beings in their very being is articulated and interpreted in such a way that *phusis* is taken as the *archē*, the source and originating principle, of natural beings. Understanding and interpreting are two ways in which human beings express their way of being. These two ways cannot be split apart but must be understood in their togetherness. Human beings always already find themselves in an interpretation of beings, which presupposes that they have in advance an understanding of being. When Aristotle turns his attention to the opinion of his predecessors, he is bringing the interpretation of beings in Greek thought back to the understanding of being from which it emerged. Only such a method can avoid the easier road that forgets the origin and attempts to draw out of the interpretation itself, whether through criticism or homage, the basis for its understanding of being. This kind of approach could never achieve the kind of truth that is appropriate to the human being's relationship to natural beings because it has no access to what is essential. Aristotle compares such an approach to the attempts of the blind man to say something about colors. In his philosophical approach to the study of what is natural, Aristotle remains true to his method and maintains himself within the "twofold" of being and beings while thinking their sameness.

The following passage from Aristotle mentions Antiphon's interpretation of *phusis* that in one way appears to conform with his own, and in another way does not. Both Aristotle and Antiphon understand *phusis* as *ousia*. According to Heidegger, Aristotle, like his predecessors, understands and interprets *ousia* as enduring presencing. For Aristotle, all beings that are truly beings have *ousia*, enduring presencing, as their way of being. Inasmuch as Antiphon's interpretation of *phusis* is in conformity with Aristotle's, he agrees that natural beings *are* to the extent that they endure and sustain themselves in presence. Yet, the problematic but undeniable character of natural beings, according to Aristotle, is that this enduring presence is nevertheless kinetic, that is, movement belongs to their very nature as beings. Since Antiphon's interpretation cannot reconcile this kinetic nature with the requirement that being must endure, he denies movement as the beingness of *phusis*, and in this regard disagrees with Aristotle. Antiphon, an Eleatic philosopher, denies the possibility of movement as belonging to the being of beings.[1] Aristotle faces the central question posed by Antiphon's views: movement implies nonbeing. But how can nonbeing be? In showing how nonbeing (change) is, Aristotle both accepts and refutes Antiphon's doctrine. That is, his refutation achieves for Antiphon what Antiphon was looking for, but had fallen away from—the vision of the being of natural, changing beings as enduring presence. Thus, Aristotle says regarding his opponent Antiphon at *Physics* 193 a 9–28 (Heidegger's translation):

But for some (thinkers), *phusis* and therefore also the beingness of natural beings appears to be what first of all lies forth in the individual and lacks all composition (*rhuthmos*). According to this opinion, the *phusis* of the bedstead is the wood, that of the statue the bronze. Antiphon explains this in the following way: If one were to bury a bedstead in the ground and it were to decay to the extent that a sprout comes up, then what would be generated (out of this) would not be a bedstead but wood. Consequently, what has been carried through in a regulated and knowledgeable way (the forming of the bedstead in the wood), is certainly something present, but it is present only insofar as it shows up in addition (*sumbebēkos*); beingness, however, lies in that which always stays the same through it all (the *phusis*), holding itself together no matter what it "goes through." Of course, if any one of these, for example, wood or bronze, should itself already have gone through this in relation to still another, that is, if it was brought into a composition—as, for example, bronze and gold in relation to water, or bones and wood in relation to earth, and similarly for whatever else among all other beings—then it is precisely these (water, earth) which *are* the *phusis* and therefore also the beingness of the others (as beings). For this reason, some say that *phusis,* and thus the being of beings as a whole, is fire while others say it is earth; some say it is air while others say it is water; and some say it is one of these, others say it is all of these. For, whatever each of them took in advance as being present in this way, whether it is simple or manifold, he extends even as far as beingness itself, whereas he takes all the rest to be modifications and dispositions of true being, and as the way in which the being is set forth (and thus entangled in relations). And so it is for this reason that each of these (whichever constitute the *phusis*) is remaining in itself the same (*aidion*). (That is, a change by which they might go out of themselves does *not* in any way belong to them.) However, the others are coming into being and going out of being "endlessly"). (WBP 335, 337–338)

Elemental Being (*Stoicheia*): Aristotle's Conception of Ontological Difference

In this passage, we are given a certain interpretation of *phusis* by Antiphon. This interpretation takes over the Greek notion of *ousia* as enduring presencing. But it attempts to understand *ousia* in terms of the beings that it encounters, and therefore ultimately as itself a being. Aristotle says the elements are themselves beings and in fact not atomic, indivisible units as Democritus contended. It has been the goal of science throughout the centuries to reduce beings to some basic unit or units. Aristotle recognizes here a certain truth in that the being of beings is a kind of unity, but he says that the nature of unity is misunderstood. Aristotle contends the "units" uncovered in such approaches are themselves composed (hot and cold, etc.) (*Met.* 986 b35). In fact, even from a materialist viewpoint, beings cannot be understood in terms of a unit but must be explained in terms of contraries. Otherwise, *kinēsis* would be impossible. But *kinēsis* is precisely what the physicist and materialist must take as given and attempt to understand (*Physics* 185 a12f). Antiphon thinks *phusis* in terms of *stoicheia*—fire, water, earth, air—the basic elements that remain throughout change, which endure change while remaining essentially unchanged. In Book I of the *Physics,* as well as Book I of the *Metaphysics,* Aristotle discusses many of his predecessors in terms of precisely this way of understanding the *ousia* of *phusis.* He acknowledges that each of these interpretations is seeking and has always sought the same, to understand

the being of natural beings. The primary reason he points to in their failure to succeed is that they did not take *motion* into account in terms of
being (*Met.* 985 b18f).

Antiphon explains the enduring presencing of being in terms of a oneness (earth or fire, etc.). All change is only an incidental result of generation out of this oneness and therefore ultimately reducible to it. Thus, all
changes are mere appearance and nonbeing (*mē on*) so that *genesis* is responsible for semblance, but not for being. "According to this understanding of the essence of being, all things—whether natural or made—
are never truly being, and yet they are not nothing. Hence they are
non-being, not fully sufficing for beingness" (WBP 337). Antiphon is unable to think the difference between being and beings except in terms of
negation. Thus, beings are nonbeing, the negation of being as permanence. Because earth, for example, endures and is permanent, it is true
being *(ousia)*. But anything that changes has no being of its own. It only
appears to be to the one who is deceived. Antiphon makes no distinction
between *genesis,* the kind of movement that is essential in natural beings,
and other kinds of movement such as locomotion and alteration. As we
will see, this distinction is crucial to Aristotle's refutation of Antiphon.
This meaning of being as permanence that Antiphon insists on has dominated in the history of philosophy.[2] Ultimately it shifts the focus of the
meaning of *ousia* to permanence and discards the primary meaning of
ousia as presencing. Being becomes that which does not appear as itself
but only in semblance. It is therefore inaccessible and something other
than beings.[3] Thus, true being must be abstracted from beings by remov-
ing the way a being shows itself to us—its *rhuthmos.*

Rhuthmos—the structure and composition of beings—changes. That
out of which it is *composed* does not. The *rhuthmos* is only sometimes
there; the element is always there. The stoicheion, then, is essential being
for Antiphon; *rhuthmos* is added on—*sumbebēkos.* Here we see that Antiphon is proposing the reverse of what Aristotle holds to be true. Aristotle
maintains that the elements are the primary way in which *phusis* has been
understood by his predecessors. In contrast, for him the elements are *sumbebēkos.* They belong to natural beings, but are not the being of these beings (*Met.* 1024 b15–33). For Aristotle, the being of beings is understood as
presencing. When a being shows itself as it is, it appears in its being. Aristotle does not deny the role that the elements play, but interprets the *stoicheia* in terms of *ousia.* Originally, the Greek word *stoicheion* meant the
shadow cast by the sundial.[4] It was the dissembling appearance whose

being is dependent on the sundial and the sun. Isolated and interpreted outside of such a context, the privative character of its being is concealed from us. The very problem that Antiphon hoped to resolve by appealing to the elemental beings—namely, this lack and incompleteness that characterizes natural beings—is here once again made problematic by Aristotle at the very center of Antiphon's philosophy. This privative character can be ignored, and it may even be useful to do so, but then the direction of interpretation is other than that required for an understanding of *phusis*. Such procedures are inherently barred from access to truth, as Aristotle says, for example, about practical knowledge: "The telos of theoretical knowledge is *alētheia,* of practical knowledge, *ergon*. For even if practical knowledge considers the how, it studies not the eternal (*aei*), but the *sumbebēkos* (along with) and the now" (*Met.* 993 b20-22). The *ergon* is a being, and thus has being. Our ability to direct ourselves toward the *ergon,* the product, presupposes a relation to *alētheia,* the being of what is. It is for this reason that Heidegger says that all essential science determines in advance the project that guides it.[5] But because the primary direction of science is toward beings, the scientist can forget this originary access and thus understand beings as mere appearance. When this happens, beings are taken as objects that are just there, which can be taken apart and examined. In doing so, the elements are discovered. The being can then be put back together into a whole that is composed of analyzable parts and the object can then be considered to be known in all details. Such a procedure can be informative, but not about what is essential. According to Aristotle, the whole is not just the sum of its parts; nor is the whole (*to holon*) constituted out of its parts. "But the whole is considered to be prior; for in *logos* the parts are named from the whole; and the whole is prior in virtue of its ability to exist independently" (*Met.* 1034 b31f).

In order to successfully address the issues that Antiphon is raising, we need to pay particular heed to what he takes to be the meaning of being. The meaning of being that he accepts in advance without questioning and that he takes over from the Greek experience and that guides his interpretation is *constancy*. Being is that which remains through change. The elemental is being because it endures. *Rhuthmos,* now identified as the condition (*pathē*), the disposition (*hexis*), and arrangement (*diathēsis*) into which these elements are placed (*Physics* 193 a25), is held by Antiphon to be nonbeing. But must not Aristotle also exclude nonbeing from beingness, and, as a Greek philosopher, only address himself to what is essential?

Despite the affinity of his thought to certain aspects of Democritean atomism, Antiphon is of the Eleatic school, a follower of Parmenides. Heidegger calls attention here and in his treatment of Aristotle's interpretation of the Megarians [see chapter four] to the fact that, for Aristotle, Eleaticism and Atomism at a fundamental level turn out to be the same. Parmenides maintained that *kinēsis* was illusion and that what *is* is an unchanging unit.[6] To change is to become what is not. Change and being are mutually exclusive. For Parmenides, it was *nous* that could see truth by separating being from nonbeing. Still, according to Aristotle, the Eleatics were unable to differentiate and think in its togetherness being and beings, and this was the source of Antiphon's error. Being comes to be understood as an elemental being out of which all other beings are composed. The original difference between being and beings, Parmenides' essential thought, gets lost in Antiphon's interpretation as well as in that of Democritus and the Materialists. "Leucippus and his associate Democritus say that the full and the empty are the elements, calling the one being and the other non-being" (*Met.* 985 b4–6). Heidegger suggests that "we can see here the origin of 'materialism' as a metaphysical position in the historical presentation of being (*seyns-geschichtlich*)" (WBP 338). For Antiphon as well as Democritus, being is the lasting and indivisible, and this is said to be the elementary matter rather than the form.[7] For the Platonists, being also means that which endures indivisibly, but this is the *eidos*.[8] Many beings share in the same "idea." What makes them different from the form and from each other, according to Aristotle's interpretation of Plato, is the *hulē*, the elementary matter (*Met.* 988 a1–5). In both cases, the individual natural being is relegated to the shadowy world of illusion. Aristotle, in contrast, does not see the natural being as a figure derived by virtue of its participation in or imitation of a being outside of it, but sees it *as* a being. Heidegger says of Aristotle:

He thinks for the first time the individual being as the *actual (Jeweilige)*, and thinks its lasting (*Weile*) as the distinctive manner of presencing, of the presencing of *eidos* itself in the most extreme present of the indivisible, that is, no longer derived, appearance (*atomon eidos*).[9]

Heidegger interprets the indivisible in Aristotle to mean "no longer derived." For Antiphon, it was the elements that are untouched by division; for Plato, it is the *eidos*. For Aristotle it is the *todē ti*, the individual being, which is present as a whole and holds itself there as such. In every case, being is understood as *aidion*—the everlasting (*Je-weilige*). In H. Paul's

Deutsches Wörterbuch, it is stated that the adverb *je* comes from the word *ewig* (forever) in German.[10] *Weilig* is from *weilen* (to dwell on or linger) and *Weile,* which originally has the temporal sense of "to rest for a time." *Jeweilig* has the meaning of "at this time" as in the sentence: "the person in charge *at the time.*" The adverb *jeweils* means "at any given time" or "from time to time." Heidegger is suggesting that Aristotle's notion of *ousia* has the temporal meaning of presencing, and the individual being (the *todē ti*) is that which holds itself there (*weilen*) for the time being and thus is. *Je-weilige* (ever-lasting) is meant in this sense, as is, according to Heidegger, the Greek word *aidion.* For Antiphon, division presupposed a limit that cannot be divided. He identifies this limit as a body—an element. But the body, Aristotle shows, is not a limit but that which is limited (*Met.* 1002 a4ff). In so doing, Aristotle brings the understanding of *peras,* limit, back to its proper foundation as the way of being of beings.

Aristotle does not look away from beings as they show themselves, in order to find, above or below them, the lasting presencing of *ousia.* Rather he seeks to understand how a being that is is what it is. For Antiphon the "that it is" and "what it is" are not the same. "What it is" is the elementary *hulē.* In his view, the fact that the "matter" is formed into this particular being is accidental, as is evidenced by the changes it endlessly endures. For the Platonists, on the other hand, "what it is" is the *eidos.* The particular being participates in and thus imitates, is an image of, this outward appearance. Its inability to hold itself in that *idea* is the result of its nonbeing. By understanding *ousia* as *todē ti,* Aristotle thinks the unity of essence and existence while thinking the difference between being and beings. For this reason, Heidegger says: "Aristotle is more truly Greek in his thinking than Plato, that is, more in keeping with the primordially decided essence (*Wesen*) of being."[11] By naming *ousia* as the enduring presencing of the individual and seeing that only here is truly found the *aidion* that the Greeks understood to be the essence of being, Aristotle refutes Antiphon's doctrine of the elements while rescuing the meaning of being that underlay Antiphon's philosophy.

While explicating the positive sense in which Aristotle is an advance over Antiphon in that he is better able to understand the ontological difference, and better able to interpret the meaning of being without reducing it to a being, Heidegger also acknowledges the limitation of Aristotle's comprehension of the question. "Now the Greeks understand *ousia* as enduring presencing. They give no reason for this interpretation of being any moe than they question the ground of its truth" (WBP 336). What Heidegger is implying here, and what he makes explicit again in his discussion of Aristotle's confrontation with the Megarians in *Metaphysics* Θ3, as we will see in the next chapter, is that Aristotle's advance in thinking enduring presencing (*ousia*) in connection with an ontological sense of *kinēsis* also covers over a failure to question the origin of the way in which this meaning of being is given to the Greeks. This is why he turns at the end of this essay to a discussion of Heraclitus and Fragment 123: "*Phusis* loves to hide itself" (WBP 370). In Heidegger's view, Aristotle corrects the tendency in Antiphon's thinking to think being in terms of beings. For Antiphon as well as Aristotle, the elementals, earth, fire, and the like, are themselves beings. For Aristotle, these atomic units are themselves bodily beings, and therefore they cannot be the basis for an account of the ground of being. But one might wonder, beyond the context of an interpretation of Aristotle, and the unquestioned acceptance of the meaning of being as enduring presencing, what account of elemental being might be possible.

The Meaning of Eternal (*Aidion*) and Its Relation to Limit (*Peras*)

We need then to discuss further two important concepts that have emerged here for consideration in these passages: what is meant by the concept "eternal," *aidion*, in Aristotle's thought, and what is the meaning of non-being, understood now by Aristotle as *sumbebēkos*, the accidental—that which is not "eternal." Both of these concepts seem to involve the key question that has guided our study of *phusis* so far: what is the meaning of *kinēsis* as the way of *ousia* of natural beings? Are motion and enduring presencing mutually exclusive? Are they not mutually exclusive but related as nonbeing to being or as mere appearance to "eternal" unconcealment? The true physicist, according to Aristotle, must be able to think *kinēsis* in terms of *ousia*, and that also means to think *ousia* in terms of *kinēsis*. The two cannot be mutually exclusive, as our consideration of *phusis* has shown. But it required the greatest philosophical exertion for Aristotle to show how we are to think their togetherness.[12]

Aidion is often translated as the eternal or eternity—*aeternitas*. But the notion of the eternal as opposed to the temporal is a later development of Christian thinking. The literal meaning of the Latin *aeternitas* is not "a-temporal," but "to return always," and in this way to be everlasting. The Greek word *aidion* comes from *aei* and *dios*. *Dios* is a word used by Homer to mean the noblest.[13] Thus, it is the word for Zeus, as well as a

[marginal note, left side, top: *Explaining elementals or a god being*]

[marginal note, left side, bottom: *eternity is not atemporal*] word for men and women of excellence and of noble nations. It is also used to depict the powers of nature. It means that which is divine-like. *Aei* means throughout time. *Aidion* means that which holds itself through time in the presence of the divine and thus *is*. The *aei* is the enduring of a being that maintains itself in its "isness." Thus, Heidegger says: "And *aei* means not only 'without stopping' and 'continuously,' but primarily that which is presently there (*das Jeweilige*)—he who is ruling at the time (*ho aei basileuon*), *not* some sort of 'eternal' ruling" (WBP 339). The question we need to deal with is the *way* in which this *aei* reveals itself, and the way in which the human being stands in relation to this view. Antiphon's way is reductive and attempts to abstract the *aei* from the illusory appearance of beings. His direction is toward beings, but not inasmuch as they *are*. His way of relating is to deny his relationship to beings *as such* and to seek out instead what is lasting and can be held onto.

For Antiphon, the elemental is that being which always remains—*aidion*. That is, it maintains itself the same. No change through which it could go out of itself belongs to it. Opposed to this being are those that are coming to be and ceasing to be without limit (*Physics* 195 a26–27). The contrast between the two kinds of beings is not between the temporal (changing) and the eternal, understood as infinite and unchanging, as later interpretations tend to present it.[14] For, as Heidegger points out, "the Christian eternal means that which lasts forever, without limits and without a beginning or end, while the temporal is that which is finite and limited" (WBP 338). But here it is precisely the opposite of *aidion* that is said to be limitless (*apeiron*). The *apeiron* has no *peras*. As such, it is *aidion*. But does that mean that everlasting being has a limit? What does *peras* mean here? Heidegger says:

But this standing there upright in itself, coming to a stand and remaining in the *stand*, is what the Greeks understood as being. Yet what comes to a stand and endures in itself thereby emerges forth freely of itself into the necessity of its limit, *peras*. This limit is not something that comes to the being from outside. Still less is it a deficiency in the sense of a harmful restriction. No, the holding which governs itself from out of the limit, the having itself in which that which endures holds itself, is the being of beings. Even more, it first makes it a being as such in differentiation from non-being. Coming to a stand means therefore: to achieve limit, to limit itself. Consequently, a fundamental characteristic of beings is to be defined by a *telos*, which means not aim or purpose, but end. Here "end" is not meant in a negative sense, as though there were something about it that did not continue, that failed or ceased. End is ending in the sense of fulfillment (*Vollendung*). Limit and end are that with which the being begins to be.[15]

In *Metaphysics* 1022 a4–14, Aristotle lists among the meanings of *peras* that it is "the primary and ultimate, out of which it is impossible to take anything (indivisible)." Limit in this sense means that which completes; nothing remains outside. As such, it is said in this passage to be the *eidos,* the outward appearance, the *telos* or end toward which beings move, and the *ousia* of beings, that which makes them always already the beings they are (*to ti ēn einai,* the essence). And finally, he says, the *archē* of beings is *peras. Archē, ousia, telos, atomon eidos, eschaton:* all these words name ways in which Aristotle understands the being of beings.

Heidegger says that what comes to a stand and holds itself as the same "emerges forth freely of itself into *the necessity* of its limits." What does Heiegger here mean by necessity? That which is named *aidion* and holds itself in its limits is opposed to that which is endlessly coming to be and passing away, and therefore does not become present as itself, as a being. "Non-being is sometimes present, sometimes absent, because it is only ever present on the basis of that which is already lying forth, that is, it merely turns up or fails to turn up along with this" (WBP 339). The contrast then is between beings that are in themselves, and the nonbeing that "is" as *sumbebēkos.* That which is in the first sense is necessary; that which merely appears along with what is is a kind of nonbeing, what "happens to be" along with what is.

For Antiphon, the elements are this primary ultimate limit. The elements are not limitless. They are rather those whose *peras* cannot be removed, and that therefore endure in this limit. They are opposed to that which sometimes looks one way, sometimes another—the always changing. The way of Antiphon's path toward being excludes change and separates the permanent from the changing, and therefore interprets changing beings as nonbeing. The criterion for this decision is permanence. He denies all attributes and dispositions to the being that has being. Thus, he excludes from his address the "merely" appearing. For Aristotle, on the other hand, the *aei* is that which comes forth of itself without assistance (*phusis*), and holds itself forth (*hupokeimenon),* and therefore endures. *Ousia* means presencing, and only for this reason does it mean constancy.

The *aei dios* is that which remains in the shining of presence, and therefore is seen (*theōria*) in unconcealment (*alētheia*). Human being is also an enduring in *alētheia,* but this way of enduring is to hold itself knowingly in the presence of being. *Theōria* is the immediate unity of the seeing and what is seen, which is prior to the separation of subject and object, and the consequent "analysis" that is based on this split. This original togetherness in which the human being dwells is named by Parmenides, and later by Aristotle, as *noein,* the seeing that always already is in the presence of the seen. Parmenides says: *"noein* and being are the same."[16] Similarly, Aristotle says in *De Anima* that noetic being is *aidion,* and capable of being in and of itself.[17] Antiphon has forgotten this original essence of the human being and, by forgetting this, he has also lost contact with the essence of beings. Instead, he seeks to recover being from beings through analysis. We have already seen that this kind of *logos,* the *logos* of demonstration, can never achieve a proof of being.

The Necessity Belonging to Beings (*Anangkē*) and the Possibility of Violence

We have seen that that which is in the way of *aidion* has the character of being necessary, whereas that which happens to come along with such a being, but does not constitute its beingness, is *sumbebēkos.* Natural beings, according to Aristotle, are both everlasting and necessary. What is the character of this necessity that differentiates such beings from nonbeing? Both Aristotle and Antiphon consider oneness (*hen*) to be a characteristic of necessary beings: "Each being itself and its *logos* are one and the same and this in no merely incidental way" (*Met.* 1031 b19-20). In search of the one, Antiphon proceeds on the mathematical model of oneness, by division into parts. Aristotle, on the other hand, understands the oneness of natural beings as that which governs the whole and being as a whole—the unifying: "For none of them (parts or elements) is a unity, but, as it were, a mere heap until they are worked up and some unity is made out of them" (*Met.* 1040 b9-10). That which is as a whole and that which belongs to this kind of unity as "that without which the whole would not be possible" is the necessary (*Met.* 1015 a20). One can indeed, according to Aristotle, proceed by dividing and collecting, itself a kind of *logos,* and discover things about beings, but what is discovered on this level is what is said to be *sumbebēkos* (*Met.* 1003 a26),[18] what happens to belong and come along with what is, but which is "neither necessary nor for the most part" (*Met.* 1026 b30-32). That which comes into view in this way does indeed come into being and is—but it does not have its being in itself but in another. As Aristotle says: "the combination is not derived from the things of which it is a combination" (*Met.* 1043 b6-7). In effect, Aristotle is presenting a critique of the method of dialectic in Platonic philosophy. We will see in chapter five that Heidegger shares this Aristotelian view of Plato. The dialectical method of synthesis and division is said to be close to sophistry in that, in itself, it has no access to being [Socratic ignorance] and is not intrinsically governed by *nous*. What distinguishes it from sophistry is its desire for truth rather than manipulation and deception.[19]

In a previous discussion, we saw that *technē* does not relate to the beings it encounters as such, or to the being of these beings as a whole, but addresses them rather as available for a coming into being that does not sustain itself, emerge out of itself, and return to itself in its sameness. This kind of coming into being is precisely what the one who knows (*nous*), the philosopher, only takes into account in terms of his vision of the whole that governs it. *Technē* presupposes this unconcealment of being (*alētheia*). Antiphon has forgotten this and therefore his way of proceeding cannot reach beyond beings to what is fundamental. He tries to discover the being of beings by going through beings—the method of synthesis and division. Antiphon relates to beings in the way Aristotle says the craftsperson looks at beings as material available for his production. He deals with what he just finds there before him, without bringing into question the source of that familiarity.

In Aristotle, there is certainly a division between the theoretical and practical, but only in both together are beings revealed. Production through *technē*, like proof through demonstration, is founded, according to Aristotle, on the originary unconcealment of *ousia* and depends on our capacity to hold this in view (*theōria*). Yet human beings do organize and structure, categorize and experiment. In doing so, they reveal ways in which beings *can* show themselves. If they *can* be revealed in these various ways, then it would seem to confirm Antiphon's belief that such beings are not necessary. Aristotle himself insists that only beings that emerge out of themselves and go forth into their being without being caused by manipulation (*bia*) or chance (*tuchē*) are necessary beings and thereby everpresencing as they are (*Physics* 199 b15–19). But for Aristotle, natural beings can be impeded from reaching their *telos*, even though the movement toward their end is a necessary movement and governed by necessity. He calls the kind of necessity that characterizes natural beings hypothetical— "if nothing interferes" (*Physics* 199 b35). Aristotle also understands compulsion and force as kinds of necessity (*Met.* 1015 a 26–27)—a necessity that is imposed from outside the beings themselves and therefore a kind of necessity that can never be the being of beings that have their being of themselves (*phusis*). Natural beings emerge out of themselves and direct themselves *toward* their being while maintaining themselves in the necessity of their limits. Their coming to be is not by chance or force, but a necessary coming to be that is continuously governed by their being. The *heneka*—that "for the sake of which" they are becoming (as *archē* and *telos*) (*Physics* 200 a8) governs the movement that is necessary "in order to" (without which a being could not be—*ou aneu ouk endechetai*) (*Met.* 1015 a20; *Physics,* 200 a6). The prepositional structure of the "towards which," "in order to," and "for sake of which" constitutes the unity of the simple (*to aploun*) (*Met.* 1015 b12) as opposed to the manifold (*pleonachōs*) that "appears sometimes one way and sometimes another" without limit (*Met.* 1015 b14). We find in Aristotle an interpretation of *aidion* and *anangkē* and *hen* that is appropriate to the being of natural beings.

At *Metaphysics* Θ5, Aristotle offers a succinct account of the various meanings of necessity. We will consider here how these various meanings are related to natural beings in order to see how the necessary character of natural beings is a cause of their coming to be. This will be done in three steps.

1. Aristotle first defines necessity in this passage as "that without which, as the accompanying cause (*sunaition*), life would be impossible" (*Met.* 1015 a20–21). Necessity is a cause in the sense of being responsible for life. Life is for Aristotle that which is governed by *phusis*. Necessity makes possible natural beings. The *sun* indicates its way of being a cause. Necessity is responsible for the being of beings by a bringing together. Natural beings are brought together according to necessity. Necessity is here further defined as "that without which life would be impossible." Necessity is the cause (*aitia)* that determines the possibility of the being-together of natural beings. Furthermore, Aristotle says, necessity is that without which the good is impossible and cannot come into being, or without which one cannot keep away or be freed of harm (*kakos*) (1015 a23–24).

2. In another sense, "necessity is the compulsory, and in fact force or compulsion" (1015 a27). In taking into itself what it needs "in order to" bring forth beings, it does violence. By enforcing its limits, necessity appropriates what is not governed by necessity and what is therefore nonbeing and limitless change. Change according to necessity is change that is directed toward and "for the sake of" the *aidion*. It holds itself within the ever-presencing of *ousia* and is this sameness with itself. Necessity is this violent holding itself together of a movement that is

governed by the need to be. Life is violence. It appropriates to itself what is necessary in order to be (Aristotle gives the example of nourishment and breathing). Aristotle says necessity does violence in this way to what lies in the path and gets in the way of the thrust (*hormē*) or the deliberately chosen direction (*prohairesis*) (1015 a28). *Hormē* is also used in the sense of the *archē* of natural beings at *Physics* 192 b20. In *Satz vom Grund,* Heidegger talks of this opposition to natural movement as the original sense of *Gegenstand* (object) in the sense of "*gegen einem über.*"[20] That something can appear in the path of a natural being and be taken over by it is a necessary ground for the possibility of *phusis*. Aristotle also points to this kind of violence as a character of *technē*. This may in part account for the origin of the human being's tendency to relate to beings in terms of subject and object. But Aristotle clearly distinguishes between the necessity with which *phusis* commands and that of *technē*. "And necessity in the proper sense is held to be something which is not able to be affected by persuasion. In this sense, necessity is contrary to the movement which is in accordance with choice and calculation" (*Met.* 1015 a33). The necessity of *phusis* refuses to yield to the power of *technē*. Its movement is not directed in the same way. *Technē* has power over only what can be affected and thus does not have a necessity of its own. It is directed toward *sumbebēkos,* that which is merely present *along with* what is and thus can be otherwise than it is. This intricate, inextricable interrelationship of *phusis* and *technē* for Aristotle is evident in his constant reliance on examples from *technē* when attempting to explain *phusis*. The refusal to yield on the part of *phusis,* as well as the ability to yield, is not only what delimits *technē,* but also a fundamental characteristic of natural beings. Natural beings can be otherwise, are such as to be able to be affected and changed, and thus make *technē* possible. There can be no *technē* without *phusis*. One wonders whether the reverse is also true, as Heidegger indicates in his essay "The Origin of the Work of Art": "True, there lies hidden in nature a rift-design, a measure and a boundary and, tied to it, a capacity for bringing forth—that is, art. But it is equally certain that this art hidden in nature becomes manifest only through the work."[21]

3. "That which cannot have its being in any other way is said to be necessarily so" (*Met.* 1015 a34–35). That which cannot be otherwise is the simple (1015 b12). It is opposed to the manifold, "which is always changing" and never holds itself as *one.* (1015 b14). The opposition

between the one and the many is not a differentiation between being and beings. The many is always such and such, but never a *this*, never a being that *is* in itself and holds itself in this way and thus maintains itself in its simplicity. In *Satz vom Grund,* Heidegger therefore says: "*Phusis* and that which belongs to it is *ta aplōs saphestera.* Being is most manifest *from out of itself.*"[22] It is in this sense that *phusis* and natural beings are simple and single. Their movement is enclosed within their being. Nor is the opposition here between that which changes and that which does not (the opposition as Antiphon understood it). Rather it is an opposition between two ways of changing, two ways of *kinēsis.*

Kinēsis that is in accord with *phusis* emerges forth and unfolds itself through an upsurge (*hormē*) that keeps it continuously in the same. Although governed by itself and thus directed by a necessity that is not violent, it can be violently impeded from accomplishing itself because its necessity is hypothetical (*Physics* 199 b33ff). In coming-to-be in its *telos,* it is not-yet there. It needs to take over and form its *hulē* in order to be. The *hulē* is that which is necessary if a being is to come to be. "The necessary in nature, then, is plainly what we call by the name matter (*hulē*), and the changes in it" (*Physics,* 200 a30). Unless the matter is there to be incorporated, a natural being will wither before it is able to fulfill itself. We have already seen that this incorporation is itself a kind of violence. It seems to me that if there is a dialectic in Aristotle, then it is governed by this notion of embodiment. The body inasmuch as it is a this (*todē ti*), and is "for the sake of" its being, takes over another. However, never as a "this," but rather as a "such." Its negation does not simply take what it negates along with it. It annihilates it in preserving itself. It appropriates to itself what presents itself as able to be appropriated. Grass, for example, as a natural being, can never by nature, that is, inasmuch as it is itself, become milk. But inasmuch as grass can be taken as other than itself—as matter for nourishment—it can be appropriated by a natural being for itself. Movement by nature and movement by violence are both possible because necessity rules over the world of nature. Without necessity, the free movement from out of itself toward its *telos* that is the essence of a natural being would be impossible. This violence that incorporates another as a "such" into another "this" is the fundamental insight that allows Aristotle to develop the categorial understanding of beings.

Antiphon's doctrine fails to give an account of the kind of *kinēsis* that constitutes natural beings. It is not every coming into being that is nonbeing, but only that which is both the coming into being of one thing and the passing away of another, as, for example, hot and cold. It is precisely these that have no being of their own, but *are* only to the extent that they are appropriated for a being that is. For Aristotle, the elemental is of this sort and not true beingness. Here Antiphon's doctrine is not totally rejected. For one thing, what he was looking for but could not find, because his *logos* was on the wrong path, is the beingness of beings. This Antiphon correctly identifies as the unitary, unchanging, necessary, and simple being that always appears as it is. In this respect, his method is far removed from that of contemporary technology, which also constitutes being on the basis of what it finds in beings and also does so by abstracting from and reducing these beings, but which understands this as a process that releases the energy that is then available to be whatever one "makes" it to be. But contemporary technology has its roots in Antiphon's "error," since he too takes a part of what is and isolates this part from the being as a whole. "And those who study these properties (*sumbebēkos*) err not by leaving the sphere of philosophy, but by forgetting that *ousia,* of which they have not a correct idea (*epaiousin*—which they do not *listen to*), is prior (*proteron*)" (*Met.* 1004 b10). Antiphon was unable to see how these characteristics belong to natural beings that change. He attempts to follow the dictum of Parmenides that says to turn away from *doxa,* the readily apparent and familiar (to us), and turn toward what is in itself true and noble and most knowable.23 But he fails because he has wandered off the path that distinguishes the true and the apparent, a path that demands that we first think the difference in its togetherness. Aristotle heeds the warning of Parmenides in the pathway of his thought. "So in the present inquiry we must follow this path (*hodos*) and advance from what is more obscure by nature, but clearer to us, over to (*epi*) what is more clear and more knowable by nature" (*Physics* 184 a16–17).24 The opposition here is not between two kinds of being—for example, the eternal and temporal—but between two ways in which beings show themselves. The kind of *logos* that Aristotle calls *noein* sees beings in the unconcealment of their being (*alētheia, eidos, ousia*); the other kind of *logos* (demonstration, experience, *aisthēsis*) sees beings only in their appearance. Heidegger says:

For the Greeks, 'being' means *presencing in the unhidden.* Duration and extension are not what is decisive but rather whether the being gives itself in the hidden of the inexhaustible, or whether presencing distorts itself (*pseudos*) into what merely 'looks like,' into mere appearance, instead of holding itself in undistortedness (*a-trekeia*). (WBP 340)

Heidegger translates *pseudos,* untruth, as *sich verkehren,* which means to change in the sense of continuously coming and going and thus to be transformed or turned into—to be dis-torted. It is this meaning of limitless trafficking with others that Heidegger wishes to evoke here in keeping with the above contrast with *aidion.* He chooses *Un-verkehrheit* to translate *atrekeia,* which means nontangled, not confused, and thus simple, certain, and true. Thus being is not a being that stands above (or beneath) beings because it is eternal, simple, unchanging, and infinite. Nor are beings, in contrast, the merely apparent that share or participate in this being. In both cases, we are talking about beings, *phainomena,* and distinguishing between a showing itself as itself, and a showing itself as it is not, but can appear to be.

The Law of Non-Contradiction

Aristotle has stated that the entire corpus of his efforts is directed by an essential insight into the meaning of being. Being is *ousia.* Aristotle's question then becomes: If *ousia* is the beingness of beings, how can beings be understood in terms of *ousia?* The problematic of the *Physics* is entirely guided by this central question. The question of *kinēsis,* therefore, is the question of how beings that are through *ousia* can have *kinēsis* as their way of being—their way of presencing. This difficulty is the crux of this work. Given a pre-understanding of *ousia* as simple, indivisible, necessary, unitary, and enduring presencing, it would seem necessary to exclude change from the realm of what is. Change can only mean infinite divisibility (Zeno), composition (the *rhuthmos* of Antiphon), the negation of permanence (the flux of Heraclitus), and the outcome of not having to be (the nonbeing of Parmenides). Yet it is clearly change and movement that let natural beings be—it *is* their way of being. Aristotle's philosophy is an attempt to rescue the Greek insight that the being of beings is *ousia.* Were the paradox of *kinēsis* to remain unresolved, then a rift between being and beings is inevitable. Being as *ousia*—pure presencing—would have to be preserved in a realm beyond or beneath beings and the human being's relation to beings would be demoted to illusion. Aristotle was keenly aware of his mission. But the mission itself was not new. Antiphon also tried to rescue the meaning of *ousia.* Aristotle's immense accomplishment rests not with the discovery of *ousia* as the meaning of being, but rather with the *path* of his thought. Antiphon goes through beings to uncover *ousia.* Aristotle grants *ousia* as the meaning of being and thinks toward beings from out of this understanding. It is this decision that is the foundation of Aristotle's thought and that governs all of his work.

In clearing a path for his understanding of the being of beings and of beings as such, Aristotle introduces a new road that cuts across an impasse in Greek thought. For Antiphon, the realm of being contradicts and excludes nonbeing. *Rhuthmos* comes and goes. Its appearance does not maintain itself, and therefore *rhuthmos* is nonbeing, mere illusion and semblance, which the philosopher must ignore. Being and nonbeing cannot be spoken together. The law of contradiction is also said to be the basis of Aristotle's philosophy. But Aristotle opens up within this law a new dimension—the dimension in which *phusis* dwells.

Aristotle calls the law of contradiction the *archē* of all understanding "which everyone must have in order to relate knowingly to beings." (*Met.* 1005 b15). It is "that which it is necessary to know in advance in order to know beings." It is "the most certain of all" in the sense that it allows beings to be seen in their being. This foundation for all understanding is the law of noncontradiction, which Aristotle states in this way: "It is impossible that the same can at the same time (*hama*) occur (*huparchein*) and not occur in the same and with respect to the same (*kata to auto*)[25] (1005 b19). Aristotle says further: "It is impossible to believe (for those who understand) that being and non-being are the same" (1005 b23). Finally, he adds: "It is impossible for the same person (who understands) to tolerate or permit it to be said in relation to one and the same being and at the same time that it be and not be" (1005 b29f).

This *archē* of understanding in advance governs all inquiry and guides Greek thinking not only because it is the basis of thinking but because it is at the same time the way in which *phusis* is seen (1005 b34). It is before all understanding and all beings because it is the original unity of thinking and *phusis* that advances before and opens the way for an understanding of beings. But this is not to say that thinking and being are identical. Rather they rest together and let that which is emerge out of this residence. The place of this unity is expressed by the phrase "*kata to auto.*" Inasmuch as the same is directed "with regard to its sameness," it cannot be present and also not present. *Huparchein,* to happen, occur, or be present has the sense of belonging to. Aristotle frequently uses it in the categorial sense, for example, to describe how the qualities or contraries belong to a being (*Met.* 1025 a14; APo 24 a27; 25 a13). In this sense, it refers to what belongs to a being in the way of *sumbebēkos. Kata sumbebēkos* is the opposite of and that which is not *kath'hauto* (*Physics* 192 b22; *Met.* 1052 a18). *To sumbebēkos* is that which belongs to and is present along with that which shows itself as such. The accidental is that which is present "under" an *archē*. The "accidental" is governed by an *archē* that is outside itself. That which is the same can never simply belong together with itself in the way of *sumbebēkos*. Its unity—the being-together of itself—is not of the sort that one could say it just happens to be together. The law of non-contradiction says that it is impossible for a being that has *phusis* as its way of being to appear in the way "properties" come and go in beings. It is possible for accidents not to be present. Therefore, they are not necessary. That which is not necessary cannot be of itself. (APo 75 a2o). That which shows itself as itself has the kind of presencing Aristotle calls *ousia*. This enduring presencing of the same is a unity that excludes the kind of appearing that can never hold itself in its being.

But is this not precisely what Antiphon and Parmenides have said? Being cannot be mixed together and confused with nonbeing. The philosopher abides by this separation and is thus able to witness the true presencing of being. It seems that the two paths have not been joined. The path of nonbeing is the illusion cast forth by *rhuthmos*—the coming into being *and* passing away of limitless change. Aristotle's law of non-contradiction seems to say the same. Being cannot be present *and* not present in the way hot and cold appear together as the presence and absence of each other in a limitless change whereby the coming to be of one *is* the passing away of the other. In *Vorträge und Aufsätze,* Heidegger points out that "*ouk* denies something to whatever is being affected by the negation. *Mē,* on the other hand, attributes something to whatever comes within its sphere of negation: a refusal, a distancing, a preventing."[26] *Mē on,* then, indicates a refusal, or a being-prevented-from achieving being. A being that achieves being is able to hold itself in presencing of itself. *Mē on* is a not-having its being of itself in this way. Aristotle remains faithful to the central thought of Greek thinking. Being and nonbeing are not the same.

Where in Aristotle's restatement of the *archē* of Greek throught has a new path been inserted that resolves the paradox that forces one to say that moving beings are nonbeing? It is found in one small word: *hama*. Derrida writes of this word:

The entire force of Aristotle's text depends on a single word which is scarcely visible because it is so evident; as obvious, it is also discreet and hidden, but it operates all the more effectively for escaping thematic attention. The tiny *hama* is that which sets the discourse in motion in terms of its articulation; from this point on, it will constitute the inner core of metaphysics; it will be the small key which both locks and unlocks the history of metaphysics—the skeletal frame on which the entire conceptual apparatus of Aristotelian discourse is supported and in terms of which it is articulated. In a certain sense, it expresses the dyad as the minimum.[27]

The word *hama* means together *at the same time.*

With the introduction of this forgotten horizon, the possibility of *phusis* is secured. Beings that emerge forth and are directed toward their being while always remaining in their sameness *can be.* Aristotle accomplishes the thinking of *kinēsis* in its belonging together with *peras. Phusis* is a way of *ousia.* Change can be *kata to auto,* in respect to the same. The *kata* here somehow holds together and yet separates. It does so through the *hama,* as Heidegger points out in section 19 of *Grundprobleme der Phänome-nologie.*[28] Through this word, Aristotle is able to articulate the structure of the being of change. Natural beings are beings whose necessity, unity, and simplicity allow for change and coming to be in time.

Aristotle's new path has been opened up by his meditation on *ousia* as the being (*phusis)* of natural beings. The structure of natural beings encloses them within this unity of being-a-whole, while opening them up to a world of contact, resistance, opposition, and growth that is made possible because their movement—their way of being a whole—is a coming to be what they already are. Antiphon was unable to think these two moments together. Aristotle does not reject Antiphon's understanding of being or nonbeing. But he looks into the abyss that separates the two in Antiphon's philosophy and discovers there the path of natural beings. In the word *hama,* Aristotle points to the path that makes possible the being of *kinēsis*—time.

For Aristotle, the elementary, as Antiphon understood it, is not a primary, formless, indeterminate being that underlies and gives meaning to beings. All beings including elements, if they exist as such, are bodies whose *ousia* individuates them. Inasmuch as they are in themselves, they presence themselves always as an individual and a *this* (*todē ti*) (*Met.* 1003 a10). This recognition that what is is individual (and as such indivisible) led many of Aristotle's predecessors including Antiphon to view only the elementary as unchanging and one. For being seems to mean precisely being a one. If it did not, then that which is would be two and an absurd regress would follow (as Zeno shows). On the other hand, if to be is to be one in Antiphon's sense, then motion is impossible—which amounts to a denial of natural beings (and ultimately even of the elements), since natural beings—or at least some of them—clearly move. Thus, others suggest that being is not unchanging, but rather constantly in motion (*Physics* 184 b17–18). In this *aporia*, Aristotle discovers an ontological sense of movement through time as the necessary way of presencing of natural beings.

The Difference Between Being and Beings

In an earlier passage, Aristotle said *phusis* is always "in" a being that lies-forth in such a way that its lying-forth is from itself and toward itself as such (*Physics* 192 b34). *Phusis* constitutes the sameness of this lying-forth from and toward itself. Moreover, this lying-forth is always already "in" its *phusis* as it directs itself toward it. This kind of movement from out of and toward itself and the holding itself together (and thus lying-forth) of this movement is the way of presencing of natural beings. But we notice something else here. A natural being is not *phusis*; it is governed by *phusis* and "in" *phusis*. Aristotle distinguishes between the presencing (*ousia*) of beings and beings that are present. He differentiates being and beings. It is only on this basis that he is able to think the sameness of a moving being with its being. This is the significance of the *kata to auto* that we discussed in relation to the law of non-contradiction. A natural being maintains itself and is maintained "in" its sameness. Therefore, it must in a way not be itself. Inasmuch as it directs itself toward itself, it *is* not itself but in relation to (*kata*) itself. Therefore, Aristotle says, a natural being is in *phusis*; *phusis* is not "in" a natural being (*Physics* 192 b35–193 a1). Antiphon tried to abstract being (*phusis-ousia*) out of natural beings and establish a difference in this way. But because *ousia* is always already there in advance of each step in this kind of method (the method of proof), it can never succeed. This is the sense in which being is said to be "a priori." Not in the sense that being stands (and exists) before beings, but in the sense that beings come to a stand and exist in their being. Thus, Aristotle says that fire, as a natural, elementary being, is directed toward the place to which it belongs. But its tendency to be carried upward, the natural *kinēsis* of fire, is not itself *phusis*. Nor is *phusis* in movement. Natural movement is rather *kata phusin*. This says simply that *phusis* is not the ontic movement of the sort we have discussed in the categories; nor is it itself a natural being such as fire. Rather, fire tends upward because it is "in" *phusis*. *Phusis* draws it to itself and encloses it, while not itself being contained by it. This means that natural beings can never "have" their being, even though it is not improper to speak of natural beings as being secured in their being, as we did earlier in terms of *peras*. The way of being of natural beings is to dwell in the security of their being while never overcoming the need for it.

Aristotle, like Antiphon, sees the difference between being and beings. Unlike Antiphon, he is also able to see the way in which they are the same, the way in which a being is its being. For Aristotle, it is this sameness that his philosophy attempts to establish. This is the originary discovery of Aristotle's thought. The horizon for that discovery remains the recognized difference between being and beings. It is this difference that constitutes the presupposition that must be recognized in reading Aristotle. If Antiphon has failed to think properly of the difference between being and nonbeing, it is because he failed to take into account their sameness. So Aristotle's philosophy must first work out the pressing question of this identity. But in doing so he is under way and in preparation for a thinking that remains presupposed but is therefore more essential—the thinking of the difference between being and beings. Every beginning that Aristotle makes and every conclusion that he reaches reminds us of this task. Thus, the present chapter of the *Physics* that guides our interpretation of Aristotle ends with the question whether there might be a way of thinking *genesis,* coming to be and ontological change, that does not show its sameness with nonbeing (understood at this point, as we will see, as *sterēsis*), but shows rather in what way they are not the same. "But whether in unqualified coming to be there is privation, that is, a contrary to coming to be, we must consider later" (*Physics* 193 b21). Heidegger leaves this final sentence out of his commentary. For it is not a conclusion at all but the gift of a task for thinking that which remains unthought in Aristotle. It is this task that distinguishes the path of Aristotle from that of Heidegger. In order to take up that challenge, one has to first walk back down the path that Aristotle opened up for us. But not in a mere repetition of what Aristotle has accomplished. Aristotle's success as an essential thinker has been such that this further reflection on the "difference" has been lost to the Aristotelian tradition. The history of metaphysics has been a persistent attempt to recover this difference, without recognizing that the difference is always already presupposed by metaphysics. Such attempts at rescue only further mire the tradition in confusions. The oblivion of being in its more radical difference from beings gets bogged down. Nevertheless, this difference as the origin and presupposition of the thinking of the being of beings remains as the hidden source of the history of metaphysics. Heidegger says: "Thus confined to what is metaphysical, man is caught in the difference of beings and being which he never experiences."[29] To take up the path that Aristotle traces for those who wish to go beyond him does not mean to throw aside the history of Aristotelian thought. Aristotle thought through the sameness of being and nonbeing because only in this way could the truth of being appear in its difference. Heidegger says: "only when we turn thoughtfully toward what has already been thought (but presupposed and then forgotten) will we be turned to use for what must still be thought."[30] It is with this question that Heidegger begins *Sein und Zeit*. [31]

The Method of Aristotle's Thought

Before continuing with his interpretation of Aristotle's *Physics* B 1, Heidegger summarizes what Aristotle has so far accomplished and outlines the importance of his confrontation with Antiphon. We have determined through *epagōgē* that natural beings are in movement. Not in the sense that they are at any given moment necessarily in motion (as regards to locomotion or alteration, etc.) but in the sense that being-moved *is* their way of being. It is this way of being that directs and makes possible the kinds of motion that beings undergo. This way of being is *phusis*. *Phusis* is the *archē* of beings that move according to their nature. *Phusis* is not motion but the *archē* of the motion in beings such that it lets them be the beings they are. The *archē* both directs and governs the emerging forth and lets that which directs and governs the upsurgence emerge into unconcealment. It is both *Ausgang* and *Verfügung* thought in their togetherness. The *telos*, that toward which a being reaches and in which it fulfills itself, directs the coming-to-be of a being. That "from which" and "out of which" a being emerges is the origin. But both the origin and the *telos* are essentially the same. *Phusis* is both. It is *ausgängliche Verfügung*. The *archē* holds a being in its togetherness and lets it come forth as a whole. The diverse moments and phases of the coming to be of a natural being do not contradict the meaning of being as *ousia*. Rather being-moved is the way in which natural beings fulfill their *ousia*. Therefore only by understanding *kinēsis* in the proper way can we understand the "nature"of *phusis* as the *archē* of the being-moved of natural beings.

Heidegger points to the beginning of Chapter III of Book II of the *Physics* in support of this seemingly circular reasoning. There Aristotle says:

Since *phusis* is the originating and governing over being-moved and thus over the upsurgence which bursts into the open, our *methodos* must not allow that *kinēsis* essentially is to remain in concealment. For whenever *kinēsis* remains unfamiliar, *phusis* also remains in unfamiliarity." (*Physics* 200 b12–15; WBP 341)

Aristotle's "method" requires both a comportment toward *kinēsis* and toward *phusis*. Unless we see what *kinēsis* is, that is, how *kinēsis* is in its being, we will not understand *phusis*. We must refer *kinēsis* to *phusis*. To do so we must already somehow be familiar with *phusis*. On the other hand, *phusis* will remain concealed unless we recognize what *kinēsis* is. We cannot resolve this circle by simply equating motion with *phusis*. We have already seen with Heidegger that this would be entirely unGreek and un-philosophical (WBP 314). Motion is not "nothing." It occurs and is the essential way in which beings, which are governed by *phusis*, come to be and are in their being. Only if coming to be can be shown as an essential way of being of natural beings can the gap between movement and being be overcome. Aristotle's "method" is such that he is able to enter into this circle—what Heidegger calls the hermeneutic circle. *Methodos*, Aristotle's way of questioning, opens up the region in which the being of beings can properly be grasped.

In *Der Satz vom Grund*, Heidegger speaks of Aristotle's task in the *Physics*:

Aristotle begins his lecture by thinking about the way in which a thinker is able to delimit beings (which are from out of and towards themselves, *ta physei onta*) in relation to their being and to comprehend this being as *phusis*. The Greek word for way is *hodos*; *meta* means after (*nach*); *Methodos* is the way we go after (*nachgehen*) a matter.[32]

Aristotle says that beings are more manifest and accessible to us, but being is in itself more manifest. The philosopher's path is from beings that are more immediately accessible to us to the being of beings that in revealing itself gives to beings their openness (*Physics* 184 a16ff). If being (*phusis*) remains concealed, so also do beings. But only by understanding beings that are revealed to us can we open ourselves to the unconcealment of being. Method is not a technique for Aristotle. It is, as his manner of inquiry, a remaining faithful to the matter that presents itself, by questioning the matter in regard to its being. This method is the philosophical method.

In our present context, Aristotle is concerned to clarify this method as the only truly philosophical path because it is being threatened by a fundamental misunderstanding, as we have seen with Antiphon. The method of analyzing a being without a view toward its being can only offer the kind of information that leads one farther astray from the truth. No claim to a genuine discovery of being can be made on this basis because the *methodos* is inappropriate. Therefore, *kinēsis* gets taken as the illusive appearance of changing forms (*rhuthmos*) that indeed can be stabilized by man (through *technē*), but that has no being in itself. Aristotle's method shows that the being-moved of natural beings, and indeed these beings themselves, are governed by *phusis* and never merely alongside or in addition to being, or accidental to it. Change is a necessary character of the being of natural beings. None of the specific categorial ways of changing fulfill this deeper meaning of *kinēsis* that Aristotle is now prepared to explore.

Aristotle's philosophical method demands that *kinēsis* be understood as *ousia*—as presencing. Heidegger points out that he translated *ousia* as *Anwesung* rather than *Anwesenheit* to avoid the tendency, a tendency that has crept into Antiphon's way of thinking, to interpret presencing in terms of the enduring and permanent, rather than understanding constancy in terms of presencing. "What is meant (by *phusis* and thus by *ousia*) is not just being-present (*Vorhandenheit*) and especially not something which is exhausted in constancy. Rather, it means presencing (*Anwesung*) in the sense of coming-forth in the unconcealed and placing itself in the open" (WBP 342). Unless we have a view toward the presencing and openness in which beings dwell, our interpretation of beings will fail. But in our immediate view of beings, this presencing is concealed. We more easily take what is present out of the horizon that gives it its meaning (and structure) and view it in regard to its being simply there before us. In this view, all structure is added on and composed of a more primary element that remains there throughout the various conditions in which it can be found. Because being is understood as what remains there unaffected by change, being must be the indeterminate "one" that underlies and determines everything that is. Aristotle has shown that this is not the case. He has thereby prepared the way for the proper understanding of the *phusis* of natural beings.

The Path of Aristotle's Thought: The Twofoldness of Phusis

Through a repetition of the central problem of Greek philosophy, Aristotle has reopened the true questionableness of the being of natural beings. He has shown that only in the proper approach to this fundamental question can we win access to the meaning of *phusis*. A natural being is understood as one in itself and *not* other than itself; it is understood as simple and *not* manifold; it's being is necessary and *not* able to be other than itself. It is the accomplishment of his path of thinking that he is able to show the beingness of this *not* which characterizes natural beings, the beingness of *kinēsis*.

This originary questioning of *phusis* inserts itself at the place of the difference between being and beings and thus sees how the unity of a being in its being occurs. It sees in this *logos* the twofoldness of being that constitutes this unity of a being as a whole. Heidegger says of the philosophical task of questioning that

It is of decisive importance, first, that we allow space for beings as a whole; second, that we release ourselves into the nothing, which is to say, that we liberate ourselves from those idols everyone has and to which one is wont to go cringing; and finally, that we let the sweep of our suspense take its full course, so that it swings back into the basic question of metaphysics which the nothing compels: Why are there beings at all, and why not rather nothing?[33]

Aristotle's Hylomorphic Theory

There is perhaps no more crucial discussion in Heidegger's commentary on *Physics* B1 than the interpretation of Aristotle's treatment of matter and form. Heidegger begins by translating the following passage from Book A of the *Physics* (193 a28–31):

According to the one way, *phusis* is *therefore* addressed as follows: it is that which primarily and from the outset lies at the basis (*hupokeimenon*) of each individual (*Geeinzelten*) and has the suitability (*Verfügliche; hulē*) for the being which has in itself the originating and governing over movement, that is, over change (*metabolē*). According to the other way, *phusis* is addressed as the placing into the figure (*Gestellung in die Gestalt, morphē*), that is, as the aspect (*eidos*) (*na*mely of that) which shows itself to the address (*kata ton logon*). (WBP 343)

We are introduced in this passage to two of the central concepts of Aristotelian thought: *hulē* and *morphē*. Here Aristotle places the two in contrast as two different ways of addressing *phusis*. Antiphon has called the primary formless element out of which beings are composed the *phusis* of beings. Aristotle names this *hupokeimenon,* this underlying substance, *hulē,* and reinterprets the essential character of matter by insisting that all underlying matter is such that it stands in a fundamental relation with that to which it belongs and for the sake of which it counts as matter, even when it is deprived of its natural form. As such it is in such a way as to be encompassed within the essential structure of what is. Antiphon rejected, as illusion and nonbeing, what he calls the *rhuthmos,* the measure that orders and structures, and thus the movement that arranges and shapes beings into certain forms. Any particular shape is at the same time both too little and too much to be called being. In contrast, Aristotle names *morphē* as co-constituting the *phusis* of beings.

In these sentences Aristotle does not simply take up and preserve Antiphon's concept of being and rename it as *hulē*. That which is always already there, and constitutes the lying-forth, Aristotle names the *hupokeimenon prōton*. We met this expression earlier when Aristotle said that lying-forth is a way of *ousia* for natural beings. That means that *hupokeimenon* and *hulē* have to be thought in terms of presencing and in terms of *phusis* and *kinēsis*. Each step of Aristotle's thinking carries along with it what has gone before. We have to ask now in what way *hupokeimenon* and *hulē* are related. *Hupokeimenon* and *hulē* name ways in which *phusis* as *ousia* can be addressed. In our present passage, Aristotle also names *morphē* as another way in which we can address the being of natural beings. How are these ways of addressing *phusis* related, on the one hand the *hulē*, which is a kind of lying-forth (*hupokeimenon*), on the other hand the *morphē*, which is addressed as *eidos*?

Aristotle calls *hulē* the *ex hou*, the "out of which" or "from which" (*Physics*, 245 b11). The *hulē* is here spoken of as that which is able to be affected (*paschein*), that is, to undergo the alteration that is caused by the sensible. He says that beings that have the *archē* of change in themselves and thus hold themselves in their structure and shape are not substantially affected by the alteration of their *hulē*. Thus, the movement that is directed toward and by the *morphē*, namely, *genesis*, is not alteration (246 a4). Affection and alteration do not alter a being as such. As long as it is governed by *phusis*, it remains what it is. When we address a being in regard to its structure and shape, we address it as it *is*.

Hulē is that from out of which a being comes to be; as such it co-constitutes the being of natural beings. But a being does not come to be due to its *hulē*, but rather its *morphē*. Thus, the *morphē*, not the *hulē*, more properly names the *archē* of natural beings. Also, there is at least one kind of *kinēsis*, alteration, that is clearly differentiated by Aristotle from that *kinēsis* that belongs to natural beings as such (*genesis*). *Hulē*, because it is sensible, that is, able to be affected,[34] is responsible for alteration. *Morphē* is responsible for *genesis*. Therefore, if we follow the path of Antiphon and only name *phusis* as *hulē*, we will only see that kind of movement that does not alone, nor even primarily, constitute the being in its being. We will, like Antiphon, recognize that qualitative movement such as alteration, that is governed by *hulē* (unlike *genesis*), does not belong to the being as such, but comes and goes while the being remains. Only when we view a being by having in view its *morphē* will we see the kind of enduring movement that can be spoken of as *genesis*. But when only *hulē* is seen as *phusis*, the *morphē* too gets distorted. The particular configurations (*rhuthmos*) in which a being is found and in which it happens to lie-forth at any given time are not responsible for the unity of the being. Here the lying-forth (*hupokeimenon*) is viewed as the "subject" that lies there as the basis for motion and change that is not directed by the being itself as such.[35] In such a light, beings can be viewed from a manifold of perspectives. In such a light, it is concluded that it is not the structures that unify a being, but that which underlies these structures. Antiphon looks at being but without having in view beforehand the meaning of being as *ousia* and without seeing the relation of being and beings. Overwhelmed as it were by the difference between being and beings, he is unable to see the sameness. Therefore he loses sight also of the difference.

Aristotle says repeatedly that this kind of change (that is involved in the categories other than *ousia*) is due to the "matter," the *hulē*: "all beings which come to be either by nature or art have matter; for each of them can both be and not be and this is the matter in each" (*Met.* 1032 a21). Aristotle does not deny or exclude natural beings from being because being must either be or not be. Natural beings are precisely those beings whose being incorporates nonbeing. This incorporation is the nature of *kinēsis*, and is due to the *hulē* of natural beings.

To understand Aristotle's resolution of the paradoxes that arise from a consideration of *hulē*, we need to recognize that *hulē* can be spoken of in different ways. Inasmuch as it is addressed from the point of view of *morphē*, *hulē* co-constitutes the being of natural beings. That is, when the *hulē* gathers itself (*kinēsis*) in its proper place and stands forth as the being it is (*eidos* as *morphē*), then *hulē* is the *ousia* of natural beings (*Met.* 1042 a32). From this viewpoint, there is no distinction between *morphē* and *hulē* (1045 b18). Rather, both together constitute the *ousia*. According to Aristotle, one of the primary meanings of *ousia*, the presencing of natural beings, is *todē ti*. It is only when we view a being as *ousia* that we can properly address the being as *a* being, as this particular being that we stand before. In this case, *hulē*, the matter, shows itself as it truly is, as the individual being itself. Heidegger translates *hekaston* (the individual) as *das Geeinzelte* instead of the more usual German word *der Einzelne*. By retaining the verbal participial form, Heidegger places the emphasis on the *Ge*, which originally indicated in German a gathering. Heidegger wants to suggest that there is a relationship between the individual and the *koinon* in Greek thought. The individual is gathered together as a whole *(katholou)*, and as such it holds itself in relation to what is common as separate (*chōrismos*).

However, it is also possible to view a being not in terms of what it is and the way in which it fulfills what it is but in terms of its nonbeing or not-yet-being what it is. A natural being has movement as its way of being. As such, it is under way toward its being and can also present itself precisely as under way. A natural being is not static in its being. It comes to be. In its coming to be, we speak of that out of which it comes to be, the *hulē*, and that toward which it is directed in its coming to be (the *eidos*). The "matter" is here presented as not yet dwelling in its *eidos*, and therefore as *not* presencing as such. *Hulē*, matter, here shows itself as a privative (*sterēsis*) way of being (*Met.* 1033 a8–12).

The individual appears as not yet in its being. When we address the individual natural being as matter, we point to a moment or phase of this being that is only properly grasped in terms of the "structure" of being as a whole. If we take this way of appearing out of this context, then our interpretation of the being will fall away from the truth. We will take this being as mere matter, without being, and we will conclude that it is semblance. The possibility of a being appearing in this way is founded on its way of being as *kinēsis* that is under way and not yet fulfilled. The movement that is governed by *phusis* is necessary, but the character of this necessity is such that the being can also not reach fulfillment. The natural movement can be interfered with. The movement can, for example, be contained within limits that are imposed from outside itself, and thus it can be impeded from its own natural self-development. To a certain extent, art is related to natural beings in this way. It takes these beings as matter that is not yet formed and is therefore available to be directed by its external formation. Such a view of beings is a distortion of their true nature, for natural beings are never mere matter, although they can be viewed in this way.

The possibility of viewing natural beings as pure undetermined matter and thus distorting their true nature must be understood both from within beings themselves and from within the human being's relation to beings. Beings must somehow be able to present themselves to us in this way–as not being what they are–and this capacity must arise somehow from an essential characteristic of the being itself. On the other hand, the human being's ability to see beings only as matter at hand must also arise from an essential aspect of our relation to being.

Aristotle makes clear that beings are never simply matter. In fact, matter itself is not a being and therefore could never be found separate from beings that have matter (*Physics* 209 b23). Matter belongs to beings, but does not in itself constitute them as beings. Beings are always already separate and individual (*Met.* 1029 a27–28). That is, they have always already incorporated matter and exist as bodies (*Met.* 1037 a5). Thus natural beings, which are under way toward and becoming what they are, are already governed by their being. Being-toward cannot be properly understood by analogy to an abstract line—for example, where the end-point and middle point are essentially separate. A natural being in its movement toward itself is always already itself and its movement is a returning or turning back upon itself. The essential characteristic of natural movement is that it originates out of and toward itself while remaining in itself. *Kinēsis* is only possible in a body, and natural movement (*genesis*) is the embodiment of a being that embodies itself. The body that grows needs to take over for itself the material for its growth.[36] To do so, it seizes beings other than itself and takes from them what it can appropriate for itself. It reduces beings to non-being so that it can derive nourishment from them. It makes them over into matter for its own becoming. Generation is only possible because corruption is also possible (*Met.* 1044 b33; also 1059 a1–8). A being is always what it is, so long as it maintains itself as itself. It can also not be, for *hulē* is a way of holding itself in its *ousia* (*Met.* 1042 a33). Only inasmuch as the matter is directed toward and delimited by *morphē* (as *eidos*) is a being embodied in its *ousia*, and one with itself. Thus, it is *morphē* that defines what a being is and determines the appropriate matter that is essential to this being.

On the basis of this discussion, we can establish that the interrelation of separate beings, and to an extent the community of separate beings, is not due to the *morphē* or *eidos* but to *hulē*. Contact, succession, combination, locomotion, and so on are due to the *hulē* (*Met.* 1068 b25; 1069 a15). It is the matter that changes and is capable of passing into and out of a being (1070 a1). Thus, the matter in two different beings can bring these beings into touch with each other, even in such a way that they remain separate beings. For the separateness, the unity of a *this* is due to its *morphē* (and that matter that belongs to it through *morphē*) rather than its matter alone. In this sense, a variety of different qualities and relations can belong to a particular being or not belong to it without affecting the being itself as such. Only as matter can a being be affected in this way. On the other hand, its being a certain kind of being and its being essentially the same as other beings in the same genus or species, while remaining separate, is due to its *eidos* and not its matter. For the *eidos* does not change. It is that which keeps a being the same throughout change. Finally, we need to repeat Aristotle's caution that neither form nor matter can be understood as independent beings on their own. The *eidos* is always the *eidos* of something. And matter is always in something. Neither *eidos* nor *hulē* alone constitute the *ousia* of the individual being, but both together. In relating to beings, we can distinguish these two moments within the structure of a particular being. But such a procedure is founded on a prior discovery of the unity that constitutes the being in its being. It is only from a prior awareness of this unity that we can even relate to beings and recognize the nature of their being.

Hulē in Greek originally means forest and woodland, and not merely the trees or wood. It never means some originally unformed and indeterminate stuff that then is formed in some way.[37] It is only because it is first a forest that it can be used for hunting or firewood or material for construction. It is due to the nature of matter, and that is, of forests and trees and so on, that they are able to be taken only as mere material available for use, but this is not what they are in themselves. In themselves they have a movement that is appropriate to their being, a natural movement by which they bring themselves into being. Natural movement is here distinguished from the movement of production in that the formation is not imposed externally but governs from within the being itself. The tree that belongs to nature is always already a tree even as it grows and develops itself. It is never first something else and then becomes a tree when it moves or is moved into a certain figure. Thus, in order to understand *hulē* properly, and that means in terms of *ousia,* the being of natural beings, we need to address ourselves to the way in which *morphē* characterizes natural beings and the *kinēsis* proper to these beings.

Aristotle has in our present passage spoken of two paths that we can take in addressing beings. Along the first path, we address *phusis* in terms of *hulē,* which is already in advance incorporated in each individual, and is appropriated for the being that has the *archē* of movement and change in itself. As incorporated, *hulē* constitutes the basis and is the ground for change. It is the *hupokeimenon,* the lying-forth of the individual. Along the second path, *phusis* is addressed as *morphē* and *eidos.* The second path does not deny the first. Rather it points to the proper way in which *hulē* is to be understood for natural beings.

We have seen that if we take the first path as the only way of access to beings, then beings are no longer seen according to their own being, but as indeterminate matter whose shape and measure in an individual are illusion and nonbeing. To view *phusis* in this way is to exclude beings and the movement that belongs to them from being. Beings get taken as nonbeing. If we take the second path and understand *phusis* accordingly, to the exclusion of *hulē,* then a similar conclusion follows. Being is *eidos,* pure form and external appearance. Aristotle suggests that Plato addresses being in this way. Being is the *idea,* that which presents itself to be seen, and gathers the seeing in itself. Thus, Heidegger says:

> But overwhelmed perhaps by the essence (*Wesen*) of *eidos,* Plato understands it as something which is in turn itself present for itself, and thus as something which is common to the individual "beings" that "stand" in such an aspect. Thereby individuals, as following after and being added onto the *idea,* the genuine being, are reduced to the role of non-being. (WBP 345)

Nonbeing, as we have already discussed, is not simply nothing but rather that which is, but has no independent being of its own, and *is* only inasmuch as it appears along with what appears in itself as itself. Aristotle refers to this kind of appearance as *sumbebēkos,* incidental. The philosopher is the one who is able to see what truly shows itself as itself, and to do so, he or she must separate (*krinein*) being from the nonbeing, which only appears to be. For Platonism, this means individual beings are not to be mixed up with being. The shadows are not to be mistaken for the true. The sensuous that changes and looks one way and then another can only be at all to the extent that true being holds these appearances to itself. Being belongs essentially only to beings that truly are. When we address beings according to their *eidos,* we turn away from particularity and change and turn toward what commonly defines all beings and makes them one. Only to the extent that they share in this oneness can individual beings be said to be. Thus, all trees are inasmuch as they share in the one idea, the aspect that constitutes them as the same. Only this *eidos* is true being; becoming and change do not belong to it. If we turn our eyes toward individuals as individuals, we will not see being, or else we will only see an image of being; being as it shows itself in something else rather than in itself. But if we address ourselves rather according to the aspect into which natural beings emerge, we will see them, not in their particular appearance at any given time, but as they truly and always are. In Platonism, this aspect is nonsensuous. The senses and the kind of vision open to the senses (*aisthēsis*) are based on the capacity to be affected. Because the senses are able to be affected and because particular beings that have matter are able to be affected, humans and beings can "touch" one another. The "touching" here is not that of contact or succession, but an encountering that itself presupposes a "recollection" of a more originary relation to the being of beings. Thus, it is a genuine kind of knowledge, ontologically distinguished from animal sensibility. But such knowledge is always knowledge of the changing, and thus of nonbeing. The human being's uniqueness is that he or she can be free from the sensuous and catch a glimpse of being itself, which must have already been seen in order to be able to *know* what beings are. Plato says: "Every human soul, rising of itself, has already viewed beings in their being; otherwise it would never have entered into this form of life."[38] This path has in common with the opposite path we have discussed that natural beings, and the *kinēsis* that belongs to them, are reduced to nonbeing. Natural beings cannot "be" in themselves but can only be in another, the *eidos*, which, as a pure being, stands on its own and is itself. The *hen* of the Parmenideans becomes in Platonism a manifold of pure beings, but this community of *eidē* excludes change, and thus natural beings are kept apart from it. Aristotle says, in contrast, that such beings, if anything, are what we mean by *ousia*. "For everything which is common indicates not a 'this' but a 'such,' but *ousia* is a 'this'" (*Met.* 1003 a9–10).

For Aristotle, the question of being is the question of what makes a particular being the being that it is. "What we are seeking is the cause (that is, the *eidos*) of the *hulē* (by which the being appears) as something. This is the *ousia* of the being" (*Met.* 1041 b7–8). The *eidos* is here said to be responsible for the belonging of the *hulē* to a particular being in such a way that the being presences itself *as* the being it is. In a natural being, the *hulē* that belongs to it is not simply or randomly grouped together into one. If it were, the being would not be one but many. Aristotle uses the example of a syllable, which is never simply an arbitrary composition of letters, but is unique in itself and cannot be reduced to its elements. What makes a man a man or a house a house is not the list of elements to which it can be reduced, but that the matter is present in a unique being, and that the matter is directed in such a way that it constitutes the unity of that being. The natural being does not come to be after matter composes it. It always already is what it is and only for this reason does matter belong or not belong together with it. The whole and being as a whole is not like a heap but is a unity (*hen*) (*Met.* 1041 b11–13). "This is the *cause* that makes *this* thing flesh and *that* a syllable. And similarly in all other cases. And this is the presencing (*ousia*) of each individual (unified) being. For this in advance is responsible for its being a being" (*Met.* 1041 b28–29). Such a being is said to gathered together in accord with *phusis* and by *phusis* and thus *phusis* governs over its being and presencing. *Phusis* is the *eidos* of natural beings. It is the *eidos* that determines a being *as* something.

We can see then that for Aristotle the path that leads to *eidos* and under-stands the being of beings in this way is more truly philosophical and closer to the truth than that which interprets *phusis* as *hulē*. But the *eidos*, like *hulē*, never exists independently of the being of which it is the aspect. "Is there then a sphere apart from the individual spheres or a house apart from the bricks? Rather we may say that no 'this' would ever have been coming to be if this were so, but that the 'aspect' means the 'such' and is not a 'this'–a delimited being (*horismenon*)" (*Met.* 1033 b20–23). The attempt to understand *eidos* as separate from beings and thus to preserve it from change and becoming results again in the interpretation of being as *a being.* Both the path downward that reduces beings to matter and the path up-ward that goes beyond beings to an eternal form stem from a failure to at-tend in the proper way to the phenomena that appear "in" *phusis.* For Ar-istotle, the present individual being that we encounter in the world is not nonbeing. *Hulē* and *morphē* are not "in" beings so that they could ever be separated out (as if they were non-essential properties). Rather, together they constitute the being of a particular being. "But as has been said, the closest matter and the shape are one and the same" (*Met.* 1045 b17–18). They are the twofold *archē* that directs and governs over the emerging of natural beings. At the same time, they are this emerging-forth itself from out of itself toward itself while remaining always in itself that is the way of being of natural beings. Heidegger translates *morphē* as "*Gestellung in das Aussehen*" (WBP 351). It is the gathering-together as a unity and the plac-ing forth of a being in its aspect (*Aussehen-eidos*) as the way of presencing of natural beings. Beings appear as what they are by holding themselves al-ways (*jeweilige*) in this presencing that constitutes their being at every mo-ment. "If therefore we simply speak of the 'aspect' in what follows, then we are always thinking of the 'aspect' which gives itself (*es ausgibt*) and inso-far as it gives itself in the present being (*das Jeweilige*)" (WBP 346). The path of Aristotle's thought follows the way in which being gives itself to be-ings and thus lets them be.

We have seen that the structure of beings is such that a being is never simply present at hand before us in such a way that it can be totally grasped in any particular concrete view that it presents. Rather, a being is always individualized in such a way that it *is* constantly related to the community of beings in which it is involved. This is true on two levels. Inasmuch as a being is constituted by *hulē* and is directed and unified according to *eidos,* it sets itself forth by taking up into itself what is appropriate to it in its be-coming. Thus, *kinēsis* is the fundamental character of natural beings. A being is necessarily, and that is to say always (in a way that is constitutive to its being), in a relation with other beings that it encounters. On one level this interrelation is governed by *hulē*. It accounts for the possibility of relations that affect a being, but not essentially as the being that it is. For example, a certain temperature is appropriate to wood, but if it comes into contact with fire, its own degree of heat will be affected by the sharing that is forced on it through this contact (*Physics* 246 b1). If the contact and force are prolonged, it may even be deprived of or prevented from fulfilling its own nature as wood. Although wood can become other than it is, its nature will always be that of wood, as long as it is. Change, on this level, is never natural change, although it is not contrary to nature in the sense that the nature of natural beings is such that they *can* be affected in this way (*Physics* 246 b10–17). The community of beings on this level presupposes first of all that there *are* natural beings and that these beings do have a movement of their own that is open to such interference. In fact, the very way in which a being grows naturally through incorporation depends on this level of community so that its own *hulē* is available to it. This interrelation of beings, and the movement therein, is determined by another level of community and another way of *kinēsis*. This other path is not that of beings, but that which first of all constitutes beings as beings so that they can at all be related in the first way. It is the being of beings, the *koinonia*, that allows beings to stand together as unique in their being—the community of *eidē*. Just as *hulē* is first of all the *hulē* of an individual being and only then able to be shared and adapted as a source of interrelation and community, so also *eidos* is always the *eidos* of something (as *morphē*), and only then can we speak of beings that have the same being (*Met.* 1045 a15–30). Being itself or *eidos* in itself does not exist and is not a being that stands above and gets shared in or participated in by other, lesser beings. Rather, beings of the same kind (nature) emerge forth and direct themselves toward and exist in accordance with what they are in common. A natural being is what it is *of itself*. Being the individual being that it is and sharing in a community of such beings are one and the same. It is the beings holding itself in that community that constitutes it as an individual. Its essence and existence are the same. In becoming what it is, it is at every moment and every phase always already what it is. Becoming what it is and being what it is are the same. It is the character of this sameness that Aristotle seeks to understand. The sameness does not eliminate the twofoldness that is characteristic of natural beings (*hulē-morphē*, existence-essence, becoming-being). Rather, it is the unity of a belonging-together of this twofoldness, the unity of natural *kinēsis* as the way of *ousia* of beings by *phusis*. Likewise, oneness and plurality, or individuality and community, are not mutually exclusive. Aristotle's entire contribution to Greek thought is guided by the insight that the being of natural beings constitutes the sameness (and difference) of these apparently contradictory poles. It is this thought that represents the philosophical task he inherited from the community of thinkers in which he lived. Aristotle's *methodos* is to hold himself open to the twofoldness of *phusis* and the oneness that belongs to this twofoldness. The twofoldness of being and beings and the twofoldness of being itself have come to light in Aristotle's investigation through the *logos* in which he pursued his path of thought. The next passage again brings the nature of this *logos* back to our attention.

The Way of *Logos* in the Discovery of *Phusis*

Just as we (loosely) call by the name *technē* what is produced in accord with this kind of knowing, and thus also what belongs to beings of this sort, so also we (loosely) call by the name *phusis* whatever is in accord with *phusis* and consequently belongs to beings of this sort. On the other hand, we would never want to say that something holds itself together (and presences) in accord with *technē* or that *technē* is there if something is a bedstead merely in terms of appropriateness (*dunamei*), but in no way has the aspect of a bedstead; nor would we do so in the address of those beings which place themselves together in a stand by *phusis*. For what is flesh and bones only in terms of appropriateness never has *phusis* belonging to it before it attains the aspect which is grasped in accord with the address—which we delimit when we say *what* flesh or bones is; nor is (that which is only appropriated) already a natural being. For this reason (then), *phusis* would in another way be the placing into the aspect *(Gestellung in das Aussehen)* for those beings which have in themselves the originating and governing over movement. Of course, placing and aspect are nothing on their own; rather they are only ever able to be shown in the addressing of a given being. However, that which stands forth from out of these (from out of the suitability and the placing) is certainly not *phusis* itself, but rather a being from *phusis*, as, for example, a human being. (*Physics* 193 a31-b 6; WBP 346-7 and 351)

In this passage, Aristotle takes a radical new step in the path of his philosophy. He introduces the notion of potentiality (*dunamis*). In Homer, the word means power or force and thus the capacity or strength to achieve something. In Aristotle, *dunamis* becomes a philosophical term that characterizes a mode of being of natural beings (and produced beings). *Dunamis* is a way in which natural beings, which are constituted by *hulē*, have their being. Thus, *dunamis* further develops the meaning of *hulē* in Aristotle's thought. Just as *hulē* belongs essentially to natural beings only when it is directed toward and governed by *morphē* (*eidos*), so also *dunamis* can only properly be said to belong to natural beings to the extent that it is a *dunamis* for the achievement of the being of these beings. Thus, *dunamis* means being-appropriated toward (*Eignung nach*) (WBP 347). *Dunamis* like *hulē* must be understood in terms of the *ousia*, the presencing. It is a constitutive moment (phase) in the structure of natural beings that achieve their presencing through *kinēsis*. If *dunamis* is translated as potentiality or possibility, then these terms need to be thought also as *hulē*. The being that is constituted by *dunamis* does not lose its potentiality (or its *hulē*) when it fulfills itself.

A natural being cannot be said to be if it is not yet what it is but only could be. Mere potentiality does not suffice to characterize the *dunamis* that *belongs to* natural beings. We have already seen that only the *hulē* that is incorporated in accord with the aspect toward which a natural being is directed can be considered the *hupokeimenon* of natural beings. Likewise, we see here that only the *dunamis* that is appropriated in accord with the aspect can be said to belong essentially to a being "that places itself together into a stand (*sunistamenois*) by *phusis*" (*Physics* 193 b1). *Dunamis* expresses more clearly this being-directed toward and in relation with the *eidos* than *hulē* does. The being that *is* is by shaping what is appropriated into its limits and containing it by holding itself together in the presencing of itself in its aspect. Aristotle speaks in this passage of *hē morphē kai to eidos* as *phusis*, and says again that *phusis* is to be understood as the *archē* of the movement of natural beings. Heidegger translates it as *Gestellung in das Aussehen*. It is the look or outward appearance that something offers. This translation is more in keeping with the meaning of *eidos* (that which is seen) than the word "form." *Gestelling* means to *place* something in a certain arrangement, and thus it means the shaping or configuration that something has. In order to retain the relation to *kinēsis* that Heidegger sees here, we have translated *Gestellung in das Aussehen* as "placing into the aspect," but the shaping or gathering into the form of the *hulē* is also intended as the meaning of *morphē*. In order to understand a natural being as it is, we need to grasp this being by seeing this delimitation—and ourselves defining a being in this way. We do so, Aristotle says, when we grasp the aspect "*kata ton logon*" (*Physics* 193 b2).

The grasping of the aspect alone (as the Platonists would demand) is, according to Aristotle, not sufficient for understanding natural beings. Nor, more obviously, is pointing out the *dunamis* or *hulē* (as Antiphon would demand) sufficient. Neither *hulē* nor *eidos,* in fact, are alone, and therefore isolating them from the togetherness in which they belong must result in a distortion of the truth. The *dunamis* is a constitutive element of natural beings. But it is so only as the incorporation of its *eidos*—as *morphē*. It is only if we first recognize the being as a whole and address it as a whole that we can see, through our relation with beings, that there are moments that constitute the being in its being. This means that the *eidos* as that toward which a being moves must already be there, and that we must already see it when we speak of *dunamis* as a characteristic of natural beings. That from out of which and with which (*hulē*) a being comes to be in its aspect must be a being toward (*dunamis*) that for the sake of which it is incorporated. In order for the *eidos* to be the *eidos* of a natural being, it cannot ever be outside of the being since it is due to its *eidos* that the being is at all. *Dunamis* and *eidos* are modes of being, of *phusis*, and not themselves beings.

Aristotle, nevertheless, does point out that we sometimes do *speak* (loosely) of *phusis* (and *technē*) in a way that would imply that the being itself is *phusis*, and that what belongs to it is physical, even though, to be exact, we would have to say that *phusis* is the being of such beings and that such beings are in accord with *phusis*. The problematic that emerges in this less precise way of speaking is that, were being entirely restricted to a particular being, then either we would have to say that only this particular being is, or else that there are lots of beings, one for each particular being that is (*Met.* 1039 b9). In order to avoid the evident problems that would emerge from such an understanding of being, we have to acknowledge a certain difference between a being and being. Yet, on the other hand, Aristotle also maintains that being is not a being that exists apart from the being. To resolve to a certain extent this difficulty, we need to recognize that being does not "exist" at all; only beings exist. Individual, separate beings *are* inasmuch as they stand forth and stand there in their being. Being (*ousia*) is this holding itself as itself. Thus, beings that emerge and become present in the same way can be said to "have" the same being. They hold themselves together and show themselves in the sameness of their being. That according to which they appropriate to themselves their own uniqueness also is the ground of their sameness with other beings. This is *eidos*. Thus, when we point to a particular being and say, "*there* is *phusis*," we do so with truth. But we never say this of a particular being if we are merely pointing to the *dunamis*. We only truly speak of a natural being as *phusis* when the *eidos* is also already there and when the being shines forth as a whole in the limits of its *eidos*—when it has attained its aspect and thus reveals itself as the being it is. Only when the *eidos* is seen as that which the

individual always already is (*to ti ēn einai*) can we see the being in its being
and define it through *logos* as *phusis* (*Met.* 1022 a26). By addressing the
being according to what it is, its *eidos,* we see the being both in its uniqueness and self-sameness (*chōriston*), and in its being of the same kind as
other beings. The boundaries that are encompassed in our grasp, through a
logos of the *eidos,* are the horizon in which a unified being unfolds and
comes to be. "The boundary is that from which something *begins its essential unfolding.* That is why the concept is discovered through definition
(*horismos*), that is, the concept names the horizon, the boundary."39 To
understand a being in its being, we need to perceive the being not merely in
the particular way it shows itself at a given time; we need also and in advance to see the being by looking beyond the being to the horizon out of
which and toward which the being is. This is the *archē* and *phusis* of the
being. We then stand in relation to the being of this being. Aristotle speaks
of this relation as a way of addressing beings (in their being). It is not simply a grasping (*noein*) of the *eidos* that is involved, but a grasping of the
eidos through *logos.* It is through *logos* that we see the being in terms of its
eidos and we see the *eidos* as that which constitutes the being as a being.

We have already seen that *morphē* has a certain priority in the structure
of *phusis* and that Aristotle thinks *morphē* as *eidos,* the way a being shows
itself to us in advance in its being. But, even here, Aristotle does not say
eidos is the meaning of being but *eidos to kata ton logon* (*Physics* 193 b2).
As Heidegger points out, "*eidos* is understood essentially as *eidos* only
when it shows itself in the horizon of an immediate address of beings"
(WBP 345). For Aristotle, the *eidos* is always the *eidos* of a being. Thus, the
human being cannot attain a relationship to being by abandoning his relation to beings. To reduce beings to nonbeing and to see beings as not belonging to being necessarily also keeps being away from view. Our relation
to beings *and* being is called *logos.* If our *logos* fails to be a standing in a
proper relation to being and beings, then our interpretation of natural beings and of *phusis* itself will fall short of the truth. The way of *logos* is not
a logic or formal system of language that we place between ourselves and
beings in order to interpret beings through language. Rather, language itself is the deposit and formalization of the discoveries about beings and
being that the original relationship of humans and beings makes evident.
Divorced from this primary meaning, language loses its force and falls out
of its element (WBP 350).

Thus, in order to understand the nature of language, we need first to
grasp who the human being is as the "*zōon logon echon*—living being to

logos not
an attribute
of the
human
being
it

whom *logos* belongs" (WBP 348). In this definition of being-human, Aristotle does not say that *logos* is an attribute of the human being. Rather *logos* defines the human being and sets him or her apart as human. For human beings, *logos* and *phusis* are the same. The being of the human being is this dwelling (*echein*) in this relation to being. It is because the human being is always in this relation that she is able to come back from it to beings and interpret them by holding them out toward this understanding of being. Because the human being not only has her being in itself but is also aware of her being and chooses her being (for herself), her highest self-expression (*aretē*) is the knowledge of *archē* and *aitia* (*Met.* I, 2). In order to be able to think *logos* and *legein* in this more originary sense (and thus in order to be able to understand the essence of language), Heidegger directs our attention to Heraclitus.

Fragment B 50 of Heraclitus says: "*ouk emou alla tou logou akousantas homolegein sophon estin hen panta.*"[40] David Krell in *Early Greek Thinking* translates Heidegger's philosophical rendition of this sentence as follows:

Do not listen to me, the moral speaker, but be in hearkening to the laying that gathers; first belong to this and then you hear properly; such hearing *is* when a letting-lie-together-before occurs by which the gathering letting-lie, the laying that gathers, lies before us as gathered; when a letting lie of the letting-lie-before occurs, the fateful comes to pass; then the truly fateful, i.e., destiny alone, is: the unique One unifying All.[41]

Here *hen-panta*, one and all, are spoken together by Heraclitus. Heidegger attempts to understand this "belonging-together" on the basis of the rest of the fragment. Heraclitus says that we will see this belonging-together of the one-all when we have listened not to the human discourse of Heraclitus, but to *the* logos and when our own *logos* is the same. The fragment points to the central significance of *logos* in determining the meaning of being.

Heidegger seeks to interpret the meaning of *logos* in Heraclitus by thinking through the original meaning of this word that he hears resonating in the verb form *legein*, which means to lay down and lay before. Among the original meanings of *legein*, Liddell and Scott cite: to lay, to pick up, to gather, to choose for oneself, to pick out. Heidegger sees in these meanings a relation to the *dunamis kata ton logon* that Aristotle discusses in *Metapysics* θ 2.[42] Here *dunamis*, Heidegger claims, means to be selected and cut out for and thus appropriated toward. To lay means to bring to lie. Laying lets things lie together before us. It gathers them together, not randomly, but with an eye to their belonging. Thus, the laying that gathers lets lie before us that which is already determined as gathered. It selects and sorts out with the "end" in view. The "end," the sheltering and safekeeping for the sake of which the gathering is accomplished in advance, guides the selection of what is laid down. The laying that lets things lie before us maintains these things in their appearing; it preserves them in presencing. "Laying is the letting-lie-before—which is gathered into itself—of that which comes together into presence."43 The laying of *legein* preserves beings in unconcealment. Heidegger's extensive consideration of the implication of the meaning of to lay down and lay before throws light on the later meaning of *legein* in the sense of saying and speaking. In its original signification, language does not mean merely the sounds and phonics of speech; rather, saying brings before us that which shows itself. "Saying is the letting-lie-together-before which gathers and is gathered."44

Heraclitus admonishes us not to listen to *him* but to the *logos*. There corresponds to every saying that is a proper gathering of what presences itself a hearing. Therefore, Heidegger also considers the nature of this hearing. Just as speaking is not fundamentally vocalization, so hearing is not in its being a mere reverberation in the ear. The same gathering that every proper saying requires is also necessary in order to hear. The gathering of what is heard presupposes also that we are gathered ourselves and attuned to that which is heard, that we belong to it. What is heard is the *logos*, the original gathering together of what lies before us in unconcealment. When we have listened to the *logos* itself, and not merely to what is said about the *logos,* then we let-lie-before, we gather, that which is already there. We let it reveal itself as it is. This is the original meaning of saying. In listening to the *logos,* we say the same, that is, we gather what already lies together.

What occurs in this saying of the same is named by Heraclitus in the final words of this fragment: *hen-panta.* In Fragment B32, Heraclitus says that the "one" is alone *to sophon.* Here is Fragment B50, *sophon* (the *hen* that shows itself and is seen by the wise) is "the way in which *logos* essentially occurs."45 It occurs in such a way that *hen* and *panta* are the same. The sameness of the one and the manifold occurs in *logos. Logos* gathers what appears into one, it lets what comes into presence appear as itself. "*Legein* lets *alētheia,* what is unconcealed as such, lie before us."46 Heidegger refers us to Fragment B112, which says that *sophon,* which Heraclitus also names the "one," occurs when we listen to the *logos,* and having gathered ourselves, let what is unconcealed lie before us and bring forth that which lies before us according to *phusis.* Here *phusis* and *logos* name the same original gathering by which beings show themselves in their being.

Phusis is a gathering that unifies and lets beings be separate in their same-ness and the same in their separateness. Separateness, individuality, multi-plicity is determined out of an original oneness. It is only in that beings present themselves as a whole that they are the beings they are. On the other hand, the oneness itself occurs not as a "one" that stands above and removed from the manifold that it governs, but as *logos,* as the original gathering unity of what emerges into unconcealment. The belonging-together of that which is the same and the difference that this sameness grants to the beings that emerge in its light are reciprocally inclined toward each other. *Phusis, logos, hen, alētheia* are all ways in which Heraclitus names the presencing of beings in their being.

In letting beings appear, presencing itself withdraws and reveals itself only as other than and not reducible to that which is present. In doing so, it grants to beings the difference that permits them to be what they are while maintaining them in its unifying oneness. Because being must conceal itself in order to reveal beings, *alētheia,* unconcealment, remains intrinsically re-lated to concealment. In appearing, beings hold within themselves the pos-sibility of showing themselves as other than they are in their being. There is the possibility that the being of these beings will remain concealed. Beings that come into presence achieve a standing and endure through the sustain-ing power of *logos.* But this enduring is not a static resting that, once achieved, continues to be. In every coming into presence, Heraclitus says in Fragment B53, there is *polemos.* Conflict is the tending apart of what is gathered together and the gathering of what tends apart. In Fragment B80, Heraclitus says: "it is necessary to keep in view the setting apart of beings (*polemos*) as bringing together (*zunon*), and joining together and ordering (*dikē*) as tending apart (*erin*).[47] It is only because they are gathered to-gether in the open that beings are able to appear as set apart from one an-other in their uniqueness. And it is because they are set apart that they must constantly be gathered back into the original unity. Heidegger tells us that this holding together of oppositions is what the Greeks experienced as beauty (*kalon*): "What the Greeks meant by 'beauty' was restraint. The gathering of the supreme antagonism is *polemos,* struggle in the sense of setting-apart. . . . For the Greeks *on* and *kalon* say the same thing (presenc-ing is pure radiance)."[48] *Logos* for Heraclitus is the gathering and joining of what tends apart. As such, it governs and keeps in its power that which it brings into the light. It is *phusis,* the power of emerging forth and rising out of concealment. In order for a being to show itself as it is and to sustain itself in its being, human *logos* must look beyond the immediate appearance of the being in such a way that its *logos* is *homologein,* a gathering back of what tends apart into the power of this original unifying unity.

Heraclitus speaks often of this task of the human being by which *sophon* comes to pass. In Fragment B43, Heraclitus says "measureless pride needs to be extinguished sooner than a raging fire." The measuring and determining of what is are tasks the human being shares, but they are only successfully and properly accomplished when they are attuned to *logos.* Because beings are capable of revealing themselves as other than they are, human beings can gather together and lay down these beings in an appearance that covers over their being. Thus, Heraclitus says in Fragment B1 that the many (the *hoi polloi*) seem to be acting according to truth, but "it remains hidden to them what they actually do while awake, just as what they have done in sleep afterwards hides itself again from them." Their deeds pass for those of Heraclitus, who determines each being by separating it in relation to *phusis;* but because they are uncomprehending, they do not bring together what is constantly together (the *logos*). "What they continually associate with most of all, with the *logos,* to it they turn their back, and what they daily encounter appears foreign to them" (Fragment B72). Heraclitus reserves his most stinging remarks for such people. In Fragment B92, he says: "dogs bark at everyone they do not know," and in Fragment B97 he remarks: "asses prefer hay to gold." In contrast to this, Heraclitus speaks in Fragment B112 of *sophronein,* proper thinking, which he calls the greatest *aretē.* When such thinking attunes itself to the *logos,* then the fateful *sophon* occurs, that is, we gather together and bring forth what appears. *Phusis* and *logos* name the same for Heraclitus: the gathering together and emerging forth in unconcealment of what is.

Heidegger emphasizes throughout his works the importance of properly understanding the meaning of *logos.* "*Legein* is the guideline for arriving at the structures of the being of the beings we encounter."[49] It is *logos* that constitutes the essence of human being. In this passage from Aristotle's *Physics* that occasions the need to question what role *logos* has in the study of *phusis,* Aristotle mentions a kind of discourse that points to a certain exemplary being and then says "*there is phusis.*" Not every *logos* of beings reveals the *phusis* of being, but only that which takes into account the *eidos* and lets the being be seen in its *eidos.* Only then, according to Aristotle, can we say nature itself is revealed as the nature of a natural being. Only when we address a being according to *what it is* do we let a being be seen in its being. Such a *logos* must somehow already have being in view in order to articulate beings in this way. And yet this pre-view (*prohairesis*) cannot be of *something* that is there outside of these beings, which *logos* adds on to beings. The foregrasping is rather a way of understanding the being of beings in which human beings always dwell, and thus it makes it possible for humans to interpret beings. This dwelling in an understanding relation to being is what Aristotle calls *noein,* the seeing of the *archē* and *eidos* of beings.[50] Just as *eidos* as one of the *aitia* and *archē* of natural beings has a special rank and can be addressed, if properly thought, as the unity of the other structural moments (e.g., the *hulē* and *telos*) so also *noein,* which sees the eidos, can be said to be the unity of knowing that gathers the structurally different moments of knowing (e.g., the relation to beings, to being etc.) into a whole and lets knowing take place. Just as the sameness of a being with itself does not contradict *kinēsis* as the character of this sameness in natural beings, so the unity and simplicity of *noein* govern over and direct the movement of the soul. Just as being does not exist outside of beings, so *nous* does not exist apart from a human being who is thinking,[51] and therefore is not a "part" of the human being. *Noein* is rather the way of being. It is the oneness and simplicity of a *logos* that listens to the *legein* of being.

The traditional interpretation of Aristotle's definition of the human being is that he is a rational animal. This implies that he is first an animal and then also has the "faculty" of thinking. Similarly, animals first are and then have the faculty of perception. These categories disguise a hidden assumption about what it means to be that is foreign to Aristotle's thought. The human being's embodiment is not separate from thinking. Rather, *legein* and *noein* constitute the way in which the human being embodies himself as a whole. Aristotle says: "It is the soul which is the *energeia* of the body."[52] Just as a being from *phusis* does not alter *itself* or become other than itself when it moves toward and rests in its being, so also, says Aristotle, the human being, "the being that holds itself knowingly (whose being is to know), becomes a knower in the fulfillment of its being by a movement which is either not an alteration of it at all (being in reality a development of its true self) or at least an alteration in a quite different sense from the usual meaning."[53] What moves a human being from the *dunamis* to know to the *energeia* of knowing, to the fulfillment of her being in knowing, is not anything outside the human being herself, but rather the source of this movement is within the soul itself.[54] Thus, Aristotle says, in agreement with Parmenides, that (theoretical) knowledge and its "object" are identical.[55] This could not mean, however, that being or beings exist in *nous* since "mind" is not a thing but the *energeia* of human being;[56] nor could it mean that mind is taken over by its object since mind (unlike appetite) cannot be affected.[57] Rather, neither *nous* nor the *eidos,* which is always there whenever *nous* is, are beings or things in themselves. The *eidos* is the unity and simplicity of being as a whole. A being can show itself as it is in itself only for a being whose being is such as to be open to grasp the being in the simplicity of a view (*noein*) that has previously gathered the being together and let it be seen as a whole.[58] The being of beings only reveals itself in this view. But this view of being only first arises and is there when being lets itself be seen in it as the being of beings.[59] When we see a being in its *eidos* and say, "there is *phusis,*" we give witness to this relation to being. The uniqueness of human being is this openness to being. The human being lives in this understanding of being in such a way that he is always in advance guided by it and guides himself by it even as he is under way toward his being.

The *logos* that defines the being of human beings is itself a gathering that allows them to be. The human being *is* in such a way that she is always reaching out toward her being. Thus, Aristotle speaks of needs and desires of the soul that, although not *logos* (*alogos*), are governed by *logos* and thus appropriated for and belonging to that toward which their striving is directed.[60] The soul moves out of itself (out of and beyond the striving) and toward itself (toward the fulfillment of its being) by holding itself (*echein*) in *logos*. Thus, happiness (*eudaimonia*) is not an activity (*energeia*) that comes at the end and is separate from desire and pleasure, but it is rather the fulfillment and unity of the human being as a whole. "For the human being, therefore, the life which is in accord with *nous* is best and most pleasant, since *nous,* above all else is the human being."[61]

The *alogos,* as desire and striving (*orexis*), shares in the *logos* by listening to it and obeying it (*Met.* 1103 a1–3). In the person who has achieved self-fulfillment (*eudaimonia*), these two "parts" of the soul are together in harmony. The *alogos* (structurally comparable to *hulē* and *dunamis* in natural beings, but distinct because the human being freely controls and chooses his or her destiny) is directed by and toward the *logos* and so co-constitutes the being of the human being. The human being is *logos,* but he does not possess it in a stagnant way as something he has accomplished. Rather his happiness is the *energeia* in which the soul rests. It is the concentration and unity of the soul in the simple vision of being. It is the *logos* that gathers itself in a sameness with itself, free from bondage to what is other than itself: "Such a person (the philosopher) has the highest degree of self-sameness" (*Met.* 1177 b1–2). The character of this sameness with herself that determines the human being as such opens her to a relation with other beings that does not depend on need or force. The "bond" of friendship is for Aristotle the full blossoming of an individual's uniqueness: "in loving a friend they love their own good" (*Met.* 1157 b33). *Noein* constitutes the self as a self. It rises into being when it lets that which is always the same be seen in its sameness. In witnessing the other in its uniqueness, the human being becomes *what* he is. The human being's separateness is always also, in an equally originary manner, a being-together with others. Heidegger responds to the charge that Aristotle's appeal to *logos* stands in the way of an originary "phenomenology" of being by saying:

But why do we lose ourselves in this wide-ranging digression into a discussion of the essence of *logos* when the question here is about the essence of *phusis*? We do so in order to make clear that when Aristotle appeals to *legesthai* he is not looking for external guidance from some linguistic usage but is thinking out of an originary and fundamental relation to beings. (WBP 350)

It is because the human being "has" *logos* that he can relate to beings and being and know the *phusis* of natural beings. The freeing of the question of *phusis* into its proper horizon and essence and thus letting natural beings emerge as the beings they are is achieved through the power that belongs to *logos*. It is through this attunement to being that the proper ontological insight into *kinēsis* as the way of being of natural beings is accomplished.

Genesis and *Sterēsis:* The Negation at the Heart of Being

"Therefore a human being is generated (comes forth) from a human being, but not a bedstead from a bedstead.". . . And furthermore, *phusis,* which is spoken of as *genesis,* that is, as drawing away from and emerging into (*Ent-stand*), is nothing less than underway towards *phusis*. (And this), of course, not as the practice of medicine is said to be the way not towards the art of medicine but towards health. For whereas the practice of medicine necessarily comes from the art of medicine, it is not directed towards this art (as its end). But *phusis* is not related to *phusis* in this way (namely as medicine is to health). Rather, a being from *phusis* goes from something towards something insofar as it is determined by *phusis* (in the movement of this being on the way). But towards what does it emerge in the manner of *phusis*? Not towards that from which (it withdraws itself at the time) but rather that towards that *as* which it is generated at the time. . . . This, then, the placing into the aspect (*morphē*) is *phusis*. Therefore *phusis* is spoken of in two ways, for *sterēsis,* privation, is also a kind of aspect (*eidos*). (Physics 193 b8–12)

We have not really looked at this peculiar kind of movement that Aristotle calls *genesis*. In fact, *genesis* is not even mentioned among the kinds of motion, locomotion, alteration, and so on that Aristotle mentions earlier. The movement that characterizes natural beings in their essence is not of the same order as that kind of motion that comes and goes within the oneness and sameness of a natural being. Aristotle names this other kind of *kinēsis*, *genesis*. *Genesis* is not from *phusis* as are the motions involved in the categories: quantity, quality, and so on. Instead, *genesis is* the essence of *phusis* (particularly of *phusis* understood as *morphē*).

It was the failure to differentiate *genesis* from the other kinds of motion that led to the failure to understand the nature of natural beings. We have seen that this inability to distinguish the two is not accidental but stems from the tendency to view beings through our involvement with them in *technē*. *Technē* is indeed a kind of becoming but not a *genesis*. For there is no *genesis* of what is produced through *technē*. Produced beings do indeed come forth and *are* as having been brought forth, but their way of coming forth is through a making. They do not come forth from out of themselves. Produced beings are not in themselves directed-toward their end. Thus, the movement that characterizes their coming forth is *energeia atelēs*. Indeed the *ergon* does not appear at all on its own in what is to be brought forth. Rather the *eidos* is brought along in the coming forth and is able to direct the coming forth only because the craftsperson holds the aspect out ahead as a paradigm that guides her work. It is the craftsperson who places the produced being in its aspect and thus lets it be a work. The being that is brought forth in this way owes its coming to be to the artist. It stands on its own as a work only because the artist has worked on it, and, having finished, withdraws.

The artist is able to lead a being forth in this way because she pays attention to the various ways in which beings move and can be moved. She knows the wood is hard and naturally holds itself in this constitution, and yet is malleable. She knows that it can be made smooth, flat, round, and so forth and thus that it is suitable as material for a table. The artist ignores the movement that is the *phusis* of wood because she is concerned only with the kinds of motion that this *phusis* permits. In ignoring *genesis*, she takes for granted what first of all makes her work possible. Thus, Aristotle is concerned throughout Book II of the *Physics* to differentiate the coming forth that is governed by *phusis* from that which is directed by *technē*. With the naming of *genesis* as the *kinēsis* that is proper to natural beings, this differentiation is completed. It is not a differentiation so much between two ontic kinds of motion as between the ordinary way in which *kinēsis* is seen and the ontological source of that motion. It is the difference between the *kinēsis* of beings and the being of *kinēsis;* the difference between being and beings.

The difference between being and beings is operative in Aristotle's philosophy and is really the horizon of his thought, but it is not so clearly demarcated (which is not to say it is confused). Therefore, it is often missed by commentators. Our confusion arises from thinking being and beings as separate and not thinking through the nature of the relationship. Part of the failure to think in terms of the ontological difference is that we have taken over our understanding of beings from *technē*. But *genesis* is a natural coming forth that the craftsperson ignores or even violates. In *technē*, the being character of beings is unimportant. But *technē* depends on *phusis*. *Phusis* is not a kind of self-making or technique. Rather, *technē* and making imitate nature.

Aristotle distinguishes the "*metabolē*" of *genesis* from motion at *Physics* V 225 a 25f:

> Therefore it is impossible for that which is not to move. This being the case, *genesis* cannot be *kinēsis* for it is that which is not which is generated. . . . So too, "perishing" is not a motion; for a motion has its contrary in either another motion or rest, whereas "perishing" (*pthora*) is the *enantion*, the contrary of *genesis*. . . . it is a change which implies a relationship of contradiction (*antiphasin*), not motion.

In order to understand what is involved in this distinction, and indeed the whole of Book V of the *Physics* that establishes this distinction, we need to consider what Aristotle means by *metabolē*. Change is a broader concept than *kinēsis*. It includes *genesis* as well. "Every *metabolē* is (a transition) from something into something" (225 a1). Thus, *genesis* is a drawing away from something beyond and into something. That from which a being comes and that toward which it becomes are not the same. Otherwise there would be no change (*Physics* 225 a2). In *genesis*, something other and separate comes into being. The difference between *genesis* and other kinds of motion (alteration, locomotion, etc.) is that motions are between contraries (e.g., hot and cold), whereas in *genesis,* the opposition of the 'from which' and the 'into which' is not between contraries but between contradictories. In *genesis,* beings come to be from not-being and not-being comes to be from being. "Change from not-being-there to being-there, the relationship being that of contradiction, is *genesis*" (*Physics* 225 a12).

Contradiction is at the heart of *genesis*. This relation between being and not-being is precisely what makes possible the being of natural beings. If *metabolē,* that is, *genesis,* were not able to hold together this radical opposition, then natural beings could not be. It was the apparently irreconcilable split between being and not-being, the fact, for example, that they cannot be said together, that led to the denial of natural beings as illusion and deception. Aristotle achieved for Greek philosophy the insight into the horizon that makes it possible for natural beings to be. At the center of his understanding of the law of non-contradiction, he introduced *time*. Natural beings are finite and temporal. It is as such that they can stand in relation to not-being and still be. But Aristotle here insists that this relation is *metabolē* but not *kinēsis*. Why is the coming from not-being into being, even if it is possible, not motion? Why is it rather, as Aristotle says, the presence and absence of change.

At *Physics* 225a 10, Aristotle says that "with respect to *ousia*, there is not motion." If a natural being is placed forth into presencing, then it *is*. If it is not, then it absolutely is not. With regard to being, a being either is or is not. Yet natural beings do have change into opposites (not-being into being and vice versa). If they did not stand in this relationship, then that which is not could not come to be, nor could that which is cease to be. Thus, Aristotle says that beings do not stay in their being as a simple unit would, but rather they endure inasmuch as their *genesis* is also an absence of change with regard to not-being (*Physics* 230 b10–11). Natural beings are able to be because their being is *twofold*. "Thus perishing is change to not-being, though it is also true that that which perishes changes from being; and *genesis* is change to being, though it is also change from not-being" (*Physics* 230 a12). In *genesis,* a being sustains itself in its being *as long as it is*. The becoming is not such that it comes to be only when it reaches its end. In its coming to be, it already is.

On the basis of *genesis,* then, Aristotle completes the contrast between *technē* and *phusis*. A bedframe is not natural. If it were, then a bedframe would be generated from a bedframe. Rather, what is natural in the manufactured bedframe is the wood. But the wood, as natural, only appears as *hulē* in the bedframe. It is for this reason that Antiphon mistakenly identified the *hulē* as true being. But to be *hulē* in the production of manufactured things is not what wood is according to its nature. This is why a bedframe is not natural, even though the artist uses natural beings in her production. The structure (*schēma*) into which wood is brought in the making of the bedframe is brought to it; it does not come forth on its own (*Physics* 193 b9–10). The natural being, in this case wood, is affected by what is outside of itself. We have already seen that it is the character of the "necessity" of natural beings that they can be affected in these ways. Still, the bedframe is what it is because of this structure that is given to it in *technē*. In contrast, as Heidegger explains, "*morphē* is the *phusis* of natural beings, for a human being is generated out of a human being" (*Physics* 193 b12). It is *morphē*, then, that Aristotle identifies as the essence of *genesis,* and thus *phusis*.

Phusis as *morphē* is the placing into the aspect and thus the coming forth into unconcealment of a natural being as what it is in itself. This is the meaning of *genesis. Genesis* is the way of being, the *ousia* of natural beings. Thus, coming to be (*genesis*) and being (*ousia*) are not separate, but the same. Becoming is the way of being of natural beings. To follow this line of thought, we must keep in mind that, as Aristotle says, *genesis* is not motion but the way of movement that is the *phusis* of natural beings. It is *morphē*.

Aristotle further characterizes this way of movement as *phusis* that is on the way (*hodos*) toward *phusis* (*Physics* 193 b12–13). Heidegger comments that we ordinarily think of a path (*hodos*) as a stretch that lies between a starting point and a goal. But this linear model is not what Aristotle means by *genesis*. Nor would Heidegger, who learned of nature by following the path of thinking while walking along the *Holzwege* in the Black Forest, mistake the nature of a pathway for this kind of commerce. "A pathway *leads* through an area, it opens itself and opens up the area" (WBP 361). To open up an area is to establish a clearing through which the light can shine, which lets beings show themselves as they are. "The clearing is the open region for everything that becomes present and absent." It is *genesis* that is the place of this opening in which the *eidos* can first be brought to light. This opening, which was made room for by the pathway of *genesis*, Heidegger says was named by the Greeks *alētheia. Alētheia*, unconcealment, is called by Parmenides that which is well-rounded because it is turned in the pure sphere of the circle in which beginning and end are everywhere the same. Aristotle says that *phusis* is a pathway from out of *phusis* into *phusis*. Here Aristotle thinks *phusis* as the opening of unconcealment that first allows natural beings to come into presence.

But Aristotle at times addresses this opening in relationship to the presencing of beings that take place within this opening, so that *phusis* is understood as a way of *ousia*. The opening itself, which is first spoken of in Greek thought by Parmenides, gets covered over. Aristotle stands at the crossroads. In his recovery of the meaning of the being of natural beings, he mostly leaves unsaid the source of his discovery.

Genesis is a going forth toward itself that is always a coming forth from itself. Yet we cannot conceive of this movement as a circle that revolves without going beyond its own revolution. For, in *genesis* we do indeed have a going beyond that from out of which the *genesis* arose. Thus, *genesis* is a movement from not-being to being, such that in *genesis* a being does come to be that is unique and separate in its being. In *On Generation and Corruption,* Aristotle speaks of the *genesis* of those beings whose *ousia* is such that it is essentially capable of not-being. "Those things whose *ousia* is perishable must go back into themselves in the sense that what recurs, though having the same aspect, is not the same numerically" (338 b17–18). Thus, Aristotle says in our present context, "a human being is generated from a human being." *Genesis* as *morphē* is the placing into the aspect such that what comes to be is of the same aspect as that from which it comes to be, but in such a way that what comes to be was not and now is. *Morphē* establishes both the sameness of beings that belong together in the *koinon* of the *eidos,* and the difference between these beings themselves as individual beings. For Aristotle, the aspect only ever is as the aspect of individual beings. Thus, the aspect alone cannot reproduce itself since it is not itself a being. The movement from out of itself toward itself is such that in this movement the being is and is what it is. "The merely spatial image of a circle is essentially inadequate because this upsurge which goes back into itself is just what lets the being arise from which and towards which the upsurge is, in each case, underway" (WBP 363).

The withdrawing of itself from its aspect as what it no longer is, and the drawing itself up into its aspect as what it is not yet, is the *phusis* that constitutes the being of natural beings. Thus, "*morphē* is addressed in two ways, for *sterēsis* too is something like an aspect" (*Physics* 193 b18–20). The sudden upsurge into being of a natural being is always an immediate abandonment of the not-being from out of which it arose. It is not a gradual linear motion that finally arrives at its end and then for the first time is. Becoming, as the abandoning of nonbeing and rising into presence is itself the being of natural beings. "If becoming *is,* then we must think being so essentially that it does not simply include becoming in some vacuous conceptual manner, but rather in such a way that being sustains and characterizes becoming (*genesis-pthora*) in an essential, appropriate manner."[62]

Genesis can only be the way of presencing of natural beings if the not-yet being of the being-on-the-way, and the no-longer being that from which the being is under way are taken up into the essence of the being itself. Becoming and perishing belong to the *being* of natural beings. Aristotle names this nonbeing that belongs to natural beings *sterēsis.* Aristotle says: *morphē,* the placing into the aspect, is also addressed as *sterēsis.* The *archē,* the *phusis,* the *morphē,* of the movement (*genesis*) that constitutes natural beings is a twofold: *eidos* and *sterēsis.* Every placing itself forth into presence is always a drawing itself away from presence into nonpresence or absence.

Thus, Heidegger says in the *Physics* B1 essay (WBP 266):

While the blossom "buds forth" (*phuei*), the leaves that prepared for and sheltered the blossom fall off. The fruit comes into appearance when the blossom dies away. The placing into the aspect, *morphē*, is *dichēs*, it is in itself twofold, presencing and absencing.

Every living being that emerges forth in itself and from out of itself and toward itself in the unity of this twofold is always also dying. But this dying is itself its way of emerging. Only by leaving itself behind can it go forth into its being.

But in this placing itself *away,* the placing itself into the aspect, *phusis* dos not exhaust itself; on the contrary, the plant as fruit goes back into its seed which, according to its essence, is nothing other than an upsurging into the aspect. (WBP 266)

The twofoldness of *genesis-sterēsis* is the enduring presencing, the ousia of natural beings.

With the concept of *sterēsis,* Aristotle achieves the summit of his thought. At the height of his thought, he reaches into the depth of Greek philosophy and draws the meaning of *phusis* out into the open. Only because the presencing of being withdraws is it able to grant to beings their way of being. The being of beings is the emerging forth out of hiddenness into the unhidden. This emerging forth maintains itself in its emerging and thus is. Unconcealment always stands in relation to and in opposition to concealment. Nonbeing belongs together with being as the being of natural beings. Thus, Aristotle's thought remains faithful to that of Heraclitus who said: *phusis kruptesthai philei,* being loves to hide itself. Hiddenness and *sterēsis* are not to be banished from being. "Rather the task that is given (by Heraclitus) is the essentially more difficult task of allowing to *phusis* in all the purity of its essence the *kruptesthai* which belongs to it" (WBP 269). It is this task that Aristotle inherited and sought to accomplish.

The culminating point of the *Physics* B1 essay was Heidegger's interpretation of *genesis* and *sterēsis. Genesis* is the name for the kind of movement that was left out when *kinēsis* was enumerated as alteration, locomotion, and so on. *Genesis* is ontological movement, so to speak. A progressively deepening understanding of the twofold, double character of the being of natural beings led to this final understanding of the twofoldness in its most radical sense, as contradictory relation, a saying from out of what is unable to be said, a being from out of not-being. That is, not just multiplicity in the sense that being has two parts, but an understanding of being as essentially divisive and agonistic. The folding of the manifold unfolds in both the sense of coming to be and in the sense of falling apart. But both becoming and falling apart are reciprocally joined. In this sense, the joining, the juncture comes before the separation into two of the co-constitutive *archē* of beings. In a sense, *archē* means precisely this jointure that opens up the span of beings. So, already here in the more radical movement that Heidegger unravels in his discussion of *genesis,* the issue of force, of *dunamis,* is central. *Dunamis,* force, is this mutual, agonistic relationality. Heidegger addresses this issue in his 1931 essay on *Metaphysics* Θ, 1–3, to which we will turn in the next chapter.

Chapter Four

THE FORCE OF BEING

In this chapter, we will take up some of the same issues as were discussed in our consideration of Aristotle's *Physics* B1, where the central problem was seen to be the explanation of the being of motion and the Aristotelian sense of the twofoldness of being. There the notions of *dunamis* and *energeia*, as well as the whole problem of nonbeing and its relation to being, were already considered in the context of an attempt to understand *physis* and the nature of natural beings. In *Metaphysics* Θ, Aristotle brings the study of *dunamis*, force or potentiality, to the fore, a notion that Heidegger considers to be the fundamental discovery and most basic insight in the entire corpus of his philosophy. Heidegger's 1931 lecture course on Aristotle's *Metaphysics* Θ, 1–3, subtitled "On the Essence and Actuality of Force,"[1] was delivered at the beginning of the same decade in which he wrote the 1939 text we just discussed on Aristotle's *Physics* B1, and offered the 1937–1938 course on *Basic Questions of Philosophy*, which included a lengthy treatment of the meaning of truth in Aristotle.[2] This decade was also the period of Heidegger's Nietzsche lectures, which focused thematically on the same subject as does the 1931 Aristotle course, namely, the problem of *Kraft* and *Macht* at play in Nietzsche's notion of the will-to-power.

In his Nietzsche lectures, Heidegger comments on the difficulty of reading Nietzsche without an adequate background, and he recommends a long apprenticeship with Aristotle before turning to Nietzsche. In the following statement, Heidegger makes explicit the connection between his reading of Aristotle and Nietzsche during this period:

Nietzsche often identifies power (*Macht*) with force (*Kraft*), without defining the latter more closely. Force, the capacity to be gathered in itself and prepared to work effects, to be in a position to do something, is what the Greeks (above all, Aristotle) denoted as *dunamis*. But power is every bit as much a being empowered, in the sense of the process of mastery, the being-at-work of force, in Greek, *energeia.* Power is will as willing out beyond itself, precisely in that way to come to itself, to find and assert itself in the circumscribed simplicity of its essence, in Greek, *entelecheia.* For Nietzsche power means all this at once: *dunamis, energeia, entelecheia.*[3]

Heidegger makes the rather startling claim that Book Θ of Aristotle's *Metaphysics,* which deals with the problem of force, is "the most worthy of question in the entire Aristotelian corpus," and that:

The Aristotelian doctrine [of *dunamis*] has more to do with Nietzsche's doctrine of will to power than with any doctrine of categories and modalities in academic philosophy. But the Aristotelian doctrine itself devolves from a tradition that determines its direction; it is a first denouement of the first beginnings of Western philosophy in Anaximander, Heraclitus, and Parmenides.[4]

In chapter two, I pointed out that one of the "oddities" of Heidegger's reading of Aristotle, from the point of view of the tradition, is his insistence that the *Physics* is no less a work of metaphysics than the *Metaphysics* is a work about physics. Here he goes further and even claims that "Aristotle never had in his possession what later came to be understood by the word or the concept 'metaphysics.' Nor did he seek anything like the 'metaphysics' that has for ages been attributed to him."[5] We shall see that Heidegger considers the failure to understand the central ontological importance of *dunamis* in Aristotle's philosophy was in large part responsible for the later reading of Aristotle as the quintessential metaphysician who reduces motion and power to the realm of becoming, and interprets being apart from these concepts. Heidegger sees at stake in his study of Aristotle's concepts of *dunamis* and *energeia* not only an effort to get Aristotle right and provide a more radical alternative reading, but also an effort to clear a space for a more originary grasp of philosophy today. Speaking specifically about the Aristotelian concepts of *dunamis* and *energeia,* Heidegger says:

To inquire into *dunamis* and *energeia,* as Aristotle proposes to do in our treatise, is genuine philosophizing. Accordingly, if we ourselves have eyes to see and ears to hear, if we have the right disposition and are truly willing, then, if we are successful, we will learn from the interpretation of the treatise what philosophizing is. We will in this way gain an experience with philosophizing and perhaps become more experienced in it ourselves.[6]

This quote links Heidegger's own thinking to his reading of the Greeks, though it is not a link that can be understood if we approach his reading of the Greeks only for the sake of looking for "influences" on Heidegger's philosophy. One can assume that Heidegger considers his own philosophy to be much more directly at stake in the efforts these lectures expend on winning back from Aristotle and for Aristotle an understanding of being that is presupposed in our ordinary ways of relating to beings.

Aristotle is said to have singled out the notion of *dunamis* and the *dunamis-energeia* relationship in Greek philosophy and raised it to the level of a philosophical concept that transforms it into his own philosophical discovery, the center out of which his own thinking flows, and the previously unspoken and sought after meaning of being that resolves the *aporia* of Greek thinking and brings closure and fulfillment to *the* question, the question of being. Against a long tradition, Heidegger is attempting to defend the claim that potentiality is not just an accidental feature belonging to beings. It is not a force that just happens to belong to the being, but is their way of being. It is Aristotle's discovery of an ontological sense of *dunamis* that allows him to think of finitude, privation, negation, and temporality as constitutive characteristics of beings as such. From Parmenides to Plato, these characteristics were excluded from the definition of being in Greek philosophy. However, in incorporating force into his understanding of the meaning of being, Aristotle does not simply reject the attributes of being discovered by his predecessors—unity, eternity, simplicity, and necessity, for example. Heidegger maintains that these characteristics of being cannot be understood as separate from or inconsistent with Aristotle's basic insight that potentiality belongs to the very being of these beings. In other words it is not so much a matter of an inversion or turning upside down of the thought of his predecessors, or overturning it, as it is a matter of coming to grips with this thought.

Aristotle's Resolution of the Aporia of Early Greek Philosophy

The primary focus of Heidegger's course aims to return us in some way to the decisive turning point in Greek philosophy at which Aristotle finally comes to grips with the question of being. Contrary to the common belief that Heidegger sees his own philosophy as an attempt to overcome the oblivion of being that starts with Aristotle's distortion of early Greek thinking, we find in this text ample evidence of Heidegger's conviction that Aristotle's philosophy is thoroughly Greek, and in fact the fulfillment of Greek thought.

Aristotle's task, one he inherited from his predecessors, was to conceive how being could be both a unity and a manifold, both simple and changing, both always there and yet always becoming. Aristotle frames the question of force in *Metaphysics* Θ1 primarily in terms of the problem of the one and the many, which rings so familiarly in our ears that we can miss the intensity of philosophical questioning involved here. A constant refrain in Aristotle's work is: *to on legetai pollachōs,* being is said in many ways. But this, Heidegger says, is not just a formula. "Rather in this short sentence Aristotle formulates the wholly fundamental and new position that he worked out in philosophy in relation to all of his predecessors including Plato; not in the sense of a system but in the sense of a task."7 One way to regain some of the force of this philosophical questioning about multiplicity is to do work on the Presocratics, for example on the Heraclitean saying of *hen-panta,* which haunts Heidegger's introductory chapter on the many senses of being in Aristotle's philosophy. It is only in relationship to the Presocratics that the force of Heidegger's reading of Aristotle becomes clear. Aristotle's thinking emerges out of his *Auseinandersetzung* with the early Greeks, especially Heraclitus and Parmenides, and Heidegger returns Aristotle to this place out of which his thought is situated.

Aristotle is not so much merely opposing Parmenides who insisted that being is simple and one, and excludes from itself all nonbeing. It is not that Parmenides insists that being is one, and Aristotle responds that it is many. Heidegger says that Aristotle does not deny and disavow the first decisive truth of philosophy as expressed by Parmenides. Rather, he first truly comprehends it by asking: if being is one, how can beings be? Must not multiplicity too belong to being as one? Must not nonbeing, the not-ness itself, belong to the essence of being? And how can this be without destroying the fundamental Greek meaning of being, and without violating the Parmenidean prohibition against mixing being and nonbeing, thereby collapsing the difference between the two? These questions about Aristotle's place vis à vis the entire Greek philosophical tradition, and thus also the history of Western philosophy, are at the heart of Heidegger's 1931 lecture course. Heidegger says that what occurs in the Aristotelian confrontation with the question of being is a transformation of the sense of being and a shift in the understanding of the question of the oneness of being.

Heidegger, then, views Aristotle's philosophy as in some way a return to the presupposition of Parmenidean philosophy, the necessary horizon for Parmenidean thought that Parmenides himself may not have completely understood, though the *aporia,* the prohibition and impasse at the heart of his thinking, certainly echoes it, namely, the difference between being and beings. Aristotle is struggling to understand this difference in the proper way, that is, as an ontological difference and not merely as an attempt to account for the differences among beings or the different characteristics of any particular being. The sense of difference here is peculiar and needs to be attended to carefully. The equation of beings and being—of *to on* and *einai*—in Greek philosophy presupposes this difference. The possibility for beings to be, their belonging to being, is founded on this difference, the otherness of being. The claim that being is other than beings, withdraws from beings, already indicates that the question of being cannot be reduced to a categorial logic of predication that has to do with beings and their attributes.

The Rejection of the Categorial Sense of Being as the Framework for Understanding Being as Force

Heidegger at the outset makes clear one of the central arguments of his course, which, if it proves true, puts an entire tradition of Aristotelian study on notice. Heidegger's claim is that, for Aristotle, the one-many problem is not addressed only or even primarily in terms of the categories. Categorial being is only one of the many senses of being. We have already seen in chapter two that Heidegger finds in Aristotle's *Physics* B1 a use of the word *katēgoria* that reflects the connection between the technical, philosophical meaning of the word and its ordinary meaning as a way of addressing something. For Heidegger, the categorical way of addressing beings is only one of the many senses of revealing being. Heidegger insists, against Kant, Brentano and many others, that *dunamis* and *energeia* are not categories of being.

Heidegger's introductory chapter in the book *Metaphysics* Θ1–3: *On the Essence and Actuality of Force* aims to clarify the sense of being Aristotle names *dunamis* and *energeia*. But much of his preliminary attention is devoted to a discussion of *logos*. Heidegger's aim is to distinguish the categorial sense of being, and the kind of *logos* this involves, from one of the other, non-categorial senses of being, namely, the one that is the subject of *Metaphysics* Θ, that is, *dunamis* and *energeia*. To prepare for this analysis, one of Heidegger's initial aims is to offset the dominant interpretation of *logos* in terms of propositional logic, and the understanding of language in terms of assertion. One needs to do this first because, as Heidegger shows in Chapter Two of his book on *Metaphysics* Θ, human *dunamis* is defined as *logos,* even though the human being has another sense of being than that found in the categories. The reduction of *logos* to assertions about objects is fundamentally tied to the erroneous assumption that all being is addressed as categorial by Aristotle.

But Heidegger also takes issue with this way of understanding what Aristotle means by category. Heidegger argues that the fundamental Aristotelian meaning of *logos,* even in reference to the categories, has the sense of a disclosing that gathers, a *sammelnden Offenbarmachen.* Gathering is the way Heidegger understands the meaning of oneness in Aristotle. Disclosing is the way he translates truth. *Logos* is the joining of oneness and truth. *Logos* is operative in the way of being Aristotle calls categorial, in *katēgoria,* which is not *logos* in the sense of judgment or predication, but *logos* as the gathering of *ousia* in terms of quantity, quality, and the like. The issue is the relationality of the first category (*ousia*) to the other categories.

Heidegger's treatment here of the meaning of *katēgoria* includes a discussion of the Greek meaning of *logos,* since Aristotle defines the categories as ways of addressing beings. But *logos* cannot be understood as the subjective, rational contribution of human beings, for then Aristotle would seem to be inconsistent, since he attributes *katēgoria* to beings themselves (*Met.* 1045 b27). Heidegger insists that the subject-object distinction, in the way we traditionally understood it, is foreign to Greek thought. Moreover, "the usual representation of the categories as 'forms of thought,' as some sort of encasements into which we stuff beings, is thereby already repudiated for having mistaken the facts."[8] Categories belong to beings and are not modes of judgment. Nor are they reducible to subject-predicate, grammatical relationships. We need to get beyond thinking in terms of subject and object if we are to understand Aristotle's problem. Or else, we need to think through what we mean by subject, by human relationality, and what we mean by object, by the beings that are ob-jects, and therefore are encountered as thrown against us, as resisting us.

In chapter three, we discussed the long digression on *logos* in Heidegger's 1939 article on *Physics* B1, where Heidegger, following Aristotle, almost suggested a kind of identity of *logos* and *physis* (*eidos*).[9] Aristotle says that *morphē* and *eidos* are only ever able to be in the *logos* of a given being. This is the same passage in which Aristotle introduces the notion of *dunamis* for the first time in *Physics* B1 (193 b6–8). Heidegger argues that the matter (*hulē*) is *ousia* only when it is incorporated in accordance with an *eidos* toward which it is directed. Likewise, Aristotle says that *dunamis,* when it is appropriated in accord with an aspect, and not a mere possibility, belongs essentially to a natural being. *Dunamis* expresses more clearly the being-directed-toward and being-in-relation-to the *eidos* than does *hulē.* But this *dunamis-eidos* (*morphē*) unity is nothing on its own, but is only ever the constitutive principles of being, shown in the *logos* of a particular being. So *logos* is crucial even in the showing of natural beings, although they move and appear on their own.

Throughout the *Metaphysics* Θ, 1–3 course, Heidegger returns to the question of the meaning of *logos* in Aristotle. In the second chapter, he examines Aristotle's definition of the human being as the one whose living is constituted by *logos.* *Logos* is not an attribute but a way of being. Our *physis,* so to speak, our being, is *logos.* *Physis* is a gathering that unifies and lets beings be separate in their sameness and the same in their separateness. Separateness, individuality, multiplicity is determined out of an original oneness. It is only in that beings present themselves in advance as a whole that they are the beings they are. On the other hand, the oneness itself occurs not as a "one" that stands above and removed from the manifold that it governs, but as *logos,* as the original gathering unity of what emerges into unconcealment.

Heidegger takes issue in the Introduction with the understanding of *ousia* as substance and the categories other than *ousia* as accidents. *Ousia* is the first category, not in the sense of a series; it is not a separable, albeit most essential part of a being, to which properties are attached; rather it is first because the other categories *are* only inasmuch as they belong together in the unifying presencing of a being as a whole. Aristotle's task is to think how this manifold can belong to a being without contradicting the oneness, the *hen,* that characterizes the being of beings. Heidegger calls "most catastrophic" the way medieval theology took for granted the equation of oneness and being and presented it as an axiom: *ens et unum convertuntur.* For Heidegger, how it is that being is one, especially in light of Aristotle's insistence that being is said in many ways, remains in question. The sameness of being and the one is not a sameness that collapses the difference but a belonging together, a reciprocal favoring, a twofoldness that involves a turning toward one another that is never apart from each other, such that the oneness of being is to be understood as a gathering into unity, a community, an original relationality.

What is important to be clear about here—and Heidegger goes to some lengths to clarify the point—is that this *koinon* of being, the sense of being as the common, is not equatable with the sum of beings or the totality of what is. The *hen-panta* is not to be thought of in terms of totality. It does have to do with being as the whole of what is, or being as a whole, but the whole here is not the sum of the parts. The relationship of the universal and the particular is also involved here. The whole in the sense of the unity of being is ontologically other than the parts; it is the prior gathering that occurs in some sense before the categorial gathering of beings in terms of *ousia*. The refusal to collapse the difference between being and the one, while nevertheless affirming the oneness of being is the philosophical decision to which he ascribes the greatness of Aristotle. It is the insight that being differs in itself, that the oneness of being is duplicitous, an insight already, of course, found in Pythagoras.

Once again, Aristotle is not here ignoring the warning of Parmenides to abide with the oneness of being and stand against the confusion of being and nonbeing. "He does not renounce it [what Parmenides says], but first truly comprehends it. He assists this truth in becoming a truly philosophical truth, that is, an actual question."[10] Aristotle gives the equation of oneness and being in Parmenides its sharpest formulation by showing how the one is in itself many. Heidegger asks:

Is this one being [*Sein*] something before all unfolding, that is, something that exists for itself, whose independence is the true essence of being? Or is being in its essence never not unfolded so that the manifold and its foldings constitute precisely the peculiar oneness of that which is intrinsically gathered up? Is being imparted to the individual modes in such a way that by this imparting it in fact parts itself out, although in this parting out it is not partitioned in such a way that, as divided, it falls apart and loses its authentic essence, its unity. Might the unity of being lie precisely in this imparting parting out? And if so, how would and could something like that happen? What holds sway in this event?[11]

These are questions that go beyond the ontic discovery of a multiplicity of categories that belong to a being, but not in an essential way. These questions hint that nonbeing, that which does not have a being of its own, belongs to the way of being of beings. *Ousia*, then, cannot be understood as excluding this nonbeing from itself, but as first allowing it to be. These questions ask about the manifold that characterizes the very being of these beings. Aristotle's attempt to understand how *ousia*, the beingness of beings, can be a unity and yet be diverse is the horizon in which the discussion of *dunamis* and *energeia* take place. The failure to interpret correctly the manifold of being that Aristotle addresses has led to the substance philosophy that reduces all multiplicity to accidental, categorial, nonessential characteristics of beings that can be excluded from the being in itself.

One way to think this togetherness of oneness and manyness is in terms of *koinon,* in terms of what is common. In each of the four ways of being as multiple, being is common. One way, the supposedly Platonic way, of thinking this commonality of being is in terms of genus. But Aristotle vehemently disagrees with the position that being is not a genus. But then nor can beings be understood in terms of species. The notion of genus is the notion of a universal class; the many that can be grouped into a class belong to the class because they share the same universal element; their specific differences determine their species identity. If being were a genus, then possibility, truth, and so on would be species-differentiating. But the true and the possible are not nothing. They too are; indeed even the nothing "is" in a sense. If the relationship of the one being to the many were a relationship of genus-species, the many would be outside being, would not be. Indeed, this is supposedly the direction of Parmenides' thought. And yet, when being is said in many ways, it is not just a sameness in name only that is involved. The commonness is not just nominal; the many in some sense do belong together; there is a oneness. We need to get a better sense of the singularity of the address that pervades the discussion of the many senses of being. How can there be a singularity of being when being is manifold?

Aristotle's answer to the question of the character of the relationality involved in the singular many is analogy. Employing a medical example, Aristotle refers to the many senses of healthy, all of which refer back to a primary sense, which sense, however, is not a genus. Like in *epagōgē,* here there is a back-and-forth relationship of healthy in the leading and guiding sense to the other senses of healthy that are understood on the basis of this primary meaning, the *archē* meaning that holds the various meanings of healthy together.

But Heidegger insists that this sense of analogical relationality is meant to explain the *pollachōs* in the restricted sense of the categories. Not every multiplicity of being is analogical in this sense. Being-possible and actual and true cannot be led back to being-substance in the same way in which being-so much and being-such, quantity and quality, can be led back to *ousia,* to being in the primary sense. The broader multiplicity also needs to be accounted for. Is this relationality in some sense also analogical, and that means in some sense a *logos* and in relation through *logos*? Or, is all Aristotelian philosophy fundamentally reducible to a substance doctrine? Or were the Medievals correct in translating this doctrine into the notion of a primary separate being, a supreme being, to which all other beings are related by analogy? For Heidegger, those senses of analogy that have been considered not relevant to metaphysics, analogy in the sense of proportion, and in the sense of metaphor, are more fundamental ontologically than the analogy of attribution.

What is the analogical character operative in the sense of being that Aristotle calls *dunamis-energeia*? To answer this question, Heidegger begins to explore Aristotle's treatment of *dunamis*. He discovers there that one of the ways Aristotle defines *dunamis* is as a cause, *aitia*. Forces are first discovered in light of causal relationships. But we need to distance ourselves from the reduction of causality to the model of cause-effect. Just as it is difficult to see force and we tend to deduce from witnessing activity that there are forces at work, so also we do not see cause but deduce it from effects. Forces do not allow themselves to be directly discerned. We always find only accomplishments, successes, effects. These are indeed what is tangibly actual. We come upon forces only retrospectively [in failures].12

But Heidegger suggests this tendency to approach things in this way leads us to a derivative understanding of things. Instead cause and effect need to be seen as mutually and reciprocally binding each other. It is not a matter of a mechanistic transfer of force onto an object. This reductive, mechanistic view of the causality involved in force views beings as owing their *dunamis* to forces outside themselves. Each of the many senses of force—power, talent, capacity, capability, competence, aptitude, skill, and coercion—then come to be understood as force inasmuch as they are referred back to a common subjective experience that runs through all of them, namely, the ability to be affected, to be subjected. In this sense, all force is an ability; nature, for example, is understood now to mean "able to be forced." "Forces of nature," understood in the active sense, becomes a meaningless term. All force is seen as a violent imposition from outside. In contrast, Heidegger views force as a cause, in the sense of a being able to be other, which belongs to the way of being of beings. What Heidegger wants us to think about is this relationality, this prior causality, presupposed in the discussion of cause and effect.

To take issue with this reductive understanding of *dunamis*, Heidegger carefully retranslates a crucial sentence of Aristotle's *Metaphysics* Θ, where Aristotle defines *dunamis* as "*archē metabolēs en allō ē ē allo*" (1046 a11). This phrase is typically translated as, "the originative source of change in another thing or in the thing itself qua other." But Heidegger renders it as, "the origin of change, which origin is in a being other than the changing being itself, or in the case where the originating being and the changing being are the same, then each is what it respectively is as a different being."[13] Heidegger says that the *en allō* should be read (on the basis of Aristotle's overall philosophical position) as connected to *archē* and not *metabolē*. He reads change, *Umschlag*, not as something happening to a being, but in an active sense.

Heidegger points to the fact that *katēgoria* here is singular. It is being according to the schemata of the category. According to Heidegger, the singular indicates the preeminent saying of the being in every individual assertion about this or that being. The category is the saying of being in the assertion (*logos*) of beings. Always along with the saying of the other categories, as ways of being, is the saying of *ousia* (being). The relationship is not genus-species because the other categories are not in themselves *kinds* of *ousia*, but ways of being. The relationship of the other categories to the first is not one of genus-species, of beings participating in universal being. Rather the relationality is analogical, one of being gathered up into the one. The schema of the categories addresses beings as the inclusive gathering.

What is the difference between the sense of being as categorial and another meaning of being that Aristotle calls *kata sumbebēkos*? It would clearly be important to Heidegger that the fourfold sense of being be preserved, and it would be equally inappropriate to collapse the schema of the categories into substance-accidents as it would be to equate *dunamis-energeia* with the categorial relationship, even though Aristotle at times speaks of the categories as *sumbebēkos*. In fact, the two senses of being are closely related, perhaps even two sides of the same coin, but the distinction is important. Heidegger points to the distinction in the context of a discussion about *eidos* in section 14 of the *Metapysics* Θ, 1–3 Volume. He says:

> The *eidos* assumes leadership in the whole process of production. It is the authority and regulator which says what the standard is. It does so from out of itself—*kath' auto* (*Met.* 1046 b13), but always in a way that excludes others. This other is, however, what is constantly running alongside and present along with it. It is what occurs with it [*das Bei-laüfig*]—*kata sumbebēkos* (b13), inasmuch as the material and each particular state in the course of production offer occasions for mistakes and failure and for being irregular.[14]

Whereas the schema of the categories emphasize the inclusive gathering, the substance-accident meaning of being involves its *sterēsis*, the potential failure that belongs to being.

Dunamis-energeia, we say, is a way of being that is non-categorial. Presumably this means that the *logos*, the way of disclosing and gathering, is of another sort. Heidegger points out that there are several domains of *dunamis*, only one of which is of concern here. That one, of course, is *duna-*

mis kata kinēsin, the force in regard to movement. There is also the notion of *dunamis* used in geometry as, for example, when we say three squared or three to the third power, and mean what can be done with something, how a length can be divided and constructed. Aristotle also calls *metaphora* a *dunamis* in the sense of what can or cannot be carried over from one thing to another, what can be affirmed or denied of something, power in the sense of being appropriate for, going along with something, being compatible with it. The analysis in section 8 shows that *dunamis* as affirming is always also denying, a *dunaton,* so that this sense of *dunamis* involves an *enantion,* a contrariness or opposition. He briefly discusses the relationship of *enantia* to *antiphasis,* to contradiction.[15] We are powerless (*adunaton*) to say at the same time both being and not being, a claim Heidegger says has to do with being and not with logical possibility. Though these considerations, this sense of *dunamis* and metaphor, are excluded from consideration in *Metaphysics* Θ1, we will see that they are at the heart of the matter as we move into *Metaphysics* Θ2 and 3. But these meanings for now are put aside in order to discuss *dunamis* in its usual sense, *dunamis kata kinēsin,* the *dunamis* that allows for an account of movement and change, *dunamis* that Aristotle defines as *archē kinēseōs* and *archē metabolēs,* the *archē* of movement and change. Force here has the sense of *Ausgang,* that from which something proceeds, that out of which change is made possible, the origin of change. Earlier we discussed Heidegger's translation of Aristotle's definition of *dunamis* as *archē metabolēs en allō ē ē allo.* "The origin, the from out of which, of change is in a being other than the being undergoing change, or if in the same being, than not in the same respect." Force is here understood as that which is responsible for movement. Heidegger claims that the matter demands that this be understood as saying that the origin is in another, not the origin of the *change* that is in another. Were we to understand *archē metabolēs en allō,* change as exchange, as meaning the origin of change in another, then an example would be the potter who changes the lump of clay into a mug. Change in this case would be the alteration that incidentally happens to a thing. But Heidegger insists that *metabolē* here also has an active sense, and does not simply mean that something is done to something else. What difference does this make? Well everything really. That which undergoes change is in some way itself a force in that it enables the change. Force itself is change, transition, transitional power, power that is in transit. So change is both active and passive and the issue is not how things that *are* get affected and changed, but about the capacity for change that belongs to the being as such. It is not about what one thing does to another but about *dunamis* and *metabolē* as the being of beings. *Dunamis* is the principle that allows for the coming to be and the coming forth into being of beings, and for their having been produced. To put it another way, Heidegger reads the genitive in *dunamis metabolēs* as both subjective and objective. Heidegger translates *metabolē* as *Umschlag*, a kind of recoiling overturning.

Aristotle also speaks of *dunamis* as *aitia*, as cause. In what sense is *dunamis* a cause? In order to understand causality, we need to distance ourselves from the reduction of causality to the model of cause-effect. We tend to view cause in terms of a mechanistic transfer of force onto an object. Instead Heidegger says cause and effect need to be seen as mutually and reciprocally binding each other. *Dunamis* is a cause in the sense of belonging to what constitutes and gives rise to beings. Moreover, cause and effects co-determine each other and cannot be thought apart from each other. What Heidegger wants us to think about is this relationality, this prior causality that is presupposed in the discussion of cause and effect.

The discussion of causality provides a frame for similarly interpreting the *poiein-pathein* structure in sections 10–11 of Chapter One of Heidegger's text. There Heidegger is analyzing what Aristotle means by *poiein*—the capacity to cause something to be brought forth, and *pathein*—the capacity of that which is brought forth to be affected. Noteworthy is the fact that both *poiein* and *pathein* are understood as *dynameis*, as causes and capacities. There is a mutuality and reciprocity involved here in the interrelationality of the change that occurs. *Dunamis* as the *archē* of *metabolē*, as the origin and cause of change, is the origin and cause of a doing, a *poiein*.

Aristotle says that all force is also *paschein*, a being affected, a suffering (*Met.* 1046 a11–16). This is usually understood as opposite to a doing (*poiein*) or effecting. Heidegger translates it as *Erleiden*, to tolerate, in the sense of not holding back, not resisting. Force as *pathein*, as letting happen, presupposes a lack, a not having and not-being, a not-standing-against. But Aristotle speaks both of letting happen (*pathos*), and not letting oneself be affected (*a-pathein*), namely, resisting. In fact, Heidegger points out, often we first become aware of the phenomenon of force when something blocks the fulfillment of an occurrence. Resistance (*Widerständigkeit*) involves the being's holding itself there as being-against, as opposing the *dunamis* of change. The being resists that with which it interacts. Thus, the being remains. Both coming to be and remaining in this active-passive sense of resisting are governed by *dunamis*.

The primary way in which we experience force is opposition. What awakens us to *dunamis* is the *not coming through,* the not-being-able. Resistance invades power both among natural beings and in relationship to human *technē.* All coming to be occurs in relationship to that which one is not. *Dunamis* opens up the *koinon,* the commonness that belongs to beings. In *Sein und Zeit,* the structure of equipmentality as well as the analysis of significance and involvement (*Bewandtnis*) parallel what Heidegger here discovers in Aristotle.

Perhaps we should return for a moment to some basic points. Remember that the discussion is about *dunamis kata kinēsin* and that *dunamis* in this sense refers to an analogical relationship that involves an *archē,* a reference back to a guiding meaning that gathers together into one. But the analysis has shown that the meaning of *dunamis* as *archē* requires that one think of *archē* in terms of a reciprocal relationality. Indeed, *archē* must be understood as both letting occur and resisting or withholding, that is, *archē* is divisive and opposing, and is the origin of a kind of twofold relationality. Heidegger says in section 10 that the notion of a *prōtē dunamis,* a guiding meaning of force, does not imply that there is a *dunamis* isolated unto itself, in addition to which we can then list further meanings. Instead, the others in their very constitution refer to the first, and in such a way that precisely this reference also gives back to the guiding meaning its very sense and content. The fragile force of bearing and resisting is just as decisive as the force of doing, of producing. *Dunamis* is the exchange of this twofold.

Heidegger offers another example of the reciprocity involved in the nature of force in his analysis of doing and tolerating in section 11:

When one speaks of the *dunamis* of doing and tolerating, are two *dynameis* meant, two modes of *dunamis,* or only one? If only one then in what sense is *dunamis* understood? If two, then how is *dunamis* to be grasped in its unity?[16]

Is the essence of force originally divergent into a twofold? That is, is *dunamis* precisely this relation and reference of *poiein* and *pathein* to each other? *Poiein* always implicates *pathein* and vice versa. *Dunamis* is this implication (*Einbezug*).[17] The whole issue can only be understood if we do not take the discussion as referring to ontic relations between beings. Aristotle is not listing types of ontic force for which he is seeking some universal definition. Rather it is a meditation on the divisive, simple essence of force.

Another complex issue for understanding and appreciating Heidegger's interpretation of *dunamis* in Aristotle involves his insistence on the priority of the question "how" in Aristotle's ontology. How the being is, its facticity, is ontologically as central to Aristotle's thinking as the question of what it is and the question of what being can only be asked in conjunction with the question how. In section 10, Heidegger claims that there is a "how" that belongs to every force, a claim to a possible completion, a being-directed toward its fulfillment. A reference to *telos* inheres within the very constitution of *dunamis*. This means that relationality already belongs to and makes cause and force possible. *Dunamis* as a being-on-the-way-toward the being is most truly manifest in its *dunamis* when its being-directed-toward, when its force is fully in play.

This not-remaining-back is therefore the essential meaning of force. This *kalos*, this beautiful display of a sameness of *dunamis-energeia*, this perfection of *entelecheia*, of holding itself in the end, is a sameness, however, that constantly exceeds itself in difference. So the "how," how a being is (its existence), necessarily belongs to all being-empowered. Heidegger denies the separation of essence and existence has already occurred in Aristotle's thought.

Heidegger's central concern is to understand and interpret the issue of opposition at the heart of *dunamis*. All force is intrinsically always also related to unforce; all force as relation always is also unforce, the privation of force, *sterēsis*. This is of course ironic, since *sterēsis* is precisely the absence and withdrawal of force. How can the withdrawal of force be the very being of force, be what makes force possible as force, what allows force to be forceful? How are we to understand the double movement of *dunamis* as *archē* metaboles? At the end of the discussion of *Metaphysics* Θ1, Heidegger suggests that we need to think of *dunamis* and *sterēsis* as middle-voiced, as *dechesthai* [a taking to oneself] and *dunasthai*, two words, receiving and giving, that Heidegger suggests at times become interchangeable in the ancient Greek language.18

The Non-Categorial Meaning of Logos *in Connection with Being as* Dunamis: *Force in Relationship to Production*

In Heidegger's discussion of *Metaphysics* Θ2, we will see that Aristotle turns in his treatment of the actuality and potentiality of moving beings to an analysis of production, of *technē*, and the structure of equipment. Then, in his analysis of *Metaphysics* Θ3, Heidegger uncovers a parallel discussion of *aisthēsis*, perception, which involves a relationship to natural beings that, in contrast to *technē*, lets these beings be disclosed in their very being.

Yet, Heidegger maintains that the relationship to beings operative in *technē* provided the framework for the Greek way of understanding the being of beings. The know-how involved in *technē* is not focused on the being as such in its nature, but on the being as *ergon,* as the work that is to be produced.

In contrast, *Metaphysics* Θ3 will discuss the *ergon,* the "work" of perception, *aisthēsis,* which does not involve a product but a way of revealing—truth. But this more fundamental relationality that primarily and fully belongs to human Dasein is operative also in *technē,* and presupposed by it. Thus, even in his discussion of *Metaphysics* Θ2, Heidegger attempts to break down the traditionally unbroachable distinction between *aisthēsis* and *logos. Aisthēsis* is the relationship a being has to its surroundings; its most basic form is *aphē,* being in touch with; the ability to feel and grasp. *Aisthēsis* is also governed by *alētheuein,* unconcealment.

Heidegger briefly pursues the interesting discussion of animal life and the concomitant question of whether animals also have some sort of *logos,* a kind of *phronēsis;* a way of comportment that allows them to explore and be cognizant of their surroundings.[19] For Heidegger, the issue is not that *logos* is restricted to humans but the difference between animals and humans has to do with how the being *has logos.* When Aristotle defines the human as *zōon logon echon,* he means that *logos* is constitutive of the being of the human. Perhaps we could say in Heidegger's terms that *logos* is an existential of Dasein. The human being's way of comportment recoils on its being as its ownmost potentiality.

Heidegger acknowledges repeatedly, both in this text and elsewhere, that Aristotle understands beings in terms of their having been produced, their standing forth in presence. So if Aristotle's thought is in the end rooted in a metaphysics of presence, then how can the conflictual character of being, the twofoldness of being, the kinetic character of being as movement, exchange, transition, and so on be maintained in Aristotle's thought. How can the nonbeing or, in other words, the not-yet and no-longer being that characterizes *dunamis,* nevertheless still be the fundamental focus and discovery of Aristotle's thought? To answer this question, which is central to an understanding of Heidegger's reading of Aristotle, we turn to Heidegger's treatment of *Metaphysics* Θ2.

It is important to keep in mind the context of the analysis of the second chapter of Book Θ. Of the many senses of being, the sense that interests us in Book Θ is *dunamis-energeia.* How are we to understand the manyness of being involved in being in the sense of *dunamis*? Heidegger uses the word

Faltung, folding or ply. He asks: "How is it that being is pleated, that being deploys itself [*Das Sein faltet sich auseinander*]?"[20] The issue is not that there are many beings and one being, but that the being itself of beings is multiplied. What then is the relational character of being that is at play in this sense of *dunamis-energeia*? How are potentiality and actuality operative in beings? This question is dealt with first in order to prepare for a higher, more fundamental sense of *dunamis, dunamis* and *energeia* in their singular meaning; not the forces and activities involved whenever there is present movement, but force and activity as such; not *dunamis kata kinēsin,* but *dunamis kinēseōs;* not the forces that belong to beings inasmuch as they move, but the being-moved, the movedness of the being as such; the being of force as such. On one level, we have here the distinction between an ontical inquiry and one that is ontological. But for Aristotle, Heidegger says, both are part and parcel of any philosophical investigation. The ontic and the ontological implicate each other. As Heidegger would say, it is only through phenomenology that there is ontology. And he would say this of the work of Aristotle.

According to Heidegger, the guiding aim of Aristotle's analysis in *Metaphysics* Θ2 is "to make more poignantly visible the essence of *dunamis* by elucidating the extraordinary relationship between *dunamis* and *logos.*"[21] Aristotle differentiates kinds of potencies on the basis of *logos.* Potencies that have *logos* are distinguished from those that are without *logos.* In the background, we need to keep in mind that the overriding question is the question about being and that *dunamis-energeia* is one of the many ways Aristotle says we speak of being. In turn, *dunamis-energeia* is a way of understanding the manifoldness, the twofoldness of being.

We have seen, in every passage on Aristotle, that Heidegger returns to a recurrent theme: being is twofold: how are we to understand this split at the heart of being, this discordance out of which beings unfold? We have suggested that we need to think this division radically. Aristotle is positioned at the site of the Parmenidean decision to sever being and nonbeing. Being is this severance, this holding away of nonbeing. But it is not Aristotle's task to repair the tear in being that Parmenides announces. Rather, what he discovers is that not only the utter separateness of being and non-being (the difference between being and beings) is involved in this rupture, but also the sameness of being and beings. Not only difference, and therefore multiplicity is implied by this separation but also unity, the unity of a gathering together, of *legein.* This, we have said, is Aristotle's fundamental philosophical project: to show, not against

Parmenides, but in a way that brings Parmenides' understanding of being to philosophical fruition, that unity, oneness, and therefore being belong even to beings.

Aristotle begins the discusssion in *Metaphysics* Θ2 with the distinction between *dunamis meta logou* and *dunamis alogos*. Elsewhere, Aristotle defines the human being as the one who "has" *logos: zōon logon echon*. The verb here is *echein*, to have, to possess. If we put these two descriptions of human being together as *dunamis* and as having, then the having of *logos* is to be understood as *dunamis*, as potentiality. To have *logos* in a human way is to be empowered with and by *logos*. If we translate *logos* for a moment as language, then what we are studying is the definition of man as the one who has the command of language, what Heidegger calls poetry, *poiesis*—the power to bring forth. Why is this *dunamis*, why is the poetic saying and gathering fundamentally distinguished by Aristotle from those beings whose power or force is without *logos*? Is the *dunamis* of the rose not also a bringing forth? Yes, but in a different sense. The rose is not conversant (*Kundschaft*). It does not deliberate and choose and direct its power. It is not worldly. Heidegger translates this worldly *dunamis* that is cognizant of its surroundings as *Vermögen*, capability.[22] What distinguishes capability from force that is without *logos*, according to Aristotle, in that capability is open to opposites, to contraries. So what makes *poiēsis*, poetic saying, possible is that human being has the power that relates to opposites, that is empowered to hold itself in relation to opposites, that commands opposition. In contrast, *dunamis alogos* is only directed at a singular.

Now we might already suspect that this openness to the twofold, to opposites, is essential for one who is conversant of being, since being is twofold. To be only directed at a singular is not to be in touch with being. Aristotle gives the example of warm and cold. Warm is only directed at warmth, though it can become cold. In contrast, the art of medicine does not aim toward itself, but toward producing health in another. Moreover, the art of curing, as such, is aimed at both health and sickness. To be successful, the doctor must know both disease and health. Why is this distinction important? For one thing, we learn from it an essential characteristic of human *dunamis*. To bring forth in a human way requires an awareness of what one is not—an awareness of what one needs to bring something about, an awareness of what is available, what is not suitable, what is contrary to and resists our working with it, and so on. It is awareness of contraries, and thereby of otherness, that opens up the neighborhood and world of involvements. In *Sein und Zeit*, Heidegger says that the "discovery of the 'world' and disclosure of Dasein are always accomplished as a clearing-away of concealments and obscurities, etc."[23] So what distinguishes human *dunamis* or conversance is that it is open to contraries. This means that there is an inner division, a discordance and finitude that belongs to this force. Finitude in the sense that it is awareness of the not, of what does not belong, of what is revealed as other than itself in one's dealings. *Wo Kraft und Macht, da Endlichkeit.*[24] Both senses of *dunamis* have the meaning of being-directed-toward, of being aimed at, in the sense that something unfolds out of it. But it is mostly through our dealings with things, through *technē*, that we become aware of *dunamis alogos,* of the *dunamis* that belongs to nonhuman beings. And we encounter these *dunameis* primarily in terms of a certain resistance, a not being able to bear the forces that encroach upon them.

In part B of section 14 of Chapter Two, which deals with *Metaphysics* Θ2, Heidegger offers an analysis of the meaning of production in Aristotle. He takes the example of the shoemaker. How is the shoemaker who makes shoes directed at contraries? Making is constantly involved in alternatives. In every affirmation, there is a leaving alone, a not affirming. The not is already taken into consideration. The producing of an *ergon*, a work, is not arbitrary. To produce requires know-how, that is, an awareness of the structure of the being to be produced and an awareness of *genesis,* coming to be. We see the *eidos* in advance (the being as a whole in its end and fulfillment, but as anticipated and therefore not-yet there). Production involves *peras*, the shaping (*morphē*) and forging into boundaries (*peras*). Heidegger emphasizes that production involves exclusion. Every production involves the including of what is essential, and the excluding of what does not work. But exclusion means exclusiveness. The being that is brought forth is exclusive. It is singled out, selected, gathered into a unity. It stands there in relation to other beings in such a way that it holds its own in relation to them. Heidegger says that we no longer have the sense organ to appreciate this exclusivity. These statements are open attacks on positivism and the contemporary scientific approach. They are closer to his work on poetry and the work of art.

In the movement of production, a world is lighted up. An opposition is uncovered, a being directed away from and toward, a conjunction of *pathein* and *poiein*, a neighborhood of beings that face one another—a disjunction. Resistance (obstinacy, obtrusiveness) unfolds a world of involvements. In section 15, Heidegger says that all movement of beings is a fleeing or pursuing. Aristotle speaks of *orexis*, desire or striving, as a lying in wait for. Beings do not simply lie apart from one another, indifferent to one another. It is not as if beings are put together by bringing together in-different matter and indifferent form. Contrariness belongs to the being of all beings. It is because the human being can relate to contrariness that it can disclose the world of beings.

Aristotle's Confrontation with the Megarians: The Way of Being-Present of Force

We should recall that Aristotle defined the human being empowered with *logos* as *zōon logon echon.* The animal who *has logos.* In *Metaphysics* Θ3, Aristotle sets out to offer a philosophical explanation of the sense of this "having" that belongs to the force of *logos,* and thereby constitutes the way human being is. But Aristotle suddenly turns to a discussion of the views of his philosophical opponents, in this case the Megarians. The Meg-arians were followers of Socrates. Their main interest was in bringing to-gether the thought of Parmenides and that of Socrates. In raising critical questions, through philosophical confrontation, Aristotle furthers the abil-ity to truly pose and understand the question, and what is at stake in the question—in this case the question of being. Heidegger understands Aristotle's relationship to his predecessors in philosophical terms. Drawing out the *aporia,* the impasse and limit of thinking are not to show how an opponent is wrong and Aristotle is right, but to raise the question anew and pose the question in an originary way. "The *aporia* point only toward the lack of originality in the posing of the question—that is, they provide the impetus toward the necessary repetition of the question."[25]

But why is it only in the third chapter, in *Metaphysics* Θ3, that Aristotle engages in this *Auseinandersetzung?* In most of Aristotle's treatises, this en-gagement comes first and it would seem on philosophical grounds that it must come first since only in *Auseinandersetzung* can the question be posed, can philosophical questioning occur. Has Aristotle forgotten his own in-sight that philosophy is essentially aporetic and can only get under way in opposition? Is he now backtracking to set up more rigorously the question we have been discussing—the question of the being of *dunamis,* namely, *du-namis kata kinēsin?* Or does the confrontation occur precisely here because a new occurrence of thinking is about to be enacted; is it for the sake of, so to speak, drawing us transitionally onto this new level of questioning? This is an especially compelling explanation in light of the fact that we have been considering *dunamis* in its ordinary sense on the way toward a philosophi-cally more important sense of *dunamis* and *energeia.*

But this way of raising the question and making the problem philosophically compelling by going through the views of others also risks having one's thinking framed by the limitations inherent in the views of others. Heidegger suggests that Aristotle may not have been able to appreciate the full depth of the challenge to his position. It may be that Aristotle misunderstood the challenge, that in this case he failed to make questionable the assumptions that both he and the Megarians shared concerning being. Specifically, according to Heidegger, both philosophical schools presuppose an understanding of being as presence. In the end, for all the efforts Heidegger makes to release Aristotle from misreadings of his thought based on Roman and medieval worldviews, he sees Aristotle as having retreated in the face of a more radical turn that nevertheless represents the true direction of his thinking, which in the tradition, for the most part, gets covered over.

Heidegger says: "One of the questions, or even the central question, of all three orientations [of Plato and Aristotle and the Megarians] concerned the essence and possibility of movement. And this means in a certain sense the question of the being of that which is not, or in other words, the question of the essence of the not and of being in general."[26] The Megarian position is that a *dunamis* is (present) only when it is at work. Only as *energeia,* only when enacted, can there be *dunameis.* But this amounts to collapsing the distinction between *dunamis* and *energeia,* and thereby denying the twofoldness of being. Heidegger translates *energeia* as "at workness" (*en-ergeia*) and not in the usual way as actuality. This is important. Heidegger says the translation guides his interpretation of the entire chapter. The notion of being-at-work implies a how, implies that force always exists *in a certain way.* The Megarians claim, in effect, that *dunamis* only is *what* it is to the extent that it is being realized. When a *dunamis* is enacted, it is available to an immediate view; it is *manifest* and thus only as such present. Aristotle disagrees. Thus, the question that is raised for Aristotle by this confrontation with the Megarians is this: "*how 'is' a capability, thought of not only as potential, but rather as actually present, although not being actualized.*"[27] In other words: how is potentiality as potentiality understood to be present and actualized when it is not activated? This question is especially poignant in that *potential* is precisely what is not present at hand. The underlying assumption of the question is that in order to be, *dunamis* must be present. Heidegger suggests that this view of being stems from the dominance of the phenomenon of production in the Greek conception of being. A being *is* when it is brought forth, when it is produced and therefore when it is completed and stands forth on its own. Both the Megarians and Aristotle presuppose the Greek understanding of being as presence.

Aristotle attacks the Megarian objection to his notion of *dunamis* by showing that the denial of *dunamis* when it is not being enacted leads to absurdity. It amounts to saying, for example, that a builder is only a builder when he is building. But it is precisely when the building is complete and he or she is no longer building that the builder can say "I am a builder" and I possess the power to build. This is just one of the senses in which we can show that the essence of *dunamis,* when *dunamis* is most truly itself, does not consist in enactment, though Aristotle would agree that what a *dunamis* is cannot be understood apart from how it is.

Both Aristotle and the Megarians claim that to be is to be present. If *dunamis* is, it must be present. But Aristotle understands the presence of force in terms of *echein,* having or possessing a force. In contrast, the Megarians understand the presence in terms of enactment. For Aristotle, then, the task is to explain the sense of this having, the holding, that defines *dunamis* as *dunamis*. "*Dunamis echein* means that something which is capable is capable in that it *has* a capability; it *holds itself in* this capability and *holds itself back* with this capability—and thereby precisely does not enact."[28] Holding itself back is understood as a way of being and a way of movement. Aristotle's project here is to offer a philosophical explanation of the sense of this having as the way of being of *dunamis*. It is his explanation in response to the Megarians of how a capability actually is, an explanation that, we will see, thinks through more originally the twofoldness of presence.

Section 19 of this chapter is devoted to Aristotle's very phenomenological explanation of this having of *dunamis* that constitutes a way of being present that demands we think through the essence of presence more originally. Aristotle's aim is to show that a potency is not absent when it ceases to be enacted. In fact, Aristotle will show, the force is most fully present as force precisely when it is not being exercised. For example, one who is practiced in something more truly has the power to do it than one who is practicing to do it. The doctor is not the one who is practicing to be a doctor, but the one who has already practiced and *become* practiced in this art. One becomes a doctor only when practicing is finished and when the work of learning is completed. The Megarians failed to see this because they conceived of being-present in terms of the *ergon,* the work with which one deals in production.

You might recall the structure in the *Nichomachean Ethics* involved in the formation of character. Habits are formed through practicing virtue. It is precisely when we become practiced in virtue, and when we are no longer practicing, that we *are* virtuous. Virtue is understood as a kind of *dunamis*. Similarly, here in *Metapysics* Θ3, Aristotle shows that non-enactment, the *Haltung* or cessation of activity, of *energeia kata kinēsin*, is a way of being-present of *dunamis*. The cessation of movement is not the end of force but rather the fulfillment of force. When force ceases to be at work, it draws back up into itself, becomes ready to act. By drawing back up into itself, it empowers the being to be on its own. In turn, of course, enactment can be shown to not be simply and solely presence. Being at work is intrinsically always also an absence, a not-yet-being-produced. Inasmuch as both the non-enactment and the enactment itself imply both presence and absence, what is required is that we learn to think of presence in a way that always also includes nonpresence. What emerges out of this discussion between Aristotle and the Megarians is the need to rethink the meaning of presence, to think presence more radically in its relationship to absence, as presence-absence.[29] In other words, to think the not-being-present that belongs to presence.

The analysis of cessation shows that the actuality of a *dunamis* as such remains independent of the actuality of that for which it is capable, though the two are intimately related. In other words, if force is most truly force when it ceases to exercise itself, we need to take a look at the peculiar interaction involved in the structure of practicing and ceasing to practice (*Aufhören*). In a sense, the drawing back into oneself of force is always involved in the exercise of force. Only by drawing back is it possible to truly be directed beyond oneself. The movement here is important. "Being trained, however, 'comes' to such practicing only if it passes over into it and is transferred (*überführen*) to it. With this, being-trained is not transported to something else, which in each case would be at hand; but rather the being-trained passes over beyond itself into something which first forms itself only in and through the passing."[30] All force involves exchange. Only because capability in advance opens up the realm of involvement can there be a transfer, an exchange, an enactment of force. "A non-enacted capability is therefore actual in such a way that a *not-yet-beginning* [a holding itself back and not being depleted] belongs to its actuality positively."[31] In other words, the transference is not forced onto the force as something new that is added to it. It is the holding back that makes the transfer possible. Heidegger describes it as a *Sichüberführung*, a leading beyond itself or transfering.[32]

Heidegger calls our attention to the way this whole issue is related to time.[33] At the heart of *dunamis* in Aristotle's sense, which involves the ceasing and withdrawing of practice, where the *dunamis* is drawn up into itself, is what I would like to call chairological temporality. Ceasing enactment, the end of the carrying out of *dunamis,* the end of the movement that occurs due to the force of being does not happen throughout a period of time or, in other words, in time, but all of a sudden, in a moment. This *kairos* which is other than *chronos* always involves ceasing, disruption, rupture, the breaking off of activity. This metabolic time of the *kairos* is on the one hand the opposite of movement and from that point of view it is rest; but on the other hand it is the essence of movement, the concentration of movement in the returning into itself, out of which *the emergence of being* is made possible. The entire discussion of the essence and actuality of force points in the direction of the need to thematically address and critically question the presupposed understanding of the temporality of being. But Aristotle does not explicitly raise the question of time. Although left unthought, it remains the horizon out of which Aristotle's philosophy evolves.

The Megarians understand being in terms of the *ergon,* the work that stands there as produced, as available and at hand in such a way that they are unable to think of being at all in terms of not yet being and no longer being, of beings in movement. Both the building and what is being built *are* present, standing alongside each other. When building is no longer occurring, then building as a possibility of being ceases to exist. But Aristotle points out that the loss of a capability is not related to whether or not it is in act. Just as building, the enactment of a potentiality, occurs over time, so it also takes time for a capability to disappear, through a process of forgetting, for example. It does not disappear in the moment when enactment ceases.

What the Megarians miss and are not capable of understanding is the being of movement as transition, *Übergang.* Because they collapse the difference between *dunamis* and *energeia* they are unable to account for the relationality of things and for the possibility of movement. They miss what we tried to describe as the twofoldness of being. In part this is because, as Eleatics, they are unable to think of privation (*sterēsis*) and incapability as intrinsically and essentially belonging to the actuality of beings. What disturbs the Megarians is that cessation, holding back, is a not-doing, which implies that the *not* can also be present. Moreover, when *dunamis* is only present as an actualization of a *work,* then no separation of *dunamis* and *ergon* is possible. The *pragma,* the work as work, can only be to the extent that it is being worked on; its being belongs to the one who is working. *Dunamis* in effect gets reduced to appropriation and the power of domination. The independence and self-reliance of beings are denied.

According to Heidegger, Aristotle offers this counterargument to the Megarians: "The actuality of the *dunamis* as such remains completely independent of the actuality of that of which it is capable—whether it has actually been produced, or is only half-finished, or even not yet begun."[34] Here, in my opinion, Heidegger has worked out the difference between the Aristotelian view of *technē* and the version of power as domination that is prevalent in modern technology. This philosophical moment of insight rescues the *dunamis meta logou,* human conversance, from its mere confinement to *technē* in the restricted sense. It also frees *technē* for a thoughtful relationship to *phusis,* and demands a consideration of the unconcealment of beings in a way other than through *technē.*

Before turning from Heidegger's discussion of the way of revealing that occurs in *technē* to his discussion of *aisthēsis* or perception, I would like— only in passing—to call attention to Heidegger's remarks on the coming to be of *dunamis* as *technē,* as the having of the capability for producing. It is a question of trying to further our understanding of the character of "having" or *echein.* In section 19, Heidegger is asking how we acquire the know-how and conversance that characterize *technē.* To have a *technē* involves acquiring it, having become practiced in it in such a way that it allows me to comport myself knowingly in relationship to what is and to stand ready to deal with things on this basis. Even before practicing my art, disclosing belongs to my way of being. It is because I am already practiced in something that I can practice it. But I must learn to be practiced through practicing, in the sense of trying to do it. There is a hermeneutic circle involved in human comportment. Heidegger here describes it as *Sichüber-führen,* passing over beyond itself. While practicing, the capability informs *itself* in the practice and thereby transforms itself. In other words, the passing over beyond itself that characterizes the coming to be of capability is not primarily a transferring of itself onto something else, but a recoiling overturning, the essential moment or movement of *metabolē* that constitutes a mode of being. But then *dunamis* is a double movement, a going forth that makes possible the production of things, and the otherness of the things that are produced. The *Reichweite,* the reach and realm of capability, is opened up in the span of *dunamis* as holding itself back in the sense of always not yet beginning and already having been in practice.

The Connection Between Force and Perception: The Capability of Disclosing Beings as Such

In conclusion, we need to look briefly at the analysis of *aisthēsis,* perception, in section 20 of the text. This is required according to Aristotle because the Megarian thesis—that *dunamis* is present only as *energeia*—implies also that only when one is perceiving is there perception; and therefore objects of perception require perception in order to be. Aristotle claims that this implication proves that the Megarians agree with Protagoras that the human being defines and measures all being, that beings only are in the *aisthēsis,* the power of the soul, and that therefore the Megarians must deny the possibility of any knowledge of beings themselves.

Aristotle's resistance to this conclusion is strongly stated. For him, "*aisthēsis* is a capability, a *dunamis,* for *alētheuein,* for making manifest and holding open, a capability for knowledge in the broadest sense."35 What is at stake then in the *dunamis* of *aisthēsis* is the question of whether human being has the capacity to truly reveal the being in itself, whether a relationality between the human being and other beings is possible that does not overpower the other in *its* being, closing off the being rather than disclosing it in its otherness, as it is in itself. To put it another way, what the Megarians implicitly assume is that all revealing essentially occurs as *technē.* In this view, beings can only be revealed as *ergon,* as products, and through the human connection to products. Our only way of being related to what has been produced is through the actual activity of producing. They believe that all knowledge of beings occurs when our *dunamis* is at work; knowledge is actual only when it is enacted. But Aristotle argues that the precondition for knowingly interacting with beings is *aisthēsis.* We do not produce things through *aisthēsis.* The capability to perceive is not actualized in the production of a product but in a disclosive openness to beings that does not interfere with their independent being. The truth of *technē,* its capacity to bring forth knowingly, depends on this prior capability for truth that is the essential *dunamis* of the human being.

Protagoras implies that we can never know beings in themselves, in their being. Similarly, the Megarian thesis that there is only perception when something is being perceived implies the denial of the possibility of independent beings. So Aristotle's task is to show that the being, the actuality, of the perceivable is not *in* perception and vice versa. Heidegger says that this issue of the mutual relation of the perceiving and the perceivable has been misunderstood because the nature of *twofoldness* has been inadequately grasped. It is not a matter of collapsing one pole into the other. No one has asked about the *Zwischen*, the between. Heidegger tries to address the *openness* that characterizes the relationship between the *aisthēton* and *aisthēsis*. He tries to show that the relationship does not destroy but founds the independent self-reliance of beings.

> Drawing oneself back out of the practice of perceiving is not the mere breaking off and disappearance of this practice, but rather has the character of a giving over of the perceived to itself as something which is then perceivable.[36]

The being in themselves of beings becomes not only unexplainable without the existence of humans, it becomes utterly meaningless; but this does not mean the things themselves are dependent on humans.

In section 20, Heidegger briefly returns to the question of the difference between animals and humans. Both are able to perceive. Aristotle characterizes the difference between humans and animals in terms of how humans have *logos*. His point is that *logos* is not something in addition to perception. Rather *logos* is a way of perceiving that is uniquely human. All perceiving beings stand in relation to and are open to beings. But human perception has a peculiar directedness toward beings that is twofold, that also holds itself back from beings and recognizes them in their otherness, that is, in their own being as such. Heidegger says: "In this perceptual relation, the relationship of the human to beings and of beings to the human is in a certain way co-determined."[37] Human perception is the *between* that belongs neither to the perceiver, nor to the perceived, that is, it belongs to both, though not in a way that collapses the difference between them. This "between" is not a third place where the two meet. For one thing, the "site" where perception occurs could never itself be present at hand. It is the thinking of this place that Heidegger says most calls us for thought today and requires the entire effort of our philosophizing. Questioning such a site for human being, Heidegger says, would begin to allow us to understand what it means that we are fundamentally *atopos*, unable to be at home in any site (*ohne Ort*). Aristotle failed to develop the questioning of this site adequately and, Heidegger says, the entire subsequent history of philosophy moves within the failure to address this question, though Aristotle takes a first decisive step toward its proper formulation.

Heidegger's confrontation with Aristotle, his deconstructive reading of Aristotle, becomes clear at this point. It is a kind of reading that involves a double movement in which destruction and retrieval implicate and co-determine each other. Heidegger shows how the traditional reading of Aristotle, like the Megarians whom Aristotle went to some lengths to refute, has misunderstood his notion of force and presupposed an unclarified understanding of being as presence. Specifically, Heidegger shows that in the history of metaphysics, a confusion between the kind of knowing involved in *technē* and that involved in *aisthēsis* inevitably mires the reading of Aristotle in problems that make it impossible to understand the greatness of Aristotle's thought.

At the end of his course, Heidegger begins the transition from the retrieval of Aristotle's philosophy, achieved during this course, to a demarcation of his own *Auseinandersetzung* with Aristotle. He writes:

Aristotle was not capable of comprehending, no less than anyone before or after him, the proper essence and being of that which makes up this *between*—between *aisthēton* as such and *aisthēsis* as such—and which in itself brings about the very wonder that, although it is related to self-reliant beings, it does not through this relation take their self-reliance away, but rather precisely makes it possible for such being to secure this self-reliance in the truth.[38]

I believe that, for Heidegger, this "between" is the unaddressed and unthematized, but presupposed, sense of *dunamis* toward which the entire discussion of *Metaphysics* Θ1–3 is under way. It is the higher, singular meaning of *dunamis-energeia* for which the discussion of *dunamis kata kinēsin* has been a preparation. This is a concept of power that is worthy of thought, one that I hope we have seen involves the privative character of force and the twofoldness of being.

Chapter Five

HEIDEGGER AND ARISTOTLE: AN ONTOLOGY OF HUMAN DASEIN

This chapter is divided into five parts. In this first section of the chapter, I want to argue that Aristotle's *Nichomachean Ethics* is primarily an ontology of human being. My intention is to offer a reading of the *Ethics* that draws it into close proximity to Heidegger's *Daseinanalytik* in *Being and Time*, though Heidegger's project was motivated by the need to overcome psychologism and epistemological subjectivity as the dominant approaches to the study of human being, whereas here the problem is more fundamentally the need to retrieve a sense of human excellence that is not reducible to normative or biological interpretations. In the second section, I somewhat reverse the task and try to show how *Being and Time,* especially in the sections on being-toward-death, does not argue for a sense of authentic human being that is solipsistic and detached from practical involvement with others, but rather opens up a way of thinking about authenticity that provides a new foundation for understanding human community. In the third section, I turn to another aspect of practical philosophy, namely, rhetoric, and a study of Heidegger's comparison in *Platon:* Sophistes of rhetoric and dialectic in Plato's philosophy. In a sense, this section is out of sync with the rest of the book, since it addresses Heidegger's reading of Plato rather than Aristotle. But as we will see, his critique of Plato and the limits of dialectic is at the heart of his attempt to retrieve, in contrast, a phenomenologically more radical reading of Aristotle. Heidegger sees Aristotle as going beyond the limitations of dialectic and directly addressing the problem of *nous,* and he sees the inability of Platonic dialectic to do this as enmeshing Platonic dialectical philosophy with sophistry. In the fourth section of this chapter, I will discuss one of Heidegger's most important studies of Aristotle, the treatment of *Nichomachean Ethics* VI, which he offers as propaedeutic to a reading of Plato's *Sophist.* Finally, the chapter ends with a discussion of the twofoldness of truth in Aristotle's philosophy, in order to show how the thematic focus of this book, the twofoldness of being, is evident in Aristotle's discussion of *alētheia*. In the section preceding this final section, I show how truth is the central concern and focus of Aristotle's practical philosophy in Book VI of the *Nichomachean Ethics*. Here in an analysis of Heidegger's reading of Aristotle's notion of truth, the inadequacy of the usual philosophical division between theoretical and practical philosophy comes to the fore.

Dasein and the Question of Practical Life

In his *Nichomachean Ethics,* Aristotle offers an understanding of human being that in a basic way is in accord with Heidegger's Dasein analytic, espousing a fundamentally nonrelational potentiality for being as the human being's way of being wholly itself. Aristotle considers *phronēsis* or practical wisdom to be primarily this kind of self-disclosure, and *praxis* or true human action to be the manifestation of this possibility of being a self in one's situatedness. I will attempt to show through an interpretation of the *phronēsis-praxis* structure in the *Ethics* that *praxis* for Aristotle means that way in which the human being factically chooses to be *for its own sake.* This apparent retreat from everyday practical involvements back into a concern for one's own being is neither for Aristotle nor Heidegger a form of solipsism but the only genuine basis for human community, and for a kind of relating to nonhuman being that cannot be reduced to the kind of relating derived from the structures of *technē* or those operative in modern technology.

Heidegger frequently states that all of Greek ontology is rooted in an overall conception of being as presence. The explication of this conception is guided by the notion of the *ergon,* the work. The work as something present in the mode of having been produced came eventually to be understood through *technē,* the kind of knowledge involved in production. We have already seen that Heidegger claims in his 1931 Aristotle course that the basic concepts of philosophy grew out of and within this understanding of a work-world. Aristotle's notions of form, matter, and end are based on this method of investigation. Heidegger says:

What the Greeks conceived as *epistēmē poiētikē* was of fundamental significance for their own understanding of the world. We have to clarify for ourselves what it signifies that the human being has a relation to the works that he produces. It is for this reason that a certain book called *Being and Time* discusses dealings with equipment.[1]

In this quote, written shortly after the publication of *Being and Time,* Heidegger indicates his awareness of the dependency of his equipment analysis in *Being and Time* on the *technē* model with which he is attempting to come to terms. It may well be that Heidegger's phenomenological commitment to the principle that "no understanding of being is possible that is not rooted in a comportment toward beings"[2] demands that his starting point be the ways things are historically and for the most part given to us. The slippage in man's relation to beings that began with Aristotle might well be what leads him to begin his own analysis with this *technē* model of the givenness of things. But it would be unsatisfactory if this analysis of equipment were his final word on the subject of human practical life. Not only would this mean that Heidegger's view of beings other than ourselves is seriously limited, but it would also imply a less than successful outcome for his analysis of Dasein's being since, as he shows, our very being becomes entangled and caught up in these equipmental structures in a way that is, in Heidegger's terms, fallen and inauthentic.

I will try to show, however, that this is not the case and that Heidegger's account of genuine *phronēsis* and *praxis* are rather to be found in Division Two of *Being and Time,* in which he discusses Dasein's possibility of being-a-whole in terms remarkably parallel to Aristotle's own understanding of the life that is characteristic of the happy person. In both the *Nichomachean Ethics* and in *Being and Time,* I want to argue, the possibility of a genuine practical life is based on a drawing back into oneself of one's ownmost potentiality. For Heidegger this takes the form of a movement of retrieval that opens up a world and our ecstatic situatedness in the midst of other beings. For Aristotle, this drawing back into oneself of potentiality is made explicit in his discussion of friendship, as I will show later. For both, it is our way of being open to the truth of beings or what Aristotle calls *theōria.*[3]

Before turning to Aristotle's *Nichomachean Ethics,* I want to bring back into the discussion a few passages from Heidegger's 1931 lecture course that we treated in chapter 4. Of particular interest to us here is the second half of the text, where Heidegger considers Aristotle's division of beings on the basis of two different kinds of *dunamis* or potentiality. Those beings that have *logos* are differentiated from those without *logos.* The *dunamis* that belongs to human beings is "*meta logou.*"

Heidegger translates Aristotle's definition of the human being, *zōon logon echon,* as the living being whose being is essentially determined by the potentiality for discourse. *Logos* constitutes Dasein's way of being, its way of holding itself in relation to itself. Heidegger says that Aristotle's phrase *dunamis meta logou* characterizes human existence. It has the sense Heidegger himself conveys when he speaks of the *ecstasis* of Dasein. The human being is always already beyond itself. Existing in the mode of *dunamis,* we do not have our being as something we possess. Rather, through the force and command of language (*logos*), we are able to rescue ourselves from the everyday "they" and say who we are. But the human being never becomes a work in the sense of a finished product. For Aristotle and Heidegger, we have our being in a different way. Our self-realization involves holding ourselves in relation to not being ourselves and thus to what is other than ourselves. With *logos* there is a dwelling in the midst of others as well as an openness to what can be.

Although Aristotle devotes the first two chapters of Book Θ of the *Metaphysics* to the explication of this human potentiality (which Heidegger calls worldliness), he takes up the question in another way in the third chapter. Here Aristotle is responding to the Megarians who charge that since to be is to be actual, no potentiality can exist except when it is actively being realized. So, for example, the builder is only a builder when he is building. But Aristotle accuses the Megarians of misunderstanding the way in which the *dunamis* is present in the human being. His point is that it is precisely when one is not engaged in the performance of a skill that one "has" the skill. Aristotle gives the example of learning. When one is learning to build and practicing how to build, one is not yet a builder. It is when one is no longer practicing that one is practiced and that the realization of the skill is most present in the person. In another example, when one is not yet running but fully concentrated and gathered into oneself at the start of a race, one's capacity to run is most fully present. So one's capability is fully present when it is drawn back into oneself and held in readiness. This is the *energeia,* the being-fully-engaged of *dunamis* as *dunamis,* the full realization and fulfillment of movement as such. To be gathered into oneself in this way is to have a way of being that embodies the temporal ecstasies of always already having been (past) and being-toward (future) the realm of one's involvements.

But what I would like particularly to emphasize here is that this openness or worldliness is first of all what makes possible specific human activities, such as building, and that it is precisely when one is not specifically engaged in this or that way that our involvement is most truly and fully our own. Likewise, there is a sense in which this drawing back into ourselves of our potentiality to be is necessary in order not to take over the being of

others. For example, in the case of the builder, it is when the builder fin-
ishes building and withdraws from skillful activity that the building is able
to be on its own. In an example that does not rely on *technē* but on
aisthēsis or perception, Aristotle says that when perception withdraws into
itself and is no longer actually being exercised, the perceivable being is
given back to itself and does not just disappear. Holding oneself back toward oneself is not a disowning of one's concrete relationship to other beings but is a way of granting to other beings a being of their own.

In the beginning of the *Nichomachean Ethics,* Aristotle argues that
logos is the *ergon* or work of human being in the sense that through *logos*
our being is most fully realized. Yet, his attention is first drawn to a discussion of the formation of character and the inculcation of virtues. Virtues
are dispositions toward acting and feeling in a certain way, namely, in an
excellent way. They constitute the general way in which we comport ourselves rather than determine particular of specific actions or feelings and
emotions determined by outside forces. So here already Aristotle is taking
a step in the direction of retrieving the person from an inauthentic involvement with beings. We have feeling because we are capable of feeling. We
are afraid because being fearful is a way of being for us, a possibility that is
open to us. The formation of virtues is a process of taking charge of those
capacities for ourselves. We can notice that having emotions—anger, fear,
joy, and the others Aristotle lists—indicates that we already stand in relation to the world around us. Anger and fear are responses to our situatedness and involvement with others. These emotions arise because we are capable of being affected. Being virtuous does not exclude being affected by
these outside forces. It is rather a question of whether we take charge of
these capacities, make them our own, concretize them in some fashion,
that allows us to stand out in relation to our involvements rather than
merely being there as part of them. Virtues open up a relationship to oneself, to one's capacities as a source for directing one's emotions and actions. I am afraid because I can be afraid, but I can also not be afraid. What
I want to point out here is that the movement is from an actual entanglement with one's surroundings to a return to oneself, and that this distancing of oneself from the immediacy of one's involvement opens up the horizon of possibilities for being oneself in that situation.

Aristotle's discussion of the mean in relation to virtue indicates again the
broader context for an understanding of human *praxis* toward which Aristotle is aiming. The virtuous person is able to see the parameters of the situation, the excess and deficiency, and choose what to do within this broader

context of understanding; thus, our natural tendencies and leanings are not allowed to distort our judgments or decisions about what to do in a given situation. For Aristotle, to be virtuous is to find pleasure in what is most worthy of being pursued. This in turn requires openness to options, a lack of immediate compulsion, a certain distance from the moment, which for the good person heightens rather than weakens the intensity of the moment. Virtue requires forethought and decision about what can be done.

Let us look briefly at the virtue of courage as an example of the way Aristotle directs the question of practical living toward the question of human being. Courage allows us to be well-disposed toward what is fearful, primarily toward what is most terrifying (*deinon*): death. The courageous person endures the end nobly. To be courageous is to stand resolutely in the face of the possibility of no longer being. Aristotle says this virtue is particularly exemplified in those situations when there is not some specific aspect of our life at issue but the whole of our life. Fearlessness in other matters, Aristotle says, resembles courage but is not the same. Thus, the citizen soldier who endures danger for honor and for the sake of the law is not, strictly speaking, courageous. He does not face death for its own sake, for the nobility or intrinsic worth of acting in this way. Aristotle goes on to say that the courageous person can fear what is fearful but endures it in an appropriate way, according to the situation, as *logos* directs. The point I would want to emphasize here is that courage is first of all a disposition toward one's own being and concomitantly a way of relating ourselves to others.

In a similar fashion, *megalopsuchia*, great-souledness, is the gift-giving virtue of one who knows his or her superiority by virtue of knowing his or her limits. Such a person, Aristotle says, would rather give than receive, so exuberant and full of life is the soul. Such a person is said to be open in hate and love, neither resentful nor gossipy. Here, as in the case of the complementary virtue of *sophrosunē*, which is described as a capacity to hold oneself back in the situation, the virtue is primarily a way of being and thereby a way of being with others.

But even if this is true and Aristotle continues to concern himself primarily with the ontology of human being and continues to draw the discussion away from the specificity of practical life, as I believe he does, I do not think this contradicts his claim to be concerned with the question of political life; rather, I think he is trying to win the proper foundation of such an inquiry. This emerges quite clearly in his discussion of justice, the paramount political virtue.

Aristotle names justice as the whole of virtue. This is because the healthy, excellent person achieves self-rule, a certain harmony between *logos* and *alogos*. Aristotle says that to be in command of oneself is also to both follow and listen. The model of the good citizen is to be able to be both a ruler and ruled in turn. To have command of *logos* is to be able to say who one is in relation to others, and thereby to face others as the kind of being who takes charge of one's being and is responsible for one's being. Thus, to be fully just is to be law-abiding, to dwell amid others in accord with *logos*. This requires knowing one's being as well as what is appropriate to one's being in given situations.

Partial justice involves having a sense of how to measure oneself in relation to others, how to differentiate oneself from others—how to determine the *isos*, what is equal to one's being, what is one's own. To do so, as Aristotle points out, requires more than a virtuous disposition. The *dianomē* or distribution that justice requires demands not only a knowledge of oneself but of what does not belong to oneself but to others. Justice is proportionate, *ana-logos*. It knows what is and is not suitable to one's being. Partial justice involves having a sense of how to measure oneself in relation to others, how to differentiate oneself from others—how to determine the *isos*, what is equal to one's being, what is one's own. To do so, as Aristotle points out, requires more than a virtuous disposition. The *dianomē* or distribution that justice requires demands not only a knowledge of oneself but of what does not belong to oneself but to others. Justice is proportionate, *ana-logos*. It knows what is and is not suitable to one's being.

Aristotle says that inasmuch as moral virtues (*aretē*) are habitual (*hexis*), they are not open to that which is other than themselves. But, like the doctor who must have knowledge of health and sickness, the distributor of justice must not only know what belongs properly to the person but also what does not. Thus, justice is the link between intellectual virtue and moral virtue. All of the virtues are through justice disposed to listen to *logos* and can therefore stand in relationship to what they are not. Justice as the highest virtue gathers the human being into a whole, but also concretely articulates and specifies what belongs to and does not belong to each human being. At this level, justice is akin to deliberation as the activity of articulating what is to be done in the realm of *praxis*. The point that I would like to draw from this discussion is that it is precisely because the human being has come to recognize his or her own limit and can see in some sense who he or she is in the whole of his or her being that the possibility of political life has emerged.

Aristotle says the work of the intellect is *alētheia*. He begins his discussion in Book VI with a twofold division of *logos,* a division made on the basis of the way of disclosure or truth, on the one hand theoretical and on the other practical. I want to address my remarks here only to the latter kind of disclosure and discuss only the kind of practical revealing that Aristotle calls *phronēsis* or practical wisdom. He defines *phronēsis* as a truthful disposition to act with *logos* in matters involving choice between good and bad in such a way that the person chooses and acts for the sake of the end, the good life as a whole, toward which he or she is directed. He says that *phronēsis* is not political because *phronēsis* is concerned more with one's own *eidos,* with the aspect in which one's own being comes to be shaped, although politics and practical wisdom do not exclude each other.

At the risk of being too schematic, I would like to suggest that in delineating the relationship between *phronēsis* and *praxis* Aristotle thinks through how the situated, finite human being can act in such a way that each action affirms his or her being as a whole and allows the person to be fully present as a concrete individual. Action, deliberation, choice, desire, and a kind of practical *nous* (the simple saying of one's being that accompanies action and the good life) are the main ingredients that come together in Aristotle's notion of practical wisdom. Aristotle indicates by his notion of *orexis,* desireful striving, that our way of being related to our end, our way of having our end, is by way of a being-toward. The end is the good life (*euzen*); this is the end that Aristotle calls *haplōs,* in itself simple and unqualified, and never a means to something else. Deliberation, Aristotle says, considers what is *pros to telos,* the means in the sense of what is in relation to or in accordance with the end and intrinsic to it. Through deliberation the end is articulated and specified and made actual for action. Human action is not like *poiēsis,* with its means-end formula. *Praxis* has to arise out of oneself and be done for its own sake because of its intrinsic nobility. The goodness of the agent determines the quality of an action. What counts for Aristotle is that the action manifests the excellence of the person. So the end of human action is not outside the human person who acts, except inasmuch as the excellent person is outside himself or herself. To sum up: In advance of acting, we are to single out, to choose what is to be done on the basis of a view toward what is involved, which is disclosed in a deliberation based on a fore-grasp of the good that is the ultimate end for which we act. So action requires a lot of advance activity. As Aristotle says frequently, deliberation takes time.

So where, then, in Aristotle's *Ethics* do we find the link between the ontology of human being and that being's practical life? I would respond that in one sense the link is there already in that the question presupposes a division between something like a theoretical life and a practical life. But Aristotle does not assume such a division. One indication of this is that his first mention of *theōria* after Book VI comes in his discussion of friendship. He says that we can observe or witness (*theōrein*) our neighbor's actions better than our own. We come to be aware of the being of our friend because, Aristotle says, we perceive, on the basis of our experience of ourselves, that human life is reflective and goes beyond itself and that life is intrinsically good and pleasant, especially for the good person. The being of another is like our own. Our awareness of our being implies awareness of being and thus the being of others. The being of another is pleasant and desirable to us. In perceiving ourselves, we perceive at the same time others like ourselves.

Aristotle says that all knowledge presupposes a certain kinship between the knower and what is known. Aristotle calls this kinship truth. *Theōria* is the activity of knowing the being of that which is other than ourselves. It implies a kind of thinking that transcends mere thinking and opens up a kinship between thinking and being. If *theōria* involves a kinship that allows the truth of beings as such to be uncovered, and if *theōria* is a characteristic of friendship, then presumably it is a kind of apprehending that mutually and reciprocally reveals the beings involved. Friendship goes beyond justice in that it takes up in a positive manner the capacity of the just person to know the difference between what is his own and what belongs to others.

I suggested earlier that the full treatment of the question of practical wisdom and action in Heidegger's *Being and Time* is not to be found in the first division of that work. The concern there is with the retrieval of human being from an inauthentic involvement with other beings. If we read Heidegger's discussions of equipmentality as his final word on Dasein's involvement with things, we will miss the import of what Heidegger has to offer vis-à-vis human practical life. Reading *Being and Time* backwards, we need to understand this analysis in the light of Division Two of the work, where Heidegger speaks of Dasein's potentiality for being a whole. Similarly, Aristotle's discussion of *phronēsis* and *nous praktikos,* as well as his discussion of friendship and happiness in the later books of the *Nichomachean Ethics,* are the appropriate context within which to understand his earlier discussion of habit and virtuous behavior.

Aristotle says that happiness as the end of human life requires self-sufficiency and a complete life. In his discussion of *phronēsis* he says that this end can never be chosen because it is always already there as that toward which action is ultimately directed. Aristotle wonders whether happiness can be attained before death and answers that being in one's end in this way is possible as an *energeia,* a being at work, that in its choices and actions chooses to choose itself and thus to disclose itself as fully and humanly present in its situation. Aristotle says: "what is always chosen as an end in itself and never as a means to something else is called final in an unqualified sense. This description seems to apply to happiness above all else" (*Nich. Eth.* 1097 a35). Happiness is not a good among others that we can choose. Happiness is that kind of human action that takes up for itself its own end as a possibility for being. In happy actions, we choose ourselves. In his discussion of practical wisdom Aristotle says: "When a person becomes corrupted by pleasure or pain, the end no longer appears as a motivating principle. The person no longer sees that he or she should choose and act in every case for the sake of and because of this end" (*Nich. Eth.* 1140 b17–20). The practical wisdom of the *phronimos* lies in the capacity to call himself or herself back resolutely, and thus to stand by this person who cannot abide by the choice he or she has made.

In speaking of conscience, Heidegger says: "The existential interpretation of understanding the summons as resoluteness reveals conscience as the kind of being contained in the ground of Dasein, in which it makes its factical existence possible for itself, attesting its ownmost potentiality-of-being."[4] In his discussion of *Nichomachean Ethics* VI in *Platon*: Sophistes, Heidegger translates *phronēsis* as *Gewissen* or conscience. The translation seems to me to be rooted in a meditation on Aristotle's *phronēsis* in the context of his discussion of moral weakness, a discussion on Aristotle's part that is comparable to Heidegger's discussion of losing oneself in the publicness and idle talk of the "they" and thus failing to hear one's ownmost self while listening to the they-self. In this regard, I see a close connection between Aristotle's notion of *orexis* or striving in his description of the *phronēsis-praxis* structure and Heidegger's discussion of "wanting to have a conscience." In 1931 course *Aristotle's Metaphysics* Θ1–3, Heidegger translates *phronēsis* as *Umsicht* or circumspection, a notion akin to Aristotle's description of deliberation. He says that *phronēsis* is the *Selbstbesinnung* of the human being, our human way of being authentically in a situation.[5]

In concluding this interpretation, of Aristotle's *Nichomachean Ethics* as an ontology of human being, I would like to quote a passage from Division

Two of *Being and Time* that specifically indicates that resoluteness in the face of one's own being is for Heidegger the basis of a free relationship with beings other than ourselves, a position that, as I have attempted to argue, is thoroughly Aristotelian:

> As *authentic being-one's-self*, resoluteness does not detach Da-sein from its world, nor does it isolate it as a free floating ego. How could it, if resoluteness as authentic disclosedness is, after all, nothing other than *authentically being-in-the-world?* Resoluteness brings the self right into its being together with things at hand, actually taking care of them, and pushes it toward concerned being-with with the others. In the light of the for-sake-of-which of the potentiality-of-being which it has chosen, resolute Da-sein frees itself for its world. The resoluteness toward itself first brings Da-sein to the possibility of letting the others who are with it "be" in their ownmost potentiality-of-being, and also discloses that potentiality in concern which leaps ahead and frees. Resolute Da-sein can become the "conscience" of others. It is from the authentic being a self of resoluteness that authentic being-with-one-another first arises.[6]

Sein und Zeit *and the Ethics of Aristotle*

In my view, Heidegger's practical philosophy is found in *Sein und Zeit,* which like Aristotle's *Nichomachean Ethics* is rooted in an essential insight into the inseparability of ontology and ethics. I will here try to offer a reading of *Sein und Zeit* that demonstrates its connectedness to Aristotelian ethical concepts and shows how it could possibly provide, in several essential respects, the appropriate philosophical basis for a contemporary, postmodern understanding of ethical relationships and political community. My primary contention is that Heidegger's analysis of death, which indeed is the constitutive existential mark of Dasein, is the precondition for a philosophy of community that remains faithful to the utter singularity and finitude of each of the members of the human community. Indeed, in his discussion of the virtue of courage, Aristotle interprets the human being's virtuous relationship to death as the earmark of the authentic individual.

The unshareability and aloneness of death, as it is analyzed in *Sein und Zeit,* have led many critics to argue that Heidegger's ontology of human being is unable to give a strong account of otherness that does not end up reducible either to an extension of the self that belongs to the being of the ontologically isolated individual or to an ontic, tool-centered encounter with other beings in the world of concern. But, as I will attempt to show, this criticism fails to take into account the transformation of the notion of selfhood (the very notion of Dasein begins with a turn from solipsism to a more original, communally-oriented notion of the self) in Heidegger's ontology, and thus fails to recognize the radical rethinking of the problem of otherness that is implicit in Heidegger's ontology. Ironically, the misunderstanding of the framework Heidegger gives for rethinking the self-other relationship replicates the misunderstanding of Aristotle's famous claim that friendship is rooted in self-love, a claim that, as he makes clear, is neither selfish nor nonpolitical.

One such critic, Jacques Taminiaux, rightfully sees the influence of Heidegger's reading of the Greeks on Heidegger's ontology. He argues in *Heidegger and the Project of Fundamental Ontology* that implicit in *Being and Time* is a Platonic bias that leads Heidegger to read Aristotelian *praxis* as if it were an intellectual *phronēsis*. He claims, "This is why in fundamental ontology transcendence prevents us from conceiving *praxis* in connection with a common realm of shared deeds and words, as did the Greek city and its Aristotelian account."[7] In Taminiaux's reading, *Being and Time* is fundamentally solipsistic, offering up a concept of world that, he says, is empty of things and people. The only contact Dasein has with others, in Taminiaux's analysis, is through the inauthentic life of fallen Dasein who allows its being to be determined by the tool-world in which it is involved. To state Taminiaux's position, as I understand it, in the strongest terms: authentic Dasein is a being unto itself, self-enclosed in a way that fundamentally isolates it from any genuine access to the other. In contrast, inauthentic Dasein is mired in the everyday world of concernful absorption in others and suffers a concomitant loss of self. The retrieval of authentic selfhood is possible only because Dasein does not truly belong with others.

Ironically, Taminiaux sees the antidote to this Platonic bias in the Aristotle-influenced emphasis on *praxis* as found in Hanah Arendt's philosophy. He reads Arendt's philosophy as a repudiation of Heidegger for having remained attached to the superiority of the life of contemplation over the life of action. Aristotle is understood as having made this turn away from his teacher Plato toward the life of action, just as Arendt has done in relationship to Heidegger's ontology. I hope to show that this reading, which is feasible only if one relies on a bifurcation of the theoretical and practical life, misses an important aspect of Heidegger's treatment of Dasein's ownmost, authentic being-itself, namely, that community and relationality, properly understood in an Aristotelian manner, apart from the modern liberal notion of a community founded on sameness, is also at the basis of the authentic experience of self analyzed in Division II of *Being and Time.* Were this acknowledged, then authentic, resolute Dasein would be seen to be at the same time both the moment of existential solitude and the ecstatic openness to the other as other. Heidegger agrees in this respect with Aristotle that self-sufficiency (*autarchēs*), the capacity to act for one's ownmost potentiality to be (*hou heneka*), is the appropriate basis for genuine friendship.

Jacques Taminiaux's reading that ascribes *poiesis* and Dasein's involvement with beings other than itself to Division I of *Being and Time* resembles, ironically, the reading of Hubert Dreyfus in his book *Being-in-the-World: A Commentary on Heidegger's 'Being and Time,' Division I*.[8] Both Dreyfus and Taminiaux share a similar assumption, namely, that there is a dichotomy between existence and facticity in the structure of *Being and Time,* a dichotomy that parallels a distinction between transcendence and entanglement. Both fail to see the centricity of Heidegger's treatment of the twofoldness of existence and facticity and the double movement between them, a "movement" that opens up the space of being in the world. As we saw in chapter one, the interconnectedness of existence and facticity was insisted on emphatically by Heidegger in his 1992 essay on Aristotle. Each author reads Heidegger in such a way as to collapse the connection between the two by privileging one. Taminiaux sees Heidegger's fundamental category as existence and therefore accuses Heidegger of a philosophy of transcendence that shares with Plato a disdain for involvement. Dreyfus on the other hand reads *Being and Time* as primarily a treatise on factical life, and he subsumes Heidegger's treatment of authentic existence into the world of everyday concern by positing the thesis that authenticity for Heidegger amounts to the realization that our existence in itself is a nullity; our being is nothing other than what we do.

Dreyfus is largely responsible for what seems to me to be an overemphasis on Division I of *Being and Time* and the assumption that it is in Division One alone that can be found Heidegger's sense of community. Thus, Dreyfus writes: "Heidegger seeks to show that the shared public world is the only world there is or can be."[9] This thesis, were it valid, would of course place Heidegger squarely against Aristotle's practical philosophy. While it is true that Aristotle emphasizes the life of politics and action as the good for humans and the avenue to human happiness, he does not at all mean the life of useful preoccupation with worldly affairs or even the pleasure humans receive from encountering others through this shared engagement with things. As I will try to show in a discussion of Aristotle's treatment of friendship, Aristotle does not appear to believe there is a conflict between the life of action and the life of theory; he in fact says both are the expressions of the happy, virtuous life.

Dreyfus argues that Division II of *Being and Time* makes explicit the primacy of Division I by demonstrating that Dasein has no other self than the one that it finds when it encounters itself as immersed in everydayness. "Anxiety reveals that the self has no possibilities of its own, and so Dasein's response to anxiety cannot be to find some resource in *itself*. . . . there is no human potential." Dreyfus goes on to claim, "Heidegger holds that (1) all for-the-sake-of-which's are provided by the culture and are for anyone and (2) Dasein can never take over these impersonal public possibilities in a way that would make them its own and so give it an identity."[10] Ironically, it is precisely the task of Aristotle's *Nichomachean Ethics* and of *Sein und Zeit* to analyze and explain this admittedly profound and unique characteristic of human being, that humans can take over their being and be wholly responsible for their actions. This is what Aristotle means by deliberate choice and what Heidegger means by anticipatory resoluteness.

Dreyfus wants to accomplish something for Heidegger that I also want to argue, namely, that in *Being and Time* Heidegger overcomes the modern concept of isolated subjectivity and provides a basis for understanding the fundamentally communal and relational character of Dasein. But the overcoming of modern subjectivity does not require one to deny the main point of Division Two, which is to show that the possibility of being whole and of being a self, far from being destroyed by the destruction of subjectivity, for the first time authentically comes to the fore. Against Taminiaux, I would also argue that Heidegger's retrieval of the existential, singular individual is premised on his philosophical destruction of the modern, transcendental subject. If *Sein und Zeit* returns to a notion of subjectivity, it is to a postmodern subject more akin to the Aristotelian praxical subjectivity of the virtuous human being. Moreover, Heidegger's sense of human community is not bound to his analysis of the world of equipmentality outlined in Division I. Indeed this world belongs to inauthentic Dasein, precisely the Dasein that tends to take itself as a subject and who encounters other Dasein only through the public realm of shared economies and enterprises. Genuine community is founded not out of this public realm of the "they," a realm in which other existential Dasein are never authentically encountered, but rather on the basis of a way of being together that itself creates the possibility for a kind of public sharing of oneself that is authentic and *existentiell*. I believe this is what Heidegger means when he emphasizes in

Division II that "*only on the basis of its ecstatic and horizonal temporality is it possible for Dasein to break into space,*"[11] the space of circumspective taking care. If even the world of concernful involvement, the work world, and this way of connecting to others, are founded on Dasein's own potentiality-for-being, then this does not indicate that significance-relationships belong to a worldless subject, but rather that Dasein is not a worldless subject at all. This double movement between entanglement and retrieve is also described in Aristotle's analysis of the formation of character and the circle-like movement between virtue and action. One cannot truly act, Aristotle says, unless one already in advance exists as disposed toward the world in such a way as to *be* ready for action. This is what Aristotle calls *hexis*. And yet, he says, one's virtuous disposition is itself drawn from one's engagement and involvement in the world, from *praxis*.

In a discussion of death that occurs in Heidegger's 1922 essay that we discussed in chapter one, one finds the following statement: "Existence becomes understandable in itself only in the act of making facticity questionable, that is, in the concrete destruction of facticity."[12] I call attention again in this chapter to this point in order to highlight the close connection Heidegger draws between existence and facticity (fallenness). Existence is described in this essay as a countermovement against the tendency toward falling; existence, he says, occurs precisely in the concrete movement of dealings and of concern. Though co-primordial with facticity in the being of Dasein, existence always arises out of a recovery from one's absorption in the they-self. Thus, existence is founded in a way of being together with others that it resists. The question, then, is whether existence, which puts facticity entirely at risk and makes Dasein's factical life entirely questionable, whether this imminent possibility of not-being that moves against concrete factical being destroys Dasein's fundamental way of being related to others, or transforms it and makes the relationality that essentially belongs to Dasein utterly unique. Heidegger emphasizes that "the countermovement against the tendency towards falling must not be interpreted as flight from the world."[13] Existence does not constitute Dasein's being as outside the world or as in any way isolated, by virtue of its authentic being, from belonging with others. If one severs the relationship between Division I and Division II of *Being and Time*, and fails to pay attention to the middle-voiced character of the movement of repetition that binds the two divisions, then any discussion of Dasein and community will inevitably miss the radical dimension of Heidegger's thought. It would be a mistake no less serious than reading the division between moral virtue and intellectual virtue in Aristotle's *Ethics* without asking about the movement that hold them together and constitutes the possibility of being a person of integrity.

On the one hand, one may understand being-with-others only in terms of specific factical ways of being thrown together. The concept of community that inevitably grows out of this view is based on my being the same as the others I encounter; in other words, it is a community based on the they-self; a community based on actualized, concrete relations in which Dasein finds itself and to which it gives itself over. It is a community that remains bound by an economy of exchange. The tendency to allow oneself to be defined by what is outside oneself is at the heart of the modern concept of community, the community of those who are the same. Fundamentally, it is also the same tendency that is at work when one understands the human being as existential to the exclusion of facticity. Heidegger's emphasis on the existential as being toward a possibility is then seen as tearing Dasein away from every actuality and from any genuine involvement with practical life. On such a reading, Dasein's mineness and radical individuation is interpreted as a fundamental solipsism, a return to the notion of Dasein as an isolated subject devoid of any substantive connection to an objective world. On this reading, the nonrelational character of Dasein's existential being makes any notion of community implausible, especially a notion of community and being-with that is intrinsic to the very being of Dasein. A community of radically subjective beings can only be established from outside, by a principle of universal law and divine authority, discovered in a realm removed from practice and dedicated to theory. On one account, this is why Aristotle turns to *theōria* in Book X of the Ethics and considers it to be the highest activity, not only because it is self-contained and precludes the possibility of letting one's being be defined from outside, but also because it is divine-like and, as superior, has authority over action.

Both these accounts of Dasein's community cloak a theological bias that insists on the need to have the human being defined by a principle outside its own being in order for the human being to encounter that which is radically other than itself. But, as we have seen in our analysis of Heidegger's 1922 Aristotle essay, Heidegger specifically criticizes this theological bias and declares that any authentic, philosophical understanding of Dasein must be fundamentally atheistic, and draw its understanding of human life from that life itself.[14] This is especially significant in that in this essay Heidegger defines philosophy as a way of standing within the movement of existential facticity.[15] The phenomenological commitment to the facticity of human life provides Heidegger with both the structure of human involvement and world, and the singularity of the existential moment. In the space of this double movement of facticity and existence, a space of repetition marked by Heidegger through his emphasis on the *je* in *Jemeinigkeit,* in this repetition that individualizes, I believe, can be found an argument for plurality in human community, a plurality of utterly singular individuals, defined by their relationships to death. This "between" opens up the space of community, a community of differing beings.

I will turn now to an explication of certain passages from Heidegger's analysis of being-toward-death in *Being and Time* in an attempt to outline a basis one may find there for an authentic, existential community of possible beings akin to the community Aristotle envisions when he turns from a discussion of the community of just people to the community of friends; a community that in a fundamental sense can never be actualized but that is for this reason neither otherworldly nor utopian, but rather fundamentally mortal.

The entire analysis of death is governed by the question of whether Dasein can in any sense have its being as a whole. Heidegger shows that Dasein's way of Being is in some sense fundamentally not accessible and ungraspable. This inability to be held in a grasp is essential to an understanding of the problem of human community. This basic point demonstrates that the kind of community to which Dasein would belong cannot be one based on appropriation and ownership. The *Jemeinigkeit* (mineness) and *Eigentlichkeit* (properness) that belong to Dasein in being-toward-death is at the same time the impossibility of ownership and appropriation. Dasein's being cannot be had or owned, not even for itself; disowning is Dasein's ownmost way of being itself. Also implied in these statements on Dasein's death, and made explicit elsewhere, is the fact that, were ownership to be taken as Dasein's authentic way of being itself and being toward others, this would presuppose that Dasein is a subject that takes what it encounters as objects and enowns them. Surely this way of establishing community can be instituted, and often is, but it is not an authentic basis for human community. Only a lack of imagination would lead us to draw the conclusion from this that therefore no community is possible. In a further comparison with Aristotle, one could easily show on Aristotelian terms that the standpoint of appropriation and ownership is the exact opposite of what constitutes the free, autonomous individuals who participate in the genuine polis.

We can conclude that any such genuine human community would have to be premised on an understanding of relationality that does not presuppose taking over the other or the place of the other. It would have to be a community in which the other remains other; in this sense a community of singular beings. One can imagine such a community in a culture that did not require assimilation. One can imagine a principle of negotiation that acknowledged the other as stranger and saw a breakdown in negotiation as the beginning of communication. One can imagine personal relationships that celebrate the other as necessarily different from oneself.

This is why Heidegger argues that one Dasein cannot in any fundamental sense represent or take the place of another, an analysis that may also be read as a critique of representational democracy. Heidegger writes: "This possibility of representing gets completely stranded when it is a matter of representing the possibility of being that constitutes Dasein's coming-to-an-end, and gives it its totality as such."[16] The fact that one Dasein cannot substitute for another, and is fundamentally not like any other, places demands on our understanding of being together, especially if we are trying to develop an understanding of a community of those who stand in relation to each other as a whole, who recognize each other in the whole of their being—an existential community, so to speak.

When Heidegger says: "*No one can take the other's dying away from him*,"[17] this does not mean that being-toward-death makes community impossible. It means rather that Dasein's being cannot be appropriated and that the possibility of exchange and expenditure between such beings cannot be thought in these terms. If we were to look back from Heidegger's analysis of being-toward-death to his earlier treatment of solicitude and care, we would find collaboration for the argument that the unshareability that defines human being not only does not preclude community but is the foundation for any truly human being-together. According to Heidegger, the analysis of care shows that for Dasein its being is for it *at issue*, that is, its being is always ecstatic, ahead of itself, uncapturable. Then Heidegger says: "Being ahead of itself does not mean anything like an isolated tendency in a worldless 'subject', but characterizes being-in-the-world."[18] Care is said to be "the existential and ontological condition of the possibility of *being free for* authentic existentiell possibilities."[19] Because Dasein's being is always possible and not actualizable in its whatness, because Dasein is always in the throes of death, its being is *free* in its relations with others, in what Heidegger calls its existentiell possibilities. Death constitutes the possibility of *free* beings. Aristotle says much the same when he maintains that a truly courageous act arises out of a sense of the beautiful and noble rather than being done for the sake of honor, or as a response to fear or compulsion (*Nich. Eth.* 1115 b3off). Aristotle defines courage as standing steadfast in the face of death. In this sense, he argues, courage encompasses all the other virtues since for it no particular situation is involved; rather courage in the face of death situates one in relationship to the whole of one's being, the greatest good of all (*Nich. Eth.* 1117 b1off).

Heidegger's analysis of truth as disclosedness rather than as embedded in the language of assertion, where truth is the predication of properties as owned by a subject, also confirms that Heidegger's thought in *Being and Time* is after a new sense of community. Heidegger says: "*Disclosedness in general* belongs essentially to the constitution of the being of Da-sein."[20] The "in general" here does not indicate that there is no content, but rather that the disclosedness is of the sort that comes in advance and does not take over the being of what is there.[21] The language of existential community is more primordial than the language of shared properties and common interests. It is fundamentally the language of the unsayable. It establishes a community of beings whose speaking acknowledges a fundamental untranslatability as the basis for human conversation. This kind of disclosive relationality is at work also in Heidegger's analysis of solicitude, where he says it is not a matter of leaping in for the other but of leaping ahead and returning (giving back) to the other *for the first time* its care, its free possibility. The peculiar character of the exchange that occurs here needs to be appreciated. How can one give something back, and yet also give it for the first time? What kind of exchange is this that gives the other what it already is—its being as possibility? Is this, for Aristotle as well as for Heidegger, the gift of friendship?

Heidegger offers us a similar paradox in his discussion of the understanding of death as something still outstanding in section 46 of *Being and Time*. Here it is clearer that the notion of possibility is transformed by death and cannot be understood as simply saying that our being is not yet actualized and present at hand for us. *Ausstehen*, we are told, usually refers to a debt that has only partially been paid up and is still outstanding. But indebtedness belongs to our very being. This means we *owe* our being; we never own it and it can never be owned. There is something always to be settled; no closure is possible. The community of such beings is one that does not aspire to closure and one in which there is always a lack of totality. The Dasein community is never without a relationship to what is outside, to otherness. But Heidegger quickly translates this discussion into a discussion of the impending character of death and says in being-toward-death all everyday relations to any other Dasein are undone. Death is non-relational and thus loosens the grip that others have on our being and that we have on others, letting each be the being it is. In this sense, being-toward-death is the basis for the possibility of a community of singular beings. Being with others, the they and the we, fails us in being-toward-death and death, Heidegger says, individualizes Dasein down to itself.22 Dasein must be on its own. Dasein is free from the tyranny of the they. Heidegger says that Dasein is brought face to face with "the possibility of the impossibility of existence in general."23 The community of possible beings stands face to face with the impossibility of all community.

In the sections of *Being and Time* on being-toward-death that seem more and more to me to speak of mortal community, the passages on anticipation (*Vorlaufen*) are particularly telling. Heidegger says: "Anticipation discloses to existence that its extreme inmost possibility lies in giving itself up, and thus shatters all one's clinging to whatever existence one has reached."24 Being-toward-death teaches us not to hold onto ourselves. But, in doing so, Heidegger says, it also frees us from the grasp of others and frees others from our grasp. Thus, Heidegger continues: "As the nonrelational possibility, death individualizes, but only, as the possibility not-to-be-bypassed, in order to make Dasein as being-with understand the potentialities-of-being of the others."25

Plato's Dialectical Philosophy and Aristotle's Recovery of Nous: *The Problem of Rhetoric and the Limits of* Logos

Martin Heidegger's 1924–1925 lecture course on Plato's *Sophist* has rightly been considered by many as one of the most important of his early manuscripts. In the course, Heidegger gives a careful and remarkable reading of this late dialogue that makes thematic the relationship between the sophist and the philosopher. Heidegger claims that the relationship between *logos,* truth, and being in Plato's thought receives its most radical treatment in this dialogue because of the struggle to finally allow the sophist and philosopher to confront each other. Of course, the struggle to distinguish the contrasting relationship to truth, speech, and being in sophistry and philosophy motivates many of the dialogues of Plato;26 however, the *Sophist* is unique in that the dialogue acknowledges that the territory of sophistry, namely nonbeing, belongs also at the center of philosophical discourse about being.

In this section, I am going to examine the portions of Heidegger's course on Plato's *Sophist* where he digresses from the direct task of reading the *Sophist*. The purpose of Heidegger's digressions is to discuss the relationship between rhetoric and philosophy in Plato's *Phaedrus* and other dialogues. These disgressions are an important clue for understanding Heidegger's peculiar claim that a treatment of Aristotle's *Nichomachean Ethics* VI is a necessary precondition for a proper understanding of the *Sophist*. In the next section of this chapter, I will discuss Heidegger's treatment of Aristotle's *Nichomachean Ethics,* which constitutes almost a third of the entire course on Plato's *Sophist*.

Heidegger's digression introduces the problem of rhetoric in Plato's philosophy. It occurs just after Heidegger's treatment of the five definitions of the sophist in Plato's *Sophist*. Heidegger points out that in all five descriptions, ending with 'eristic', "there is also an accompanying *legein*."[27] The art of eristic and other sophistic forms of *logos* is studied in rhetoric. In order to get some access to what is at stake in this framing issue for any understanding of the *Sophist*, Heidegger examines the treatment of rhetoric and its relationship to dialectic in the *Gorgias and Phaedrus*. This choice to divert from the task of studying the *Sophist* in order to treat this issue in the these other dialogues is motivated by Heidegger's claim that Plato's thought progresses from a totally negative view of rhetoric as an art mired in corruption and deception,[28] to a more positive account of the place of everyday rhetoric and its concern with nonbeing in the *Sophist*. The *Phaedrus* is contrasted with both the *Gorgias,* as the negative account of rhetoric, and the *Sophist* as the place where Plato works out a positive account of how dialectical speech emerges out of and overcomes the tendency of rhetoric toward deception. Thus, the *Phaedrus* is the dialogue in which the transition to a positive view of rhetoric can be traced. It is in this dialogue that Plato accounts for the possibility of a correlation between human speech and truth. Going through the discussion of rhetoric and dialectic in this dialogue, therefore, is a necessary preparation for the reading of the *Sophist*. When Heidegger returns to his analysis of the *Sophist*, the outcome of his discussion demonstrates that the philosopher who dwells on being cannot escape the intrinsic relationship of being and nonbeing which lies at the foundation of dialectic (GA19, 568). Thus, the philosopher in the end also has to take into consideration, albeit in a positive way, negation and nonbeing, inasmuch as they belong to being. As Heidegger points out, the "positive" account of negation in the dialogue takes the form of a recognition of beings in their otherness and in their presence with others (GA 19, 560). In the *Sophist,* Plato no longer sees division and the separating out of what is other as a contribution to the task of gathering into one what belongs to the matter being addressed. Difference comes to be understood in its essential connection to the understanding of being.

These digressions are not unrelated to Heidegger's discussion of Book VI of Aristotle's *Nichomachean Ethics,* with which Heidegger begins his course before turning to Plato's *Sophist.* They both appear to Heidegger to be required by a consideration of the theme of his course and of the dialogue around which the course is centered. Both are related to Heidegger's central thematic concern, which is the relationship between *logos* and *alētheia.* Heidegger often insists in his *Sophist* course that Aristotle brings to fruition and radicalizes the thought of Plato from the point of view of "scientific" philosophy, which Heidegger explicitly understands as the philosophy of existence (GA19, 218). This is partially because, according to Heidegger, Aristotle demarcates the limits of human speech (*logos*), whereas Plato sees dialectic per se as the essence of philosophical activity. But also, Aristotle, according to Heidegger, worked out for the first time the character of a positive account of everyday rhetoric, the necessity of which Plato clearly came to recognize but never explicitly made thematic. In the *Gorgias,* rhetoric, and the sophists who practice it, remain utterly cut off from the truth, without any possibility of access through the kind of speech they practice. In the *Sophist,* the limits of Plato's philosophical methodology, established in the *Phaedrus* in contrast to sophistry, are marked, and Plato's understanding of the problem of philosophy begins to undergo a transformation. But this delimitation of the inadequacy of dialectical philosophy only foreshadows the more originary understanding of the truth of beings that Heidegger attributes to Aristotle. For Aristotle, and already for Plato in this late dialogue, written, Heidegger suggests, in conversation with Aristotle, the question of truth and the possibility of ontological disclosure involves the force of community, the possibility of copresence. But this *dunamis koinonia* implies that what is, according to its nature, is empowered by its way of being to stand in relationship to what is other than itself and what it is not. In a certain sense, the utter separation of the sophist and the philosopher thereby comes into question. The problem of nonbeing, formerly ascribed to the domain of the sophist, now is seen as intrinsically also the concern of philosophy.

This sketchy overview of Heidegger's treatment of the development of Plato's understanding of rhetoric and dialectic leading up to the *Sophist* makes evident why Heidegger needed to turn to the *Phaedrus* and the relationship between sophistry and philosophy that is worked out there. An understanding of the problem of truth and being in the *Phaedrus* is necessary for an appreciation of the intellectual struggle required to carry out the rethinking of dialectic that occurs in the *Sophist* and that allows philosophy to undergo such a radical transformation. And finally, the confrontation between Aristotle and Plato not only sheds light on the movement of Plato's thought toward its most radical limits, but it also helps Heidegger to clarify his own sense of phenomenology vis-à-vis the treatment of *logos* in Plato and Aristotle. The *Sophist* course makes clear that Heidegger sees the turn to a phenomenological orientation as at the very heart of Plato's understanding of philosophy, especially in terms of the recognition by Plato that *the* question of philosophy is the question of the existence of the human being who is asking about being. Heidegger's reading of the *Sophist* also brings to the fore the problem of intentionality and Plato's and Aristotle's implicit, but unthematized, discovery (in the notion of community) that the question of intentionality (*nous*) needs to be worked out in terms of the problem of world and time.

The Ontological Status of Dialectic

Heidegger's thematic focus in every one of his works that deal with Plato is *alētheia* and the place of truth in Plato's thought. What he discovers in each of his considerations is that the site of this philosophical disclosure of beings for Plato is *logos*. Specifically, Plato locates the truth of beings in *dialegesthai*. *Logos*, therefore, is of paramount importance in Plato's philosophy. It is the way to truth and being for humans. This, according to Heidegger, is why Plato writes in dialogues and Socrates is always announcing his erotic attraction to discourse. The *Phaedrus* beautifully depicts this attraction in the beginning of the dialogue:

> You must forgive me, dear friend; I'm a lover of learning, and trees and open country won't teach me anything, whereas people in the city do. Yet you seem to have discovered a recipe (*pharmakon*) for getting me out (230d).

The lure of course that draws Socrates is *logos*. For Plato, language is not just a vehicle to express something that is actually disclosed outside of discourse. Nor does Plato, as Heidegger points out, write in dialogue form for merely aesthetic reasons, as if the form was incidental to the content. Beings are not just reported upon and examined in the discourse; rather, the disclosure of what is first occurs through *logos* and *dia-logos*. The Socratic conversation and his dialectical interchange with his interlocutors *is* the

practice of philosophy. In this sense, Heidegger sees Platonic philosophizing as thoroughly and unabashedly logocentric.

Nevertheless, within Plato's philosophy, there is a certain tension with
regard to the limitation of *logos* as the bearer of truth. This is altogether
evident in the constant struggle against the deceptive power of language
that is part and parcel of Socratic dialogue. *Logos* cannot in and of itself
be defined as truth, for *logos* for the most part covers over what truly is.
This indicates that in some way *alētheia* and *logos* are not the same, that
truth is not indigenous to language, that there can be a truth beyond ordinary language. According to Heidegger, Aristotle was the first to look beyond *logos* to *nous,* whereas Plato's thinking is tethered to the possibility
of truth that can belong to language, once deceptive language is distinguished from the language of philosophy. Philosophical language is described by Socrates as genuine assertion that is spoken out of the soul.
Therefore, what frames Plato's philosophical approach is the problem of
truth and the capacity to distinguish truth from falsity and deception. Dialectic aims "to pass from *logos* as prattle, from what is said idly and hast-
ily about things, through genuine speaking, to a *logos* which, as *logos*
alēthēs, actually says something about that of which it speaks" (GA 19,
195). *Dialegesthai* is a passing "through speech," departing from what is
idly said, with the goal of arriving at a genuine assertion, a *logos,* about
beings themselves. Dialectical truth is won in the battle to overcome the
way *logos* for the most part, in its ordinary, everyday practice, drags us
away from truth into untruth.

In contrast, Aristotle does not see *logos* as the ultimate source of truth,
though most of the various kinds of truths that are humanly possible are
meta logou, accompanied by *logos.* The exception for Aristotle is *nous.*
However, this pure perception in no way can belong to human language.
Heidegger says, "*logos* can therefore take upon itself *alētheuein,* yet it does
not do so on its own but from the *noein* and *dianoein* in each case, that is,
from the respective *aisthēsis*" (GA 19, 196–197). Dialectic for Aristotle is
in the same domain as rhetoric; both are *logoi* and both involve the human
capacity or incapacity to address what is as such. In both cases, language is
shown to provide a genuine opening for truth. But the success of that address cannot be ascribed to *logos* itself in the way it is, according to Heidegger, in Plato's philosophy. Dialectic cannot on its own reach the truth.
Heidegger calls it an attempt (*Versuch*).[29] To attempt means that a certain
movement and risk is enacted that propels one in the direction of truth, but
that cannot itself produce truth. Thus, Heidegger says:

Dialegesthai therefore possesses immanently a tendency toward *noein*, seeing. Yet insofar as the consideration remains in *legein* and as *dialegesthai* continues on in and through discussion, such "speaking through" can indeed relinquish idle talk but cannot do more than *attempt* to press on to the things themselves. *Dialegesthai* remains a matter of speeches; *it does not arrive at pure noein* (GA19, 197).

Aristotle sees Platonic dialectic as a preparatory stage of *theōrein*. Dialectic is a *"wanting* to see" (GA19, 200) that assists one's interlocutor to open his or her eyes. This intrinsic connection of dialectic with desire and striving for something beyond itself is evident in the erotic appeal that is always associated with Socrates' practice of dialectic. It is, for example, the context for his claim in the *Theaetetus* that he is incapable himself of possessing true knowledge, but is rather the one who practices midwifery, and has a divine gift in assisting others who are pregnant to give birth.[30]

The *Sophist*, Plato's most radical dialogue with regard to the dialectical approach to being, is situated by Heidegger as "a remarkable turning point between the position of Parmenides and the one of Aristotle, which consummates all these projects of Greek ontology" (GA19, 205). The *Umschlag* that occurs with Plato centers on the transformation of Greek rhetoric and opinion (*doxa*) into a philosophically grounded *logos*. In turn, it was Aristotle, on the basis of Plato's accomplishment, who brought the question of how one addresses beings back to the Parmenidean insight into the noetic character of being and it was he who first thought through the double sense of *logos*. The two senses of *logos* pertain to the twofold way in which beings are disclosed. The first pertains to the way in which beings for the most part are revealed as addressed and encountered in their belonging with other beings. This is the *logos* that addresses beings inasmuch as they are related to something. "For Aristotle, *logos* manifests itself in its peculiar relational structure: *legein* is always *legein ti kata tinos*" (GA19, 206). In contrast to this *logos* that says something about something, Aristotle identifies, in *Metaphysics* IV and elsewhere, a *logos* that addresses beings as such (*kath' auto*) and sees (*theōrei*) them in their being (GA19, 208). For Aristotle, this seeing of the being in itself requires, in advance of any particular, categorial way of addressing beings, that one has being as a whole in view. The back-and-forth relation of these two ways of addressing what is, such that every disclosure of beings presupposes a knowledge of the whole of beings, allows Aristotle to conceive of the difference between being and beings in a way that advances beyond Plato. Plato, according to Heidegger, thinks through to the question of being, but thinks being in terms of beings and thus as itself a being. This is particularly reflected in the

notion of unity that Plato associates with being. Plato ascribes to being itself and the ideas a numerical oneness, and thus thinks of the whole of
what is in terms of the community of unique kinds (*ta genē*) (GA 19, 522).
In contrast, Aristotle distinguishes between oneness and number, associat-
ing numerical integrity with beings rather than being.

Aristotle considers all three, rhetoric, dialectic, and philosophy itself to
be aiming for the same thing; that is, all three are understood "to have beings as a whole for their theme" (*Met.* 1004 b20). He even states that sophistry and dialectic move within the same field of beings (*genos*) as does philosophy (*Met.* 1004 b22). As Heidegger says, all three "claim to deal with
the whole" (GA 19, 214). In light of this, the difference between each is
telling. For, it is an indication, at least from what I understand to be
Heidegger's perspective, of the enormous philosophical struggle in which
Plato was engaged in his rethinking of dialectic in the *Sophist*. Philosophy
alone among the three is said by Aristotle to be able to stand in relationship
to the matter being addressed in its *Sachlichkeit*. This is what Aristotle
means by *theōrein*. The person who engages in *theōria* chooses a life that is
in touch with the true uncovering of what is. In contrast, dialectics aims
also for this, but is incapable of achieving it on its own. Its way of relating
to the task of exhibiting the whole of what is is an appropriate preparation
for philosophy. That is, the method of going through the *logos* aims for the
being in its being, but cannot itself reveal it. It sets the being apart and gathers what belongs to it on the basis of a prior attunement to being that does
not emerge out of its practice. But its method is serious and on the way toward this disclosure.[31] In contrast, the sophist does not attend to the matter and speaks without being in touch with what is spoken about. The art
of sophistry amounts to a clever use of words that are detached from their
orientation toward revealing what is. It educates people to speak well, but
not to be responsive. This is why its method is particularly hostile to the
dialogical pursuit of truth, which requires that one's partner be heard in
the give-and-take of the investigation. The rhetoricians have the ability to
speak well without the attentiveness to the matter that characterizes philosophy and dialectic. Heidegger says: "The sophist has made a decision in
favor of this formal-aesthetic ideal of human existence, i.e., in favor of an
unconcern with the matter" (GA19, 215). The sophist has no concrete, factical commitment to what is being spoken about. It is the art of mere persuasion. In this light, dialectic occupies a peculiar middle ground. It shares
with sophistry a commitment to *logos* as its way of approaching the region
of its concerns. And it also shares with sophistry an inadequacy within itself

with regard to its ability to address beings in a way that reveals them in their being. Yet, it is also akin to philosophy in that it strives for the truth and takes its measure from its attempt to reach the truth.

Plato's Negative Account of Rhetoric in the *Gorgias*

For the most part, Plato identifies rhetoric with sophistry and the practice of public oratory. Rhetoric was the art of correct speech. It was this practice that had come to define the very character of excellent speech and therefore the very significance of *logos* in Greek culture. Plato's initial challenge to the sophists was uncompromising. Rhetoric was mired in mere opinion and was unable to give an account of the matter it claimed to address. Heidegger particularly calls attention to the *Gorgias* as an example of this negative view of rhetoric. Rhetoric could not even be considered an art, since "it precisely refuses to deal with that about which it is supposed to teach others to speak. It is a know-how that is not oriented toward any substantive content but instead aims at a purely extrinsic, or, as we say, 'technical,' procedure" (GA19, 310).

Yet, despite this negative view of rhetoric, Plato did not call into question the priority of *logos*, nor did he deny the insistence on the importance of excellence and correctness in speech. Rather, Plato tried to redefine the conditions on which speech can be said to carry out its genuine intention to produce truth. Thus, Heidegger concludes, "Plato sees his dialectic as the only fundamental science, such that in his opinion all other tasks, even those of rhetoric, are discharged in it" (GA19, 337–338). It is because of this common commitment to *logos*, which even Aristotle shared for the most part, that Aristotle views rhetoric and dialectic as being on the same level. Despite the explicit difference and opposition that Plato establishes between rhetoric and dialectic, such that rhetoric comes to be associated with untruth rather than truth, nevertheless Aristotle considers both rhetoric and dialectic incapable of truly disclosing beings in their being. Philosophy requires a movement beyond the gathering that occurs in human *logos*, an attunement to something that cannot be discovered in *logos*, namely, an openness to the pure givenness of the being as such that is seen in *nous*. *Nous*, divine-like rather than human thought, is the place in which originary truth occurs. And the immediate givenness of being to thought that occurs here is presupposed by ordinary *logos*. There is of course a kind of *logos* involved in *nous*, but the *logos* is the direct saying of the being as such (*kath' auto*) and not a saying something about the being (*ti kata tinos*). In Aristotle's view, dialectic, with its method of collection and division, remains rooted in a way of revealing things that presupposes their original givenness. Its territory, therefore, is the same as that of the rhetoricians. Heidegger refers to a passage in Aristotle's *Rhetoric* at 1354 a1 to support his interpretation:

Aristotle emphasizes that dialectic is the *antistrophos* of rhetoric, or vice versa; they are opposites. That means they are both on the same footing. For Plato, on the contrary, we have seen that *dialegesthai* and dialectic are in principle preordained to rhetoric, they are what first make it possible, whereas for Aristotle rhetoric is *antistrophos*, it resides on the same level, as regards its epistemic character, as dialectic itself. (GA19, 350–351)[32]

The fact that dialectic is committed to overcoming the tendency toward deception involved in this way of speaking about what is constitutes the greatness of dialectic and its gift to philosophy. But in the *Sophist* dialogue, Plato comes to recognize that the tendency toward being covered over, toward not-being disclosed as what it truly is, belongs to the very nature of beings and therefore is of intrinsic concern even to the philosopher. Thus, Heidegger says that in the *Sophist*:

Plato actually understands sameness as sameness and otherness as otherness, and on the basis of insight into the *tauton* and the *heteron* he is able to grasp the concept of *mē on*. Accordingly he explicitly emphasizes that the dialectician must attend to the sameness and otherness of any given being. (GA19, 527–528)

Here we can see that Plato's position has moved from a purely negative assessment of the status of nonbeing (in the *Gorgias*) to one that takes it up into a positive, philosophical approach to the question of being as such. From this discovery, Aristotle's own philosophy emerges such that, Heidegger says, "Aristotle says what Plato delivered over to him, only in a way that is more radically and more scientifically developed" (GA19, 11). In Heidegger's view, one indication of the fact that Aristotle's philosophy is the culmination of the most radical and scientific direction of Platonic and Greek thought is his ability to offer a positive and detailed articulation of the legitimate domain of rhetoric. For Aristotle, the beginning point of philosophy lies in the proper relationship to the everyday. Rhetoric for Aristotle is a legitimate pursuit in that it addresses the way for the most part things appear to us and the various affects through which the soul of the human being is disposed toward things.

In contrast, for Plato, even in a late dialogue such as the *Theaetetus*, the hustle-bustle of the sophists, their inability to stay with the matter being discussed, is a symptom of their enslavement to mere opinion.[33] In this dialogue, the perspective of the sophist is narrow-minded, whereas that of the philosopher is governed by a vision of the whole. This is why the philosopher is said to make out poorly in the everyday goings-on of the sophistic regime. The philosopher spurns the skill of the rhetorician as dangerous to his soul. The whole dialogue is about the purposeful substitution of power and deception for truth, and how the soul becomes tense and shrewd and dried up in the process of gaining skill in this pursuit. But the scathing attack in the *Theaetetus* on the rhetoricians and lawyers (who are, according to the ending of the dialogue, about to put Socrates on trial) is not only to do with the philosopher's disdain for false opinion and the tendency to deceive. It is also about how the souls of those who practice rhetoric and vie for court victories become "small and warped."34

Plato's Positive Account of Rhetoric in the *Phaedrus*

Heidegger begins his discussion of the *Phaedrus* with an argument that the second part of the dialogue should be viewed not as a theory of rhetoric through which one can discriminate with regard to the relative quality of the speeches in the first part of the dialogue. It is not a treatise on oratory at all. Rather, "the theme is speaking in the sense of self-expression and communication, speaking as a mode of existence in which one person expresses himself to another and both together seek the matter at issue. We saw earlier that Heidegger equates what he calls scientific philosophy with a philosophy that is rooted in existence. What is at stake for Aristotle, according to Heidegger, is the *bios* of the philosopher. This is why Aristotle says in the *Metaphysics* that wisdom, the life of *theōria*, makes us free. And this is why *logos* and the capacity to address what is belong to the very definition of what it means to be human. Heidegger sees already reflected in the philosophy of Plato and Aristotle an understanding of the ontological significance of the study of human being. Beings are truly revealed only in the context of a lived experience. The question of being cannot be divorced from the question of life. For the Greeks, the question of life is that of the soul and the possibility of its being beautiful. It is for this reason that Plato connects dialectic with dialogue, because all disclosure of beings also always involves self-disclosure and the opening of oneself to another. Thus, the problem of rhetoric for Plato always circles around the problem of who it is that is engaging in discussion. This is why he says "as regards myself, I want knowledge" and why he worries about becoming "like Typhon with a much-confused form."35 For Socrates, the love of *logos* is intrinsically tied to the desire for self-knowledge. Thus, rhetoric, inasmuch as it is a *logos,* can provide a space for encountering others, providing it is engaged rhetoric that reveals both the soul of the one who is speaking and that being that is under discussion and with which the speaker is in touch. Thus, under these conditions, Plato says that rhetoric can have a certain justification. One can understand, given the centricity of this orientation with regard to speech in Platonic philosophy, why Socrates condemns writing as an intrinsically false *logos* that can never be in touch with that about which it attempts to give an account. The problem of deception and its relationship to truth is examined by Plato in this dialogue in terms of this fundamental commitment to a living discourse. It is not so that the person who speaks can be around to answer questions that Socrates insists on dialogue. It is because truth is intrinsically connected to existence. The sophist fails to see the importance of this dimension of truth, and in fact his art attempts to preclude it in two ways. First, the art of persuasion requires that one not be caught, that one not be revealed, that one's own genuine "position" not be exposed. Second, the art depends on the confusion and mixing up of things that allow the sophist to more easily make things appear own way or another, according to his design. In contrast, Platonic dialectic attends to the soul of the one conversing and tries to sort out the tendency for things to be mired in confusion so that the truth can be exposed in its singularity. The aim of dialectic is to make visible the *mia idea,* the whole of the being in its concrete totality (GA19, 331). This gathering of what belongs to the address in light of this vision of the whole is the task of *sunagōgē* and *diairesis.* To speak in this way is to speak well. The beauty of such speeches is related to the attunement to the matter and not to some external principle of harmonious organization. In this sense, the dialogue is about the question of how one speaks well, and how one differentiates beautiful speeches from those that are deceptive. Finally, Socrates concludes that even deceptive speeches, if they are to be purposeful and effective as an art rather than haphazard and only coincidentally successful, presuppose a relationship to truth, albeit one that is covered over. In other words, even one who wishes to deceive effectively must first of all be in touch with what she wants to keep hidden. And one who wants to be taken as knowledgeable when they have no relationship to the matter must be able to know themselves well enough to be able to resist communication. Moreover, they must know the matter well enough to detect and combat the deception of others that will make them successful debaters. Then if one is "putting a face on things that does not correspond to the true state of affairs, such an opponent can detect the deception and bring to light the fact that he is speaking about the things themselves but is precisely concealing them and covering them over" (GA19, 327). Thus, Heidegger claims, the Platonic adherence to the question of existence "finally places the rhetoric of the time back on its most proper foundation" (GA19, 325). Even successful rhetoric, when success is defined by its intrinsic ability to deceive, which Socrates continues to spurn, requires a relationship to the truth. The practice of rhetoric feeds off genuine *logos* and is dependent on it. Thus, for Plato, rhetoric remains at best a derivative art that is and should be subordinated to philosophy. But this also means that those who engage in opinions and play with the confusion of apparent reality are able to be subject to, and perhaps, if they have a good soul, are prepared to be affected by, the genuine search for truth in the practice of dialectic. The need to affect and produce a movement toward truth in the soul of the learner points also to the intrinsic connection between dialectic and rhetoric. In Plato's view, one's ability to dwell in the truth is something that is always in need of being regained and dialogue is for the sake of recovering one's original connection to what is. The process of conversing about what is can occasion, although not produce, knowledge of what is among those conversing. This requires *anamnesis*. The seeing of the being in its oneness "is accessible only to one who has the possibility of *anamnēsis*, i.e., to one who possesses genuine *mnēmē* and genuinely retains what he once already saw" (GA19, 333). The fact that this original, already given sense of what is, in terms of which dialectical philosophy proceeds, must be recovered and can only be recovered through a careful retaining of the matter at issue throughout the investigation, indicates again that deception is not an accidental phenomenon but belongs to the very nature of human being. Dialectic "requires an overcoming of definite resistances residing in the very being of the human being" (GA19, 334). In this sense, as compared with the treatment of rhetoric in the *Gorgias* and elsewhere, Plato discovers a positive way of appropriating rhetoric and its engagement with falsity, and of transforming it into a genuine art. This art he calls dialectic.

The importance of this positive appropriation of the place of rhetoric and its situation with regard to dialectic can be appreciated in regard to Plato's treatment of the rhetorician's tendency toward deception. A definite and important relationship is thereby established between the everyday way in which things are deceptively revealed and the task of philosophy as a genuine love for and pursuit of truth. This view of rhetoric implicates the movement of dialectic in a relationship with opinion and appearance. It indicates that a movement from appearance to truth is possible. It opens up a difference between appearance and semblance, semblance coming to be understood as a way of appearing that cuts off this movement. In this way, an intimate connection between the sophist and the philosopher is established. Here in the *Phaedrus* this connection is not made thematic and the actual practice of dialectic is not demonstrated. But that is precisely what the dialogue *Sophist* accomplishes. And so, Heidegger's digression to study the *Phaedrus* is not accidental but necessary in order to establish the horizon of Plato's question when he writes this dialogue.

The Sophist *Course: Aristotle's Recovery of Truth after Plato*

In his lecture course on Plato's *Sophist,* Heidegger makes a remarkable claim that in fact governs his entire discussion of this Platonic dialogue. He says: "There is no scientific understanding, that is, no going back historically to Plato without passing through Aristotle" (GA19, 189). Aristotle is said to be the philosopher who comprehends in a radical fashion the problem with which Plato and his predecessors were grappling (GA19, 190). No Plato interpretation can be legitimate that does not measure up to Aristotle! Aristotle is supposed to have sorted out and distinguished the various ways of seeing and questioning that run together in Plato's philosophy, sorted them out on the basis of an understanding of the guiding orientation of Greek philosophy—namely, the question of the sense of being and the concomitant question of truth. Plato's primary aim in the *Sophist,* according to Heidegger, is not to unmask the sophist but to discover the philosopher who can only be indirectly traced through the *logos* of dialectic. Heidegger claims that the Platonic, dialectical arguments employed in this dialogue are on the way toward the discovery of "a higher level of philosophizing" (GA19, 165). But dialectic can only disclose this stage negatively, by pointing to what is not available through the rhetoric of the sophist. Aristotle's greatness, Heidegger says, is that he is able to take up in a positive manner the implicit direction of Plato's thought, toward a kind of saying of being that is not a *dialogos,* and make this authentic disclosure of being thematically explicit. Plato's thought remains, in the end, according to Heidegger, confined to and dependent on the less primordial saying at work in dialectic. In the *Sophist* dialogue, the primary distinction is between dialectical thinking and sophistry. Aristotle in contrast unfolds a further distinction that distinguishes philosophical thinking from both sophistry and dialectic, equating dialectic with the *logos* of affirming and denying—*kataphasis* and *apophasis*.

However, more is at issue here than a mere making explicit of what is already contained in Plato. Aristotle's capacity to think through dialectic to its aim and end accomplishes a transformation of Platonic philosophy. The new, Aristotelian level of philosophical thinking about language and truth is attained, according to Heidegger, precisely by being made thematic, since the truth of being cannot appear through an investigation of beings. Plato's thinking remains caught in the limitations of its approach. Primarily this limitation has to do with the failure to properly distinguish being and beings. Heidegger says that Plato tended to search for being by going through beings and defining being as beyond beings, and, in the end, thinking of being as itself a kind of being. Aristotle penetrates more deeply into the question of being as such. Thus, Heidegger says:

Plato did obtain a certain sense of being, although not as radically as did Aristotle later on, but then it "happened" to him that he addresses this being as *das Seiende* so that what genuinely are beings must be set down by him as non-beings. Aristotle saw through this peculiar mistake completely. (GA19, 85)

Heidegger views the *Sophist* dialogue as Plato's most radical attempt to confront in a scientific way, that is, to bring to conceptual clarity, the question of being inherited from Parmenides. In this dialogue, the *mē on*, nonbeing, is shown to be. Being and not being, sameness and otherness, tautological identity and multiplicity, are shown to be intrinsically woven together. Plato introduces the notion of *dunamis koinonias*—the power of community, of coming together and separating, as belonging to the character of being. But for that which is to affect and be affected in this way, it is required that what is other than being also be. The intermingling of being and nonbeing (falsity) is made manifest and occurs in *logos, that is, in the movement of the soul that addresses something as something. The sophist, the one who discloses falsely and shows things as they are not, exists because the power to be covered up and thus shown as false belongs to being and because human beings dwell in truth and falsity. The philosopher, in Plato's view, is distinguished from the sophist as the one who moves away from not being and appearance toward the truth. However, Plato still thinks of being as a being, and, therefore, he implicitly conceives of both being and nonbeing as *eidē* that are present together, that are mixed or woven together in an ontic fashion. Thus, Heidegger claims that with Plato's limited conception of *koinonia* "the difference between the essentially still ontic treatment of motion and rest in Plato in contrast to the ontological treatment in Aristotle becomes clear" (GA19, 515). The *Sophist* dialogue is viewed as the place where Plato comes to the edge of a breakthrough to ontology but falls short because he has not discovered the ontological difference. Heidegger seems to me to attribute this breakthrough to Aristotle, at least to the extent that Aristotle's understanding of being and presence is said not to be derived from beings.

The *Sophist* is also the dialogue in which, for the first time, according to Heidegger (GA19, 483), Plato takes into account the being of bodily beings, perceived beings (*aisthēta*), and concedes that they too in a way are able to be. Heidegger considers this concession to also be an Aristotelian moment in the dialogue, a likely indication that Plato and the young Aristotle are here in confrontation with each other. What it indicates for Heidegger is that Plato, under the shadow of Aristotle, has made the turn to phenomenology (GA19, 484), has recognized the philosophical power of staying with the matter being addressed and not leaping beyond it in order to impose a structure onto it from outside. Heidegger's reading of *Metaphysics* I of Aristotle in Chapter Two of GA19 centers on an interpretation of the movement from *aisthēsis* to *sophia* that allows what is encountered in *aisthēsis* to reveal itself from itself in its being. He sees this as distinguishing first philosophy, in Aristotle's sense, from sophistry: "The *bios,* the life of the philosopher, is dedicated to pure *Sachlichkeit*. The philosopher has decided absolutely, as the proponent of this radical research, in favor of pure *Sachlichkeit*" (GA19, 215). In contrast, the sophist speaks *about* the thing but does not speak from out of the matter itself. Philosophy, unlike sophistry, is not restricted to a concern for human being alone. Philosophy, the *theōrein* of being as being, goes beyond the *eu legein,* the *logos* that defines human being as the *zōon logon echon*. First philosophy is about the possibility of reaching beyond the limits of human *logos,* of reaching a divine saying of the *truth* itself. This is one of the reasons Heidegger gives for Aristotle's insistence, in the end, that *sophia,* theoretical wisdom, is higher than *phronēsis*. *Phronēsis* is the revealing of human being whereas *sophia* is the kind of thinking and disclosing that arises out of the possibility of a kinship between thinking and being, a kinship that is open to human being as a possibility, but does not arise out of human being itself. In *theōria,* the otherness of being, the holding and retaining of the being as such in *its* being, is preserved.

Before turning to Heidegger's analysis of Aristotle's explication, in Book VI of the *Nichomachean Ethics,* of the many senses of truth and the access to these ways of disclosing through *logos,* it may be helpful to give at least one further example of how Heidegger will situate Plato's philosophy in the context of the Aristotelian distinctions we are about to consider. Heidegger claims that *technē* is the ground of the Platonic interpretation of being as *eidos,* as the presence in the soul of the idea (GA19, 47). This is a particularly striking assertion in that the sophist is the one who claims to practice an art, the art of rhetoric. In Heidegger's view, it is another indication of the close proximity of sophistry and dialectical philosophy. In distinguishing the sophist from the philosopher, Plato is said to have left unchallenged the approach to being through *technē,* the *art* of speech—*dialektike.* The sophist engages in false art by putting together what only appears but does not truly belong together. In contrast, for Plato, philosophy as dialectic is the art of speaking correctly, *orthos logos.*

Why, then, is Aristotle so much greater than Plato? What has Aristotle accomplished that allows *him* to discover, in a positive sense, the philosopher for whom Plato was searching, and that in turn allows us to offer a proper interpretation of Plato? To answer this, Heidegger insists, requires that the seminar on Plato's *Sophist* dedicate the weeks up to the December holidays to Aristotle. Heidegger turns to Aristotle in order to grasp better the sense of being and truth that is operative in Plato's ontology. In identifying the sophist as the one who covers over being, Plato places the issues of truth and being at the center of the dialogue. Thus, Heidegger announces in the first lecture: "What Aristotle says is what Plato handed over to him, only more radically and more scientifically developed" (GA19, 11). This gift to Aristotle is a question, the question of *logos* as *alētheuein.* Heidegger, in turn, brings to his reading of both Plato and Aristotle these same questions concerning *on, alētheia,* and *logos.* The primary texts of Aristotle that Heidegger turns to for assistance in understanding these fundamental philosophical issues are the *Nichomachean Ethics* VI and *Metaphysics* I.

In Book VI of the *Nichomachean Ethics,* at 1139 a1, Aristotle says: "In discussing the excellence of the soul, we said some are of character and others of understanding (*dianoia*). In what follows, we deal with excellence in *dianoia.*" *Dianoia* is not just the seeing of the being (*nous*), but also the ability to interpret beings in the light of this view. Even though the entire chapter is said to be about *dianoia,* it is not specifically discussed in the chapter. This is because *dianoia* names the interrelationship of the various ways of knowing. At 1139 a6–9, Aristotle speaks of two paths of knowing: "On the one path, we see beings whose *archē* is not able to be other [natural beings, e.g., are to the extent that their being arises out of themselves and does not belong to another]; on the other path, we see what is able to be governed by another [e.g., beings from *technē* and accidental being]. *Dianoia* opens up the relationship between these two paths. *Dianoia* is understanding in the sense that it is directed toward and holds in view what it grasps but moves away from the immediacy of the grasping toward the being of what is understood. In *Sein und Zeit,* Heidegger describes *Verstehen* in similar terms and chooses the word ecstatic to covey the sense of movement and temporality at work in this way of disclosing what is. *Ekstasis* is the opposite of *stasis.* Its way of being in place is to always be outside and beyond itself, to always be displaced. It dwells at the site of *phusis,* the placing of a being in its limits.

[handwritten marginal note: Ekstasy]

Aristotle makes clear that Book VI of the *Nichomachean* Ethics is not only a study of intellectual virtue, but also a treatise on truth, on ways in which human beings stand in relation to being. The virtuous intellect is virtuous precisely inasmuch as it engages itself with beings and discloses them in their being. It is in this sense that Aristotle understands truth. But, according to Aristotle, it is not just theoretical thinking that has to do with truth. Truth is the aim of both theoretical and practical knowledge. The usual framework for reading the *Ethics,* the division between moral virtue and intellectual virtue, is problematic. Moral virtue has to do with *hexis,* habit or disposition. But Aristotle clearly indicates that intellectual excellence is also a matter of disposition and comportment (*Nich. Eth.* 1139 b13). *Sophia* and *phronēsis* in this regard are like the moral virtues; they are ways of being in which the human being is disposed truthfully toward what is. Aristotle's treatment of intellectual virtue is more akin to the phenomenological sense of intentionality than it is to any concern with some notion of an internal, purely intellectual activity that has no relationship to being. When this involvement with beings and this kinship with being are defective, then intellectual excellence is destroyed.

Aristotle distinguishes five modes of truth: *epistēmē, phronēsis, technē, sophia, nous.* He begins Book VI by suggesting that the *logos* that defines human being as the *zōon logon echon,* the living being who by its very being has *logos,* is double, divided in two. Heidegger seems most of all to want to glean from Aristotle on his way to a reading of Plato this character of twofoldness that Aristotle considers central to *logos.* In the end, Heidegger sees the Aristotelian philosopher not so much in terms of either one of these two senses of *logos,* but as the one who can move between the two and thereby open up the horizon for being.

The two *logoi* are the one by which we contemplate beings whose *archai* do not admit of being other and the one by which we apprehend beings that can be other. Aristotle designates the one that encompasses both *epistēmē* and *sophia* by the word *epistēmonikon* and the other that includes *technē* and *phronēsis* by the word *logistikon*. Heidegger points out that in this division *nous* has been left out. This is because *nous* itself is twofold and also has two senses, corresponding to the two *logoi*—the *nous* involved in the disclosing of beings that have otherness, and the *nous* that discloses the *aei on*, the beings that are always-being, that hold themselves always, as long as they are, the same in their being.

The close proximity of *technē* and *phronēsis* as both being involved in the disclosing of what can be other is important to note. But *technē* has to do with produced beings whose *archē* is in another, whereas *phronēsis* has to do with human being itself. Human being is also fundamentally constituted by otherness, not by virtue of being dependent for its being on another being but because it is characteristic of human being to be embedded in its situation and expressed in *praxis*. The apprehension of eternal being in *epistēmē* and *sophia* is the way of disclosing natural beings, *phusei on*, beings that have their *archē* in themselves and not in another, as well as divine being, the movement of the spheres, and so on.

In each case, in both the case of *sophia* and *phronēsis*, theoretical and practical wisdom, *nous*—an immediate grasp of what is—is required. While Aristotle does privilege *sophia* over *phronēsis*, Heidegger does not see Aristotle as tying *phronēsis* to *sophia* in a hierarchical way so that *sophia* would be the disclosure of the being while *phronēsis* would be the equivalent of an apophantic disclosure of beings through synthesis or division. Both *sophia* and *phronēsis* are activities that involve *nous*. The philosophical closeness of *phronēsis* and *sophia* that is established in this way does not deny, according to Aristotle, that *sophia* has a certain priority as a higher way of apprehending beings. This priority takes on an added importance in the context of Heidegger's project of reading Plato. To the extent that Plato's primary orientation is in the direction of *phronēsis*, his thinking will be limited to the one sense of *nous*, the kind of noetic knowing that is relevant to practical wisdom.

Phronēsis, Heidegger says, is only possible because it is primarily an *aisthēsis*, an ultimately simple view of the moment, an *Augenblick* of the moment (the *kairos*) (GA19, 174). It is in *praxis* where the phronetic moment is revealed in its fullness and brought to fruition. In other words, it is not a question of a division within practical life between prudence or wisdom and choice or action. Heidegger makes this point strongly in the *Sophist* volume. *Phronēsis* is intrinsically an *aisthēsis* and fundamentally a disclosure that occurs in action. It immediately leads to and issues in resolute choice and prescribes action. Indeed, Heidegger translates *phronēsis* at one point as *Gewissen,* conscience. This practical being called back to the situation and situating oneself out of an overview of one's being is for Aristotle a noetic activity, a *nous praktikos.* As Heidegger shows, this way of having its being that is disclosed in *phronēsis* is peculiar. Though noetic, there can be no pure, atemporal beholding of such being since the resolute moment of *praxis* is always already caught up in coming to be, in the character of its being able to be other than it is.

Before turning briefly to *sophia* and the higher *nous* that occurs in this way of truth, let me highlight what I think is important here in the context of Heidegger's Aristotelian reading of Plato. What Heidegger tries to show is that *phronēsis* involves a close relationship between *nous* and *aisthēsis,* a pure, even noetic, perception that uncovers the being in its ultimate particularity. We have, Heidegger says, "two possibilities of the *nous: nous* in the extreme concretion and *nous* in the extreme *katholou,* in the most general *Allgemeinheit*" (GA 19, 163). *Phronēsis* aims at the *eschaton,* the ultimate particular, the fullness of being in the moment as revealed in its singularity. In this sense, *phronēsis* is a revealing, an *alētheuein* that is without *logos,* though, as we will see in the next section, Aristotle also sees the saying of being in a twofold sense, so that *phronēsis* is without *logos* in one sense, but remains a simple saying of being in a higher sense. Heidegger argues that the limitation of *phronēsis,* according to Aristotle, can be traced to its confinement to this one sense of *nous.*

Phronēsis is directed toward and has its end in action. But action is impossible unless the person is already good and dwells in the understanding of what to do that is disclosed by the good. The good, the *agathon,* is not disclosed in *phronēsis.* Thus, *phronēsis* is dependent on a prior disclosure that is higher in rank than itself (GA19, 167). Heidegger argues that the good is not meant here in an ethical sense but in fact gives expression to the being of world and what he later calls being in the world.[36] But the discovery of this requires not the *aisthēsis* of an *eschaton* but the seeing of *katholou,* beings as a whole.

Plato's thought, emanating out of *phronēsis,* remains rooted in the vision of singularity. He sees the need to move beyond the peculiar aspect of appearance to a vision of being that goes beyond *aisthēsis.* But his appeal to *eidos* remains committed to a vision of being as singular and one. In this regard, Heidegger's discussion of the difference between arithmetic and geometry is important. Platonic metaphysics is rooted in an arithmetic sense of the one rather than in the geometric, relational, more ontological sense of the one that is found in Aristotle. It is because Plato conceives of being as utterly singular in this way, because the Platonic neglect of the noetic vision of the whole has begun to be challenged by the concern about the *koinonia*, the community of being, that the *Sophist* dialogue is so interesting to Heidegger.

Heidegger's treatment of *sophia*, of the disclosure of being that cannot be other, is complex. He identifies several senses of *sophia* in Aristotle. *Sophia* is seen as the contemplation of divine being—in the theological sense. *Sophia* is also seen as that which apprehends the *archai*, the ontological structure of beings. And as we have seen in chapter one, *sophia* rather than *phronēsis* is seen as the way of disclosing that governs *technē*.37

But the sense of *sophia* that allows the philosopher to emerge is outlined by Aristotle in *Metaphysics* Θ, 1–2. Philosophical *sophia* is governed by and open to the *nous* of the *katholou*, of beings as a whole, but it also, unlike in *technē*, remains faithful to the particularity of being. Philosophical wisdom stands between the double *nous* of the *eschaton* and the *katholou*, the individual and the whole—and opens up the horizon on which beings are revealed in their being. *Sophia*, like *phronēsis*, is a noetic activity, a kind of free and pure perceiving of what is as such. While *phronēsis* is a noetic view that holds in view the particular being that appears in the fullness of its being at the moment, *sophia* looks beyond the *eschaton*, the thisness, the *ousia* in the sense that Aristotle ascribes to *ousia* when he defines it as *todē ti*, *sophia* looks beyond this to the *katholou*, to beings as a whole, to the *archai* that are always there, not just in the moment, but whenever the being is. This twofold look of the philosopher, this questioning *sophia* and *theōria*, is understood by Heidegger as the releasement of beings into what lets the beings be revealed. Philosophical *sophia* is the way of disclosing that gives beings over to their being. Aristotle calls such philosophizing *archē* questioning. For Aristotle, the *archē* is itself twofold and thus the movement of thinking that would heed the *archē* must itself be twofold.

What Heidegger shows is that for Aristotle philosophy is the desire to know more, *mallon eidenai*, to see more, to go beyond, to explore. This pursuit is not in opposition to concern and productive involvement with beings. On the contrary, it is the desire to propel oneself more deeply into the thick of things. *Sophia* is not some sort of abstract theoretical activity.

Heidegger says: "The why of *sophia* has a primordially practical sense" (GA19, 32). That is, the why that the philosopher asks is practical and not theoretical. *Sophia* is the intellectual disposition of one who sees more than what is given, the one who sees beyond experience in the sense of experiencing more deeply. Philosophy asks the question why. To question why is *sophia*. Philosophical wisdom is staying by what one observes and making it questionable. It is this sense of staying with what one observes that Aristotle calls *theōria,* contemplation or pure observing of the being as such, for its own sake. In other words, philosophy releases itself from its concern for the beings it encounters and experiences in order to open up an encounter with beings that offers *more*, that discloses the being as such, in its being. Inasmuch as it is a freeing, a questioning, and a projecting beyond, this divine-like *theōria* is a pure movement and the highest movement. Aristotle does not have locomotion in mind here, but rather a movement that stays with itself, as, for example, the tautological movement of thought thinking itself.

We have seen the double sense of being as both able to be otherwise and not able to be otherwise than it is. We have also seen the twofold sense of *nous* as both the truth of being as a whole and the truth of individual being as such. Now I would like to return briefly to one of the questions that Heidegger asks in the beginning of the *Sophist* course, that is, the question of *logos* and its relationship to *alētheia*.

Aristotle differentiates between two different ways of being and thus two different ways of revealing beings. Beings that can be other than they are have their being as a being-together-with. Synthesis is one of the ways these beings are revealed in their togetherness. However, beings that have their being in themselves cannot have their being as such revealed in this way. Their being is *aei on*, an always being, always (as long as they are) not being other than they are. Such beings are made manifest in their being, not through *kataphasis*, not by a saying something in respect to something else (*kata*), not in a bringing together of something in terms of something else, but in a simple saying (*phanai*) and being in touch with (*thigein*) that is given by *nous* and to *nous* in the selfsame showing of the being that is uncovered. Heidegger says in his 1925 *Logik* course that Aristotle here posits the identity of thinking and being in a way that has yet to be understood, but which Aristotle insists cannot be understood as in any way parallel to the uncovering of being in the synthesis of assertion (GA21, 190). In synthesis, the uncovering and discovering that take place are also a covering over. Being false as well as being true belong to this way of disclosing.

Whereas, in the truth of *noein* and *thigein*, in the disclosing that takes place in the nonmediated thinking of being in itself, no being led astray (no *tauschen*) is possible. One either sees it or one does not. Here the alternative is not between a knowing that discloses truly and a knowing that fails to disclose what is intended, but between knowledge and ignorance. For Aristotle, the possibility of revealing something falsely lies in the *synthesis* character of assertion, which does not belong to the seeing of the being as what it is in itself.

We see, then, that Heidegger also discovers in Aristotle a twofold *logos*. If this is the case, then would not the movement between the two *logoi* after all have to be a *dia-logos* or dialectic—a certain reinscription of Plato that would go beyond Aristotle and discover the philosopher as the one who dwells in the between. It seems to me that Heidegger's reading of the *Sophist* dialogue is guided by his attempt to think through philosophically the limits of dialectical thinking. He sees in Aristotle, who achieves his insight only by going through Plato, a philosopher who more radically addresses the question of beings as a whole. We are left with the need, however, to once again readdress, after Heidegger's analysis, the notion of singularity and particularity that is central to Platonic philosophy. Perhaps Heidegger's treatise has opened up a way of returning to this singularity in a manner that goes beyond the Aristotelian framework that contrasted it with beings as a whole. Perhaps yet another reading of Plato, one that reads Plato against Aristotle, would permit a discussion of the singularity of the whole, a singularity that, in Platonic terms, would necessarily be doubled and disseminated (*dia*).

The 1925–1926 Logik *Course: Aristotle's Twofold Sense of Truth*

Heidegger's most sustained and direct treatment of the question of truth in Aristotle is found in sections 11–14 of *Logik: Die Frage nach der Wahrheit* (GA 21). Prior to these sections, Heidegger shows the contribution that Husserl made to a genuine, philosophical understanding of truth through his critique of psychologism. However, in section 10, Heidegger discusses what he takes to be the inadequacy of Husserl's own approach to the question of truth. As Husserl has shown in his critique of Brentano, the question of truth is not a question that belongs to psychology. Rather, truth must be understood by returning to the matter itself (*aus den Sachen selbst*) that is to be uncovered. In other words, *Die Sache selbst* is not given by representation (*Vorstellung*), that is, truth is not determined primarily in propositions or in relation to assertion, but in respect to the kind of knowing Husserl called intuition (*Anschauung*). But Husserl did not adequately or appropriately address the question of the connection between the truth of assertion and the truth of intuition and to do this requires a return to Aristotle (GA21, 109).

According to Heidegger, Husserl establishes that the proposition, as the structure of relation, is founded on the truth of the intuition of identity. Heidegger says of Husserl's sense of the truth of identity uncovered in intuition:

> With Husserl's typically encompassing and fundamental formulation of intuition, namely the giving and having of a being in the fullness of its bodily presence (*Leibhaftigkeit*), a formulation that is not restricted to any particular field or possibility but instead defines the intentional meaning of the concept of intuition, Husserl has thought through to its end the great tradition of Western philosophy. (GA21, 113–114)

But the critical point that Heidegger raises is the question of why intuition is held to rank prior to the logic of assertion in the matter of truth and what the nature of this *Vorrang* is. In other words, what is the relation between the truth of intuition, the immediate givenness of the being fully in itself, and the truth of assertion, the givenness of the being in this or that way, as this or that? Despite Husserl's claim of priority for intuition, the character of the relationship between intuition and assertion is determined out of the model of propositional relationships. Thus, the kind of truth that is held to be a founded mode comes to dominate the way of thinking about truth in general. Husserl has uncritically taken over the structures of assertion, such as synthesis and correspondence, into his way of thinking about what is uncovered in all modes of truth, even those he ranks higher than assertion.

Before turning to Aristotle in an effort to untangle this confusion, Heidegger goes through a destruction of the history of philosophy to show that philosophy has, throughout its history, stood in one way or another under the dominance of two fundamental starting points of ancient thought: *logos* and *nous*. Yet, Heidegger calls the equation of the truth of *nous* with the truth of intuition and that of *logos* with *Satz* (logical proposition) "a somewhat comical linkage of Greek and German" (GA21, 110).

Heidegger's project in investigating Aristotle, particularly his interpretation of truth in *Metaphysics* Θ10, is an attempt to win back in an originary way an access to the phenomenon that lies before the truth of *logos* and the truth of *nous* and constitutes the sphere in which both are brought into relation and, in fact, the horizon out of which both emerge. This turns out to be time. Thus, in the second division of this text, Heidegger exposes how time governs the meaning of *nous* and *logos*, of the truth of being and the being-true or being-false of beings in relation to their being (GA21, 207). This recognition, developed out of a rethinking of Aristotelian notions, provides the basis for Heidegger's treatment of time as the central focus of *Sein und Zeit*. His investigation of truth in Aristotle leads him to raise the question of time as the central issue of phenomenology.

Aristotle begins the discussion of truth in *Metaphysics* Θ10 with another reminder about the many senses of being. But the formulation here is different than it is elsewhere in two important respects: Aristotle says not just being but both being (*to on*) and nonbeing (*to mē on*) are said in many ways. And then he also says that of the many senses of being and nonbeing, the most authoritative sense is that of truth and falsity. So, with regard to the question of the interrelationship of the many senses of being, Aristotle indicates that the meaning of being as truth has a certain precedence (*Met.* 1051 b2). Werner Jaeger and others have insisted that Chapter 10 is misplaced because it is about truth and not about potentiality and actuality. Heidegger in contrast says this chapter, far from being spurious, is the pinnacle of Aristotle's thought and the appropriate culmination of what is at issue in *Metaphysics* Θ. Clearly Heidegger's argument hinges on the central importance of nonbeing that is at the heart of the discussion of potentiality. The question of truth emerged already in Book VI of the *Metaphysics*. The context in which the discussion of truth emerged was an analysis of *sumbebēkos,* the accidental. That there can be accidental cause, Aristotle says, is implicit in the fact that not everything comes to be by necessity and things can be otherwise than they are (*Met.* 1026 b30). So the notion of the accidental is connected to chance and especially to the fact that not-being belongs to the possibility of being; things can be other than and apart from what they are. Aristotle often equates the relation of substance to the other categories with the notion of substance and accident. But categorial relations have primarily to do with synthesis, what belongs together; *sumbebēkos* has to do with falling apart, not belonging, privation. The connection between the discussion of accident and of truth occurs because truth and falsity are said to be concerned with the question of what is together and what is apart, synthesis and division. In *Metaphysics* E, Aristotle mentions yet another sense of truth, the truth that addresses what is simple and the *ti esti,* the being in its whatness. Of this sense of truth, Aristotle says, there is no truth and falsity (*Met.* 1027 b29). But he then says the discussion of this sense of truth must be postponed until later. Aristotle's promise to discuss this sense of truth that excludes falsity is fulfilled in *Metaphysics* Θ10.

There are two different ways in which beings can be approached: in terms of their empirical movements and in terms of their ontological disclosure. Correspondingly, there are two sense of truth, noetic truth and the truth of predication (*kataphasis*). In order to retrace Heidegger's path in analyzing these two senses of truth and their interconnection, I will first consider his treatment of Aristotle's sense of the *logos* of assertion, which is the kind of saying (*kataphasis*) that is related to beings and a thinking (*dianoia*) about beings (GA21, 138). Then I will turn to Heidegger's reading of Aristotle's sense of the saying that is always presupposed and that has already occurred in the disclosure of assertion, namely, the simple saying (*phasis*) and thinking (*nous, noein*) that reveals the being as such, as it is in itself, that is, the being of what is. Finally, I will try to pose the question of the relation of these two ways of thinking and saying, a question that provides the impetus for Aristotle's, and, I believe, Heidegger's thought.

Both Aristotle and Heidegger attempt to situate their thinking about truth in confrontation with Parmenides who forbade those who would truly think from bringing together the two paths of speaking in regard to being. This is why Heidegger says that it is only through Aristotle that Parmenides' fundamental thinking can be understood.[38] For Aristotle, it is precisely this contra-diction, this prohibition, that is the matter for thinking for the philosopher. He calls it "the *archē*, the source of all understanding that everyone must have before he can relate knowingly to beings" (*Met.* 1005 b15). He calls this *archē*, this principle, "the most certain of all" in the sense that it allows beings to be seen in their being. Aristotle has several formulations of this law of non-contradiction, all of which are important, but I will call attention to that at *Metaphysics* 1005 b29: "It is impossible for the one who understands to tolerate or permit it to be said together in relation to one and the same being, and at the same time (*hama*), that it be and not be." Heidegger's discussion of this *aporia*, this impasse, at the heart of thinking hinges on the question of the relationship of *nous* to the *logos* of assertion. He shows that the issue at stake in Aristotle's discussion of *nous* and *logos* is truth, the disclosure of the being of beings. In turn, falsity, nonbeing and nondisclosure, is central to Aristotle's concern about truth. What Heidegger finds in Aristotle is, first of all, a radical separation of the saying of *nous* and the way of addressing beings involved in assertion. He then traces in Aristotle the decision to rank *nous* higher and prior to the other kind of discourse. Finally, he identifies the source of the untraversable difference between these two, a source that Aristotle himself failed to articulate but which he nevertheless stood near to, and which can be deciphered in the formulation of the law of non-contradiction. The source is there named *hama,* a word for time and togetherness in time. In other words, with the importation of time into the Parmenidian radical separation of these two discourses, Aristotle uncovers the horizon of the twofoldness of Parmenides' thought, a horizon that, in turn, went unnoticed and unthought in the metaphysical tradition that followed Parmenides.[39]

The *hama* opens up the relationship of being and nonbeing. Nonbeing can be disclosed precisely because being, the *eidos,* is always already uncovered before we come to the disclosure or nondisclosure of beings in time. The not being said together and the not being at the same time indicate the derivative character of the *logos* of assertion, which always follows after an original disclosing and is true to the extent that it brings together what can and does belong together in this disclosure and keeps apart what is not together (GA21, 146). But, although derivative, this kind of *logos* does uncover beings, those whose way of being is such that they can be with other beings in the way of being-together or synthesis. Aristotle differentiates beings on the basis of their way of being revealed. Thus, there are beings that can be only in that they are together with another, namely, those whose way of being is *sumbebēkos,* accidental. Black can only be, for example, in that it belongs to another being. Other beings such as natural beings do have their being in themselves and are therefore always already what they are, before they are together with others. These beings are *aei on,* enduring being in itself, one and unchanging (GA21, 180). They do not have their being as a coming and going with another. Nevertheless, natural beings, while dwelling simply in their being, do have their being in a way that can be shaped and determined in different ways. But it is only by being directed out from their *eidos* that they become determined in this or that way. It is in the *logos* of assertion that the disclosure of a natural being as having this or that characteristic takes place. This disclosure first of all takes the form of addressing the being as something, a making specific and thematic what the being is and keeping it in this disclosure. Such a disclosure takes the being as already disclosed in its present-at-handness and identifies it as something.

Naming can be an example of this kind of uncovering—a horse, a dog, a deer, and so on. What is presupposed and taken for granted in naming is the prior disclosing that makes it possible for me to recognize this particular being as having such and such a being. This requires that I already know and be in touch with (*noein* and *thigein*) the being of beings (GA21,

182). The being-true of my identification depends on the being's truly having the kind of being I have ascribed to it. For, I could be mistaken. Heidegger uses the example of a man walking in the woods who sees something approaching. It is a deer, he says. But he is mistaken. Upon getting closer and focusing his attention toward the object, he discovers that it is after all only a bush (GA21, 187). Thus, according to Heidegger's analysis, both the naming that identifies what the being is and the activity of ascribing properties to the being are part of apophantic discourse or assertion. Neither are the kind of noetic revealing of being that it always presupposed in this other way of revealing. Husserl's treatment of truth remained, therefore, confined to a mistaken assumption that all truth is found within the framework of assertion.

It may not be immediately clear how it is that naming involves *sunthesis* and *diairesis,* the primary characteristics of the *logos* of assertion. But, for example, in exhibiting the being as a deer, there is a denying to it all those ways of being that are not what a deer is. Likewise, letting the being be seen in this way ascribes to the deer those characteristics that it can have and that are appropriate to its way of being. Such affirmation and denial belong to naming precisely because synthesis and division are the ways in which beings such as natural beings give themselves to us to be disclosed. Assertion involves first of all the making present of a being. Only on the basis of such a way of disclosing a being can it further delineate the being in terms of categorial properties. The statement, "the board is black," says that being-black is something that belongs to the board. Something, namely a board, is seen as something else, as black. In being seen as black, the board is seen as not gray or yellow.

But the structure of this kind of revealing is even more complex in that two beings—board and black—must be already disclosed before putting them present at hand together. Why must this be so? For one thing, being black does not belong necessarily to the being of the board. It could still be what it is if it were a green board (GA21, 137). The board must already be seen as separate and other than in its blackness before it can be put together with it. Also, the mode of being of these two kinds of beings is different. Black never is except as together with a being that has its being in itself, whereas the board has its being in itself, albeit not in the same way that natural beings do.

The upshot of Heidegger's analysis of the *Metaphysics* up to this point is that both the revealing of substantial being and of accidental being belongs to the *logos* of assertion. Naming, as well as ascribing properties to what is named, belong to apophantic discourse. But both presuppose another disclosure, one that is prior to the representation of something as something. The simple saying of *nous* is not what occurs in the disclosure of substances in relationship to accidental properties. The revealing of beings as present at hand, substantial beings, is a derivative meaning of truth.

The possibility for the being true and false of beings arises with the *logos* that is operative here, as well as with the way of being that is uncovered in this way of revealing beings. In Heidegger's rendition, Aristotle says:

> For it is not for the reason that we in our uncovering take you in your being present at hand as white that you are white, but it is on the basis of your being at hand as white, that is, because we let this being at hand as white be seen in our speaking, that our comportment uncovers. (*Met.* 1051 b6–9/ GA21, 175)

What makes our comportment toward a being such that it is false is that our discourse does not reveal the being as it truly is in its togetherness with others. It covers over the being. It lets the being be shown as other than it is. But, even in being led astray in this manner, there is only a partial closing off of the being. All being false is always also a letting the being be seen in a privative way. The not being seen is due both to the *logos* and to the being that is disclosed. It can be true when I say it that the board is black and yet false tomorrow after the painters come.

On the other hand, it can never be true, as Aristotle points out, that a triangle has two right angles. The way of being of a triangle resists such determinations (GA21, 177). The being in itself, the *eidos,* directs what can and cannot and what does or does not belong together with it. But for this to be so, nonbeing must, in fact, belong to the very character of the *eidos* that is disclosed in advance. The privative character of being cannot be only a factor of apophantic discourse or synthetic judgment. A more deep-rooted, prior falsity belongs to the very heart of being. This nonbeing is the source of the failure to disclose that lies at the heart of the kind of uncovering that Aristotle describes in his treatment of *apophansis,* the propositional statements of assertion.

Aristotle differentiates between two different ways of being and thus two different ways of revealing beings. Beings that can be other than they are have their being as a being together with. Synthesis is the way these beings are revealed in their togetherness. However, beings that have their being in themselves cannot have their being as such revealed in this way. Their being is *aei on,* an always being, always (as long as they are) not being other than they are. Such beings are made manifest in their being, not through *kataphasis,* not by a saying something in respect to something else (*kata*), not in a bringing together of something in terms of something else, but in a simple saying (*phanai*) and being in touch with (*thigein*) that is given by *nous* and to *nous* in the selfsame showing of the being that is uncovered. Heidegger says that Aristotle here posits the identity of thinking and being in a way that is yet to be understood but which Aristotle insists cannot be understood as in any way parallel to the uncovering of being in the synthesis of assertion (GA21, 190). In synthesis, the uncovering and discovering that take place are also a covering over. Being false as well as being true belong to this way of disclosing. Whereas, in the truth of *noein,* in the disclosing that takes place in the thinking and seeing of being in itself, no being led astray (no *tauschen*) is possible. One either sees it or one does not. Here the alternative is not between a knowing that discloses truly and a knowing that fails to disclose what is intended, but between knowledge and ignorance. For Aristotle, the possibility of revealing something falsely lies in the synthesis character of assertion, which does not belong to the seeing of the being as what it is in itself. One must always already have the being as a whole in a predeterminate way and retain the being as it is in itself in advance of any determination of the being as having this or that specific character. The calling attention to the being as manifest in a determinate way presupposes the prior disclosing of the *eidos,* the aspect in which it shows itself as such. The being together of something as something requires a turning back to the being as it is in itself, which must always already be disclosed in order for the truth of synthesis to occur. But what is turned back to cannot itself be disclosed in a synthesis, for it is because of this prior disclosure that synthesis is even possible at all.

For Heidegger, it is here that the essential question lies. Dasein's *Besorgen,* its concern for beings, involves this coming back to that with which Dasein is always already dwelling, that which governs and first of all makes possible the unity of thinking and being, the *logos* of synthesis, and the relationship of the two. Aristotle did not make this thematic, although it is the horizon on which his philosophy is based. In Aristotle's presentation, the relationship between *nous* and *logos* and between being and beings is one of priority. The presentation of being is prior to and governs the manifestation of beings. Aristotle's question and problem—really the entire question under which Greek philosophy emerges—involve the question: how can beings be? This question attempts to expose the being's way of being. The Greeks, Heidegger says, already dwelled in an understanding of being itself, and therefore left unspoken the meaning of being.

From the point of view of any knowledge of beings, the prior disclosure—the prior presence—of being is necessary. Thus, for Aristotle, the truth or disclosure of *eidos* must always come before and be independent of the truth of beings. Yet as the *archē* and *aitia*—that out of which beings emerge and that which is responsible for their being what they are—it lets beings be. It gathers beings into the oneness of being. This oneness with being is what Aristotle calls truth. How then are we to understand this *thigein* that is in touch with being and this *nous* that occurs as always the same as being, in a togetherness that is not a synthesis? Aristotle says that no falsity or deception is possible in this way of seeing (*nous*). Only ignorance, *agnoia*, is possible (GA21, 185). He points out that ignorance is not the same as not being able to see at all, that is, being incapable of knowing. It is only the one who can see—whose way of being is to see—who can fail to see. But this indicates an incompleteness in the identity of *noein* and *eidos*, thinking and being. It is a sameness that does not have to occur, but without which no truth, no disclosure, is possible.

The possibility of not seeing has two sides. That which is to be seen can be there and I can fail to see it as it truly is. Likewise, I can be looking for it and it can turn out not to be there at all. In the latter case, we need to ask: what is the character of this complete not-being and not-having that Aristotle says is not the same as the partial being true and being false we have already discussed as the combining and dividing that occurs in assertion and the *logos* of propositions? This possibility of a complete not-seeing, as in the example of something that is simply not there to be discovered, must be prior to the other kind of truth and falsity, which sees something but sees it wrongly, or as coming to be in this way or that. This example of an absence of truth is not the same as falsity. This prior concealment and not-being (*ouk on* rather than *mē on*) must be a simple not-being-there that is different from the coming together and departing of a being that is already there. This primary sense of truth and untruth is the ground of the possibility of truth and falsity.

The always being there as it is in itself of the being in its *eidos* is what makes possible the movement and passage of beings. But even though the being can be disclosed in its constancy as the being it is (in its *eidos*), and this prior disclosure precludes but also makes possible motion and coming to be, this does not imply that there is no possibility of its not being or no longer being what it is. The movement from not being to being that characterizes the being itself in its original upsurge into being is not of the same order as that kind of motion that comes and goes within the oneness and sameness of a being. Aristotle names this other kind of movement that is prior to motion in the more narrow sense "*genesis.*" The difference between these two kinds of movement is not of the same order as the difference between the movement of alteration and locomotion. It is the difference between the *kinēsis* of beings and the being of *kinēsis,* the difference between being and beings. In chapter three, we discussed the following quote from Aristotle's *Physics,* but it bears repeating here in relation to this discussion of truth:

> Therefore it is impossible for that which *is not* to move. This being the case, *genesis* cannot be *kinēsis,* for it is that which is not which comes to be. It is a sudden change (*metabolē*) which implies a relation of contradiction (*antiphasin*), not motion. . . change from not being there to being there, the relation being that of contradiction, is *genesis.* (225 a25ff)

Aristotle has said that the *eidos* is what being is. The *eidos* cannot be lacking in the fullness of being. But he also says in *Physics* B1, as we pointed out earlier, that *sterēsis,* privation and not being, is a kind of *eidos.* In the *Metaphysics,* at 1004 b27, he says:

> Thus the other of opposition corresponds to *sterēsis;* that is to say, everything leads back to being and not being, and oneness and manyness. And nearly all thinkers agree that beings that are present are and endure out of opposition. At any rate, all address the *archē* as this kind of opposing.[40]

In *genesis*—the movement of *eidos* from not being to being—a being comes forth into presence and sustains itself in its being as long as it is. Thus, Aristotle says of natural beings that "they endure inasmuch as their *genesis* is also an absence of change with regard to not-being" (*Physics* 230 a10, b11). The twofoldness of *genesis* and *sterēsis* is the enduring presencing of beings. The being of beings is the sudden emerging forth out of untruth or hiddenness into the truth. The being that is is as long as it sustains itself in this emerging. But unconcealment, the emergence and being of a being, always remains in relation to and in opposition to concealment. These opposites do not exclude each other, but grant the disclosure of beings. *Alētheia,* truth, belongs to being and is a way of being because the human being stands essentially in relation to the twofold character of being. This prior disclosure, this oneness of "seeing" and being, is the basis for the *logos* of assertion and propositional logic. In *Sein und Zeit,* Heidegger analyzes in detail the derivative character of the truth of assertion and the primordial meaning of truth as unconcealment. The indebtedness of his analysis to his reading of Aristotle is only alluded to in that text. His earlier courses make this debt manifest.

CONCLUSION

There is much that remains unsaid in this book. It is by no means comprehensive, and the ongoing project of publishing Heidegger's *Collected Works* means that there will be still other texts than those considered here that will add new material, as well as amplications of some of the more innovative aspects of Heidgger's interpretation that are sometimes only cryptically presented in the currently available literature. Especially important is a text that I have only considered in passing here, since it was only recently published, his 1924 course, *Basic Concepts of Aristotelian Philosophy*. This course offers an extensive treatment of Aristotle's *Rhetoric*, which Heidegger reads in conjunction with a treatment of *hexis* and moral virtue in the *Nichomachean Ethics*. The analysis of *pathos* there is important for an understanding of the decisive sections on mood in *Being and Time*, and gives further evidence to my claim that Heidegger sees Aristotle's practical philosophy as an ontology of human Dasein.

In the end, perhaps there is need for critical assessment, for another book that would offer more evaluation of Heidegger's interpretation than I have provided. It is after all important for a philosopher to attain some distance from the author he or she is studying. In retrospect I appreciate this point, but I also believe that a genuine encounter with the thought of Heidegger can only be based on a careful presentation and understanding, and this attempt has proved formidable in its own right. While the voice of the author is always present in the text, I have tried not to infuse the reading of Heidegger that I have presented with an agenda of my own that would interfere with the analysis rather than support it. At the same time, I have tried to avoid proselytizing, preferring instead to expose the work of Heidegger and let it speak for itself. There is an interpretative strategy that I did bring to this work, however. I tried to set up an encounter between Heidegger's reading and the text of Aristotle, to situate Heidegger's claims in a broader context of passages from Aristotle, so that the legitimacy of

Heidegger's interpretation could be judged on the basis of a return to the texts of Aristotle. I believe this was the motivating principle and goal of many of Heidegger's readings, and it provides the appropriate basis for a critical discussion of his interpretation.

Although I consistently return to the thematic focus of the book, the twofoldness of being, I think this theme in the end remains underdeveloped, and it is my hope that it provides a starting point for further study. It is especially important to return to this topic on the basis of what has been presented here, and to take up the question of the implications of this theme as a question for philosophy. Granted the claim that for Aristotle being is twofold, how is this twofoldness to be understood and what might one learn from it about the meaning of being? There is no doubt that this task for thinking was the gift that Heidegger received from Aristotle, and that spurred Heidegger onto his own philosophical path. Heidegger takes up in particular the issue of time and the finitude of being, and the issue of *sterēsis,* nonbeing, in addressing these questions as projects.

The central topic that pervades Heidegger's interpretation of Aristotle, and the one above all others that demonstrates his knowledge and insight, is the topic of *kinēsis.* For Heidegger the problem of movement and the question of the ontological character of moving beings was the fundamental question of Aristotle's philosophy. Aristotle's metaphysics entered into this basic *aporia* that governed the experience of being in ancient Greece, the difficulty of thinking of the being of motion, the denial of ontological *kinēsis.* He was able to grasp, on the basis of this question, the meaning of being and thereby to bring to its end the philosophical struggle of his times. The ensuing history of philosophy is the witness to his accomplishment. In our time, called by some the time of the end of metaphysics, we are once again required to return to the beginning, not out of what some consider to be a Heideggerian nostalgia for the Greeks, but to stand once again prepared for a new beginning.

NOTES

Chapter One: Martin Heidegger's Relationship to Aristotle

1. Martin Heidegger, "Mein Weg in die Phänomenologie, in *Zur Sache des Denkens* (Tübingen: Max Niemeyer Verlag, 1976), 86.
2. Helène Weiss, *Kausalität und Zufall in der Philosophie des Aristoteles* (Basel: Haus zum Falken, 1942), 1.
3. Walter Bröcker, *Aristoteles* (Frankfurt: V. Klostermann, 1964); Ernst Tugendhat, *Ti Kata Tinos* (Freiburg: Alber, 1971); Karl Ulmer, *Wahrheit, Kunst und Natur bei Aristoteles* (Tübingen: Max Niemeyer Verlag, 1953).
4. Most notably, Theodore Kisiel and John Van Buren.
5. See especially Theodore Kisiel, *The Genesis of Heidegger's* Being and Time (Berkeley: University of California Press, 1993); William J. Richardson S.J., *Heidegger: Through Phenomenology to Thought* (The Hague: Nijhoff, 1963); Thomas Sheehan, "Heidegger's Early Years: Fragments for a Philosophical Biography," in *Heidegger: The Man and the Thinker,* ed. Thomas Sheehan, pp. 3–19 (Chicago: Precedent, 1981); John Van Buren, *The Young Heidegger: Rumor of the Hidden King* (Bloomington and Indianapolis: Indiana University Press, 1994).
6. Martin Heidegger, "Mein Weg in die Phänomenologie," 86.
7. See especially chapter five, "Heidegger and Aristotle: An Ontology of Human Dasein."
8. This course has appeared in Heidegger's *Gesamtausgabe* [hereafter GA] as Volume 61. *Phänomenologische Interpretationen zu Aristoteles: Einführung in die phänomenologischen Forschung* (Frankfurt: V. Klostermann, 1985).
9. Martin Heidegger, GA18, *Grundbegriffe der aristotelischen Philosophie,* ed. M. Michalski (Frankfurt: V. Klostermann, 2002).
10. For an important discussion and chronological account of the Aristotle courses leading up to *Being and Time,* see Theodore Kisiel, *The Genesis of Heidegger's Being and Time,* Part II.
11. Martin Heidegger, *Sein und Zeit* (Tübingen: Max Niemeyer Verlag, 1972). *Being and Time,* trans. Joan Stambaugh (Albany: State University of New York Press, 1996). A much more detailed and nuanced reading of Aristotle's treatment of time in the *Physics* was given by Heidegger in a 1927 course, just prior to the appearance of *Being and Time.* The course has appeared in Martin Heidegger, GA24, *Die Grundprobleme der Phänomenologie* (Frankfurt: V. Klostermann, 1975). *The Basic Problems of Phenomenology,* trans. A. Hofstadter (Bloomington: Indiana University Press, 1982).

12. See, for example, Werner Marx, *Heidegger and the Tradition,* trans. Theodore Kisiel and Murray Greene (Evanston: Northwestern University Press, 1971).

13. See Kisiel, *The Genesis of Heidegger's Being and Time.*

14. Kisiel, *The Genesis of Heidegger's Being and Time,* 248–271; Sheehan, "Heidegger's Early Years: Fragments for a Philosophical Biography."

15. Martin Heidegger, *Sein und Zeit,* 2.

16. Franco Volpi, "Being and Time: A Translation of the *Nicomachean Ethics?,*" translated by John Protevi, in *Reading Heidegger from the Start,* ed. T. Kisiel and J. Van Buren (Albany: State University of New York Press), 1994, 195–213.

17. Martin Heidegger, "Platons Lehre von der Wahrheit," in *Wegmarken* (Frankfurt: V. Klostermann, 1967). "Plato's Doctrine of Truth," in *Pathmarks,* ed. William McNeill (Cambridge: Cambridge University Press, 1998).

18. Martin Heidegger, GA33, *Aristoteles, Metaphysik Θ, 1–3: Von Wesen und Wirklichkeit der Kraft* (Frankfurt: V. Klostermann, 1981), 4. *Aristotle's, Metaphysics Θ1–3: On the Essence and Actuality of Force,* trans. Walter Brogan and Peter Warnek (Bloomington: Indiana University Press, 1995), 1.

19. Martin Heidegger, GA 20, *Prolegomena zur Geschichte des Zeitbegriffs* (Frankfurt : V. Klostermann, 1979), 184. *History of the Concept of Time,* trans. T. Kisiel (Bloomington: Indiana University Press, 1985), 136.

20. GA33, *Aristoteles, Metaphysik Θ, 1–3,* 82.

21. Though copies of this essay circulated among his students, the manuscript was eventually lost. It was rediscovered and finally published in 1989 as "Phänomenologische Interpretationen zu Aristoteles (Anzeige der hermeneutishchen Situation)" in *Dilthey Jahrbuch für Philosophie und Geschichte der Geistwissenschaften,* 6: 235–274. An English translation by Michael Baur, "Phenomenological Interpretations with Respect to Aristotle: Indication of the Hermeneutical Situation," appeared in 1992 in *Man and World* 25, 355–393.

22. Martin Heidegger, "Hegel und die Griechen," in *Wegmarken,* 266. "Hegel and the Greeks," in *Pathmarks,* 331.

23. Martin Heidegger, "Phänomenologische Interpretationen zu Aristoteles," 244.

24. Martin Heidegger, GA20, *Prolegomena zur Geschichte des Zeitbegriffs,* 9.

25. Martin Heidegger, "Recollection in Metaphysics," in *The End of Philosophy,* trans. J. Stambaugh (New York: Harper and Row, 1973), 79.

26. Martin Heidegger, *Nietzsche Volume I: The Will to Power as Art,* trans. D. Krell (New York: Harper and Row, 1979), 203.

27. Martin Heidegger, *Einführung in die Metaphysik* (Tübingen: Max Niemeyer Verlag, 1953), 30.

28. Martin Heidegger, *Was ist das—Die Philosophie?* (Pfullingen: Neske Verlag, 1976), 22.

29. Martin Heidegger, "Recollection in Metaphysics," 75.

30. Martin Heidegger, *Einführung in die Metaphysik*, 12.
31. Martin Heidegger, *Einführung in die Metaphysik*, 137. For a full treatment of the notion of originary thinking in the context of what Heidegger calls the first beginning and the other beginning, see Martin Heidegger, GA65, *Beiträge zur Philosophie (Vom Ereignis)* (Frankfurt: V. Klostermann, 1989).
32. Werner Marx, *Heidegger and the Tradition*, 11. In this work, Marx consistently presents the basic words and thoughts of Aristotle from the point of view of later Latinized interpretations. Heidegger himself has said that this Roman interpretation of the primordial Greek experience is a pile of distortions, no longer recognizing itself. See Martin Heidegger, *The End of Philosophy*, 14.
33. Martin Heidegger, "Phänomenologische Interpretationen zu Aristoteles," 235–237.
34. Martin Heidegger, "Phänomenologische Interpretationen zu Aristoteles," 249.
35. Martin Heidegger, "Phänomenologische Interpretationen zu Aristoteles," 250.
36. Martin Heidegger, "Phänomenologische Interpretationen zu Aristoteles," 246.
37. Martin Heidegger, "Phänomenologische Interpretationen zu Aristoteles," 246.
38. Martin Heidegger, "Phänomenologische Interpretationen zu Aristoteles," 246.
39. Martin Heidegger, "Phänomenologische Interpretationen zu Aristoteles," 251.
40. Martin Heidegger, "Phänomenologische Interpretationen zu Aristoteles," 238.
41. Martin Heidegger, "Phänomenologische Interpretationen zu Aristoteles," 242.
42. Martin Heidegger, "Phänomenologische Interpretationen zu Aristoteles," 25.
43. Martin Heidegger, "Phänomenologische Interpretationen zu Aristoteles," 374; also see GA18, *Grundbegriffe der aristotelischen Philosophie* (Frankfurt: V. Klostermann, 2002), 24–36.
44. Martin Heidegger, GA18, *Grundbegriffe der aristotelischen Philosophie*, 24.
45. See the next two chapters for a discussion of Heidegger's reading of Aristotle's *Physics* B1, which deals with *phusis* and its relationship to *technē*.
46. Martin Heidegger, GA21. *Logik: Die Frage nach der Wahrheit* (Frankfurt: V. Klostermann, 1976).
47. For a discussion of this controversy and its historical context, see Robert Bernasconi, "Heidegger's Destruction of *phronēsis*," in *The Southern Journal of Philosophy* 28, Supplement (1989): 127–147.
48. Martin Heidegger, "Phänomenologische Interpretationen zu Aristoteles," 258.
49. Martin Heidegger, "Phänomenologische Interpretationen zu Aristoteles," 259.
50. Martin Heidegger, "Phänomenologische Interpretationen zu Aristoteles," 259.
51. Martin Heidegger, "Phänomenologische Interpretationen zu Aristoteles," 260.
52. Martin Heidegger, "Phänomenologische Interpretationen zu Aristoteles," 246.
53. Martin Heidegger, "Phänomenologische Interpretationen zu Aristoteles," 243, note.
54. Martin Heidegger, "Phänomenologische Interpretationen zu Aristoteles," 243.
55. Martin Heidegger, "Vom Wesen und Begriff der φύσις : Aristoteles' *Physik* B,1. *Wegmarken* (Frankfurt: V. Klostermann, 1967), 367. [hereafter

WBP]. There is a more detailed discussion of this point at the end of chapter three.
56. "Phänomenologische Interpretationen zu Aristoteles," 266.

Chapter Two: The Doubling of Phusis: Aristotle's View of Nature

1. Martin Heidegger, GA45, *Grundfragen der Philosophie: Ausgewählte Probleme der Logik* (Frankfurt: V. Klostermann, 1984). English translation by R. Rojcewicz and A. Schuwer, *Basic Questions of Philosophy: Selected Problems of Logic* (Bloomington: Indiana University Press, 1994).
2. Martin Heidegger, "Vom Wesen und Begriff der *Phusis:* Aristoteles' *Physik* B1," in *Wegmarken* (Frankfurt: V. Klostermann, 1967). Hereafter, references to this essay will be cited as WBP and placed in parentheses directly after the quote. The page numbers refer to the original edition of *Wegmarken.* The *Gesamtausgabe* edition of this text contains no changes from the original edition. An English translation of this essay by Thomas Sheehan is available in *Man and World* (1976) and reprinted with changes in *Pathmarks.* I have benefited from this translation, though often I have offered my own English rendition. Though written in 1939, this essay first appeared in 1958 in *Il Pensiero,* vol. 3, #2–3 (Milan-Varese), and it was first published separately in 1960 in *Testi Filosofici (Biblioteca "Il Pensiero").*
3. Werner Marx, *The Meaning of Aristotle's Ontology* (The Hague: Nijhoff, 1954).
4. The implication that there is an etymological connection between the Latin *natura* and the Greek root from which *genesis* and *gignomai* are formed is borne out by Cornford: "So, too, in Latin *na-tura* is derived from *na* of *na-scor* and *na-tivitas.* In fact, *(g)natura* is derived from the same root as *gi-gno, gi-gnomai.* Cf. *Met.,* 1014 b17." See footnote C, 114 of Aristotle, *Physics I,* trans. by F. Cornford and P. H. Wicksteed (Cambridge: The Loeb Classical Library, 1970).
5. For an amplication of this point, see Martin Heidegger, "Die Frage nach der Technik," in *Vorträge und Aufsätze* (Pfullingen: Neske Verlag, 1978), 9–40. "The Question Concerning Technology," trans. W. Lovitt, in *Basic Writings,* ed. D. F. Krell (New York: Harper & Row, 1993), 307–343.
6. Aristotle, *Metaphysics* 985b19.
7. Aristotle, *Physics* 191 b30–35.
8. Martin Heidegger, *Sein und Zeit* , 34.
9. Martin Heidegger *Sein und Zeit,* 29.
10. See chapter five.
11. Martin Heidegger, *Sein und Zeit,* 31.
12. Martin Heidegger, *Sein und Zeit,* 34.
13. Aristotle, *Posterior Analytics,* 99 b20–21.
14. Aristotle, *Posterior Analytics,* 100 b12.
15. Joseph Owens, *The Doctrine of Being in the Aristotelian Metaphysics* (Toronto: Pontifical Institute of Medieval Studies, 1951), 382.

16. Martin Heidegger, "Mein Weg in die Phänomenologie," 87.
17. Anaximander, DK12, in *The Presocratic Philosophers,* ed. G. S. Kirk, J. E. Raven, M. Schofield (Cambridge: Cambridge University Press, 1983), 106–107.
18. Martin Heidegger, *What Is a Thing,* trans. Eugene Gendlin (Chicago: Henry Regnery Co., 1967), 236.
19. Martin Heidegger, "Bauen Wohnen Denken," in *Vorträge und Aufsätze,"* 149.
20. Martin Heidegger, *Sein und Zeit,* 243.
21. Martin Heidegger, "Bauen Wohnen Denken," 154.
22. Cf. *What Is a Thing,* 26–38 and 62–64; see also *Wegmarken,* 273–309.
23. Friedrich Nietzsche, *The Will to Power,* trans. Walter Kaufmann and R. J. Hollingdale (New York: Vintage Books, 1968), 12 (B), 13.
24. I am introducing Aristotle's word *ousia* without comment at this time since we will be considering its meaning shortly. It is on the basis of the difference between the relation to natural beings in *technē* and the way *phusis* governs beings that Aristotle first introduces this term. What gives priority to *ousia* in the discussion of the categories is not its negation of movement as eternal and permanent being, but rather its radicalizing the entire meaning of *kinēsis* and placing the question on an ontological level.
25. Aristotle, *Categories,* 3a-6b.
26. Aristotle, *Categories.* 3 a7.
27. Aristotle, *Categories* 5 b1–6 a25.
28. Martin Heidegger, *Nietzsche II* (Pfullingen: Neske Verlag, 1961), 72.
29. Martin Heidegger, *Was heißt Denken* (Tübingen: Max Niemeyer Verlag, 1971), 51. "What Calls for Thinking," trans. F. Wieck and J. Glenn Gray, in *Basic Writings,* 381.
30. Martin Heidegger, *Nietzsche II,* 76.
31. Cf. Aristotle, *Nichomachean. Ethics,* 1103 a30 ff.
32. See Aristotle, *Nichomachean Ethics* E, 4.
33. See also Aristotle, *Physics* 184 a16 ff and Heidegger's commentary on this in *Der Satz vom Grund* (Pfullingen: Neske Verlag, 1978), 112 ff.
34. In the context of a discussion of the relationship between etymological transformation of language and the history of being, Heidegger discusses the interrelation between the different names for being in various languages. There he points out that the Indo-European radical "*bhû*" and "*bheu*" are related to the Greek *phuo* (to emerge, to rule, to come to a stand and endure) and thus to *phusis* and *phuein.* In turn, these are related to the Greek root "*pha*" as in *phainesthai* (from these stems come the Latin "*fui,*" the German "*bin*" and the English "been"). Heidegger concludes: "*Phusis* would therefore be emerging into the light; *phuein* would be to radiate, to shine (*scheinen*) and thus to appear (*erscheinen*)." Martin Heidegger, *Einführung in die Metaphysik,* 54–55. When Heidegger suggests *Aufgang* here as a possible translation of *phusis,* he means to convey these interrelations that are lost in the word for growing (*wachsen*). Aristotle also mentions the relation between *phusis* and *phuo* and its meaning as *genesis* at *Metaphysics* V, 1014 b16.

35. The various meaning of *aufgehen* and the etymology of this word can be found in Hermann Paul, *Deutsches Wörterbuch* (Tübingen: Max Niemeyer Verlag, 1968), 47.
36. Cf. Martin Heidegger, *Einführung in die Metaphysik*, 46–47.
37. Liddell and Scott, *A Greek-English Lexicon* (Oxford: Clarendon Press, 1968), 1274
38. Plato, *The Republic*, 329e.
39. Martin Heidegger, GA 26, *Metaphysische Anfangsgründe der Logik* (Frankfurt: V. Klostermann, 1978), 183.
40. Cf. Hermann Paul, *Deutsches Wörterbuch*, 38.
41. Martin Heidegger, *Einführung in die Metaphysik*, 46–47.
42. Martin Heidegger, "Was heißt Denken," 144–145.
43. Martin Heidegger, *Sein und Zeit*, 94.
44. Cf. Martin Heidegger, *Einführung in die Metaphysik*, Chapter III.
45. Martin Heidegger, *Einführung in die Metaphysik*, 47.
46. Aristotle, *Nichomachean Ethics* 1141 b4 ff.
47. Martin Heidegger, *What Is a Thing*, 10.
48. Cf. above, Chapter I, section 3.
49. Cf. Aristotle, *Metaphysics* IV, 4–8.
50. Martin Heidegger, "Brief über den Humanismus," in *Wegmarkens*, 150. "Letter on Humanism," trans. F. Capuzzi and J. Glenn Gray, in *Basic Writings*, 223.
51. Aristotle, *Nichomachean Ethics* 1139 a1–3.
52. Aristotle *Nichomachean Ethics* 1139 a6–9.
53. Martin Heidegger, GA24, *Grundproblem der Phänomenologie*, 466.
54. Cf. Liddell and Scott, *A Greek-English Lexicon*, 521.
55. Cf. Aristotle, *Categories* 10 a1, *Posterior Analytics* 1455 a33 and *Rhetoric* 1390 b29.
56. Martin Heidegger, *Einführung in die Metaphysik*, 125.

Chapter Three: The Destructuring of the Tradition

1. On Parmenides' denial of the being of motion, see Parmenides, Fragments B1 and B15, in H. Diels and W. Kranz, *Die Fragmente der Vorsokratiker I* (Berlin: Wiedmannsche Verlag, 1956); cf. also Wolfgang Schadewaldt's discussion of Parmenides in *Die Anfänge der Philosophie bei den Griechen* (Frankfurt: Suhrkamp Verlag, 1979), 311–351.
2. The search of modern Physics for the ultimate nuclear particle continues this understanding of being as permanence, although it has been distracted in contemporary science by the discovery of the energy that is released in the process of reducing matter to the primary elements.
3. Cf. Martin Heidegger, *The End of Philosophy*, 4.

4. Liddell and Scott, *A Greek-English Lexicon*, 1647.
5. Martin Heidegger, "Die Zeit des Weltbildes," in *Holzwege* (Frankfurt: V. Klostermann, 1972), 71.
6. Diels-Kranz, *Die Fragmente der Vorsokratiker I*, Parmenides Fragment B8, 237-238. Also cf. Heidegger's essay on Parmenides in *Vorträge und Aufsätze*.
7. Aristotle, *Metaphysics* 987 a2-10.
8. Cf. Aristotle, *Metaphysics*, Book A, 6.
9. Martin Heidegger, *The End of Philosophy*, 8.
10. H. Paul's *Deutsches Wörterbuch*, 330.
11. Martin Heidegger, *The End of Philosophy*, 7-8.
12. Cf. Martin Heidegger, "Vom Wesen und Begriff der *Physis,*" 313 and 343 ff.
13. See Liddell and Scott, 434, for confirmation.
14. Cf. *Physics* 203 b1 ff for Aristotle's rejection of the notion that the being of beings is infinite.
15. Martin Heidegger, *Einführung in die Metaphysik*, 46.
16. Aristotle, *On the Soul* 413 b24-27.
17. Cf. Heidegger's interpretation of this saying from Fragment B5 of Parmenides in *Einführung in die Metaphysik*, 104ff.
18. Cf. also *Metaphysics* Book E, 4 and Heidegger's discussion of this in GA21, *Logik* (Frankfurt: V. Klostermann, 1976), 163 ff.
19. See Martin Heidegger, GA 19 *Platon:* Sophistes (Frankfurt: V. Klostermann, 1992), sections 27- 28 and sections 50-55. See also GA 18 *Grundbegriffe der aristotelischen Philosophie*, 6-7.
20. Martin Heidegger, *Der Satz vom Grund* (Pfullingen: Neske, 1986), 141.
21. Martin Heidegger, "The Origin of the Work of Art," trans. A. Hofstadter, in *Basic Writings*, 195.
22. Martin Heidegger, *Der Satz vom Grund*, 113.
23. Parmenides, Fragment B4; cf. Heidegger's remarks in *Einführung in die Metaphysik*, 89 ff.
24. We have already seen that this is the meaning of *epagōgē* through which Aristotle first establishes the meaning of *phusis*.
25. This translation is based on Heidegger's, which can be found in *Die Frage Nach dem Ding* (Tübingen: Max Niemeyer Verlag, 1975), 139.
26. "*alētheia* (Heraklit, Fragment 16)," in *Vorträge und Aufasätze*, 261.
27. Jacques Derrida, "*Ousia* and *Grammē,*" trans. Edward Casey, in *Phenomenology and Perspective,* ed. Joseph Smith (The Hague: Martinus Nijhof, 1966), 80.
28. Martin Heidegger, GA 24, *Grundprobleme der Phänomenologie*, 335, 357ff.
29. Martin Heidegger, *The End of Philosophy*, 87.
30. Martin Heidegger, *Identity and Difference*, trans. J. Stambaugh (New York: Harper & Row, 1969), 41.
31. Martin Heidegger, *Sein und Zeit*, 2.

32. Martin Heidegger, *Der Satz vom Grund,* 111.
33. Martin Heidegger, "What Is Metaphysics," in *Basic Writings,* 112.
34. On the relationship between *paschein* and *poiein,* cf. Martin Heidegger, GA33, *Aristotle,* Metaphysik Θ, 1–3 section 10. This work is the subject of the next chapter.
35. On the way in which this understanding of *hupokeimenon* came to the fore in the history of metaphysics, cf. Martin Heidegger, *Nietzsche* II, 429–436.
36. Cf. Aristotle, *On Generation and Corruption* 321 a 3Off: "The *ousia* of the one (of the body) remains unchanged, but that of the other (of the food) does not."
37. Cf. Liddell and Scott, 1847.
38. Plato, *Phaedrus* 249 e₂
39. "The boundary is that from which something *begins its essential unfolding.* That is why the concept is that of *horismos,* that is the horizon, the boundary." Martin Heidegger, "Bauen Wohnen Denken," 149.
40. Heidegger's translation of this fragment is found in his essay "*Logos* (Heraklit, Fragment 50)" in *Vorträge und Aufsätze,* 217–218. It is a transliteration of the meaning of the fragment and requires a consideration of the interpretation of the fragment found there on pp. 199–221.
41. Martin Heidegger, "*Logos* (Heraclitus Fragment B 50)," in *Early Greek Thinking,* trans. D. Krell (New York: Harper & Row, 1975), 75.
42. See the next chapter for an extended commentary on this question in relation to Heidegger's reading of *Metaphysics* Θ1–3.
43. Martin Heidegger, "*Logos* (Heraclitus Fragment B 50)," 63.
44. Martin Heidegger, "*Logos* (Heraclitus Fragment B 50)," 64.
45. Martin Heidegger, "*Logos* (Heraclitus Fragment B 50)," 70.
46. Martin Heidegger, "*Logos* (Heraclitus Fragment B 50)," 70–71.
47. Cf. Martin Heidegger, *Einführung in die Metaphysik,* 127.
48. Martin Heidegger, *Einführung in die Metaphysik,* 100–101.
49. Martin Heidegger, *Sein und Zeit,* 25.
50. Aristotle, *Nichomachean Ethics* E, 6.
51. Aristotle, *On the Soul* 429 a23. For Heidegger's extended consideration of Aristotle's *On the Soul,* and especially his analysis of the soul in relationship to perception, see GA18, *Grundfragen der aristotelischen Philosophie.*
52. Aristotle, *On the Soul* 414 a18.
53. Aristotle, *On the Soul* 417 b6–7.
54. Aristotle, *On the Soul* 417 b23.
55. Aristotle, *On the Soul* 430 a4.
56. Aristotle, *On the Soul* 429 a24.
57. Aristotle, *On the Soul* 433 a18–20.
58. Aristotle, *On the Soul* 417 b22–23.
59. See WBP 347.
60. Aristotle, *Nichomachean Ethics* 1102 b30.
61. Aristotle, *Nichomachean Ethics* 1178 a6–7.
62. Martin Heidegger, "The Anaximander Fragment," in *Early Greek Thinking,* 31.

Chapter Four: The Force of Being

1. Martin Heidegger, GA33, *Aristoteles, Metaphysik* Θ, 1–3: *Von Wesen und Wirklichkeit der Kraft* [hereafter in this chapter cited as GA33]. Page references are given first in the German edition and then in the English edition.
2. Martin Heidegger, GA45, *Grundfragen der Philosophie. Ausgewählte "Probleme" der "Logik"* (Frankfurt: V. Klostermann, 1984).
3. Martin Heidegger, *Nietzsche* I: *The Will to Power as Art,* trans. D. Krell (New York: Harper & Row, 1979), 64.
4. Martin Heidegger, *Nietzsche* I: *The Will to Power as Art,* 65.
5. Martin Heidegger, GA 33, 4; 1.
6. Martin Heidegger, GA 33, 10; 7.
7. Martin Heidegger, GA 33, 13; 10
8. Martin Heidegger, GA 33, 7; 4.
9. Martin Heidegger, "*Vom Wesen und Begriff der Physis,*" 348–352.
10. Martin Heidegger, GA 33, 27; 22
11. Martin Heidegger, GA 33, 31; 25.
12. Martin Heidegger, GA 33, 78; 65.
13. Martin Heidegger, GA 33, 80; 67.
14. Martin Heidegger, GA 33, 142; 121.
15. Martin Heidegger, GA 33, 65; 54.
16. Martin Heidegger, GA 33, 104 ; 88.
17. Martin Heidegger, GA 33, 105; 89.
18. Martin Heidegger, GA 33, 114; 96.
19. Martin Heidegger, GA 33, 126; 107
20. Martin Heidegger, GA 33, 14; 11.
21. Martin Heidegger, GA 33, 131; 112.
22. As with most translations, capability is not an adequate translation for *Vermögen* . We should know that the word, as was true of *ousia,* has a commonly used meaning of procurements or property. In a sense, what we mean by capabilities are those forces that most truly belong to us. *Vermögen* is also used technically to mean faculty—the faculty of perception, for example.
23. Martin Heidegger, *Sein und Zeit,* 129.
24. Martin Heidegger, GA 33, 158; 135.
25. Martin Heidegger, GA 33, 161; 138.
26. Martin Heidegger, GA33, 163; 139.
27. Martin Heidegger, GA 33, 171; 146.
28. Martin Heidegger, GA 33, 183; 157.
29. Martin Heidegger, GA 185; 158–159.
30. Martin Heidegger, GA 33, 191; 164.
31. Martin Heidegger, GA 33, 192; 165.
32. Martin Heidegger, GA 33, 191; 164.
33. Martin Heidegger, GA 33, 187; 160.
34. Martin Heidegger, GA 33, 187; 161.

35. Martin Heidegger, GA 33, 195; 167.
36. Martin Heidegger, GA 33, 206 ; 177.
37. Martin Heidegger, GA 33, 197; 169.
38. Martin Heidegger, GA 33, 202; 173.

Chapter Five: Heidegger and Aristotle: An Ontology of Human Dasein

1. Martin Heidegger, GA33, *Aristoteles, Metaphysik* Θ1–3, 137.
2. Martin Heidegger, GA24, *Grundprobleme der Phänomenologie,* 466.
3. In the *Nichomachean Ethics,* at 1170 a2 and after, Aristotle says that the supremely happy person will need friends since such a person chooses a *theōrein* of actions that are good and that are one's own, and such are the actions of a good person who is a friend.
4. Martin Heidegger, *Sein und Zeit,* 300.
5. Martin Heidegger, GA33, *Aristoteles, Metaphysik* Θ1–3, 126.
6. Martin Heidegger, *Sein und Zeit,* 298.
7. Jacques Taminiaux, *Heidegger and the Project of Fundamental Ontology* (Albany: State University of New York Press, 1991), 131.
8. Hubert Dreyfus, *Being-in-the-World: A Commentary on Heidegger's "Being and Time," Division I* (Cambridge: MIT Press, 1991).
9. Hubert Dreyfus, *Being-in-the-World,* 301.
10. Hubert Dreyfus, *Being-in-the-World,* 305.
11. Martin Heidegger, *Sein und Zeit,* 369
12. Martin Heidegger, "Phänomenologische Interpretationen zu Aristoteles," 245.
13. Martin Heidegger, "Phänomenologische Interpretationen zu Aristoteles," 245.
14. Martin Heidegger, "Phänomenologische Interpretationen zu Aristoteles," 246.
15. Martin Heidegger, "Phänomenologische Interpretationen zu Aristoteles," 247–250.
16. Martin Heidegger, *Sein und Zeit,* 240.
17. Martin Heidegger, *Sein und Zeit,* 240.
18. Martin Heidegger, *Sein und Zeit,* 192.
19. Martin Heidegger, *Sein und Zeit,* 193.
20. Martin Heidegger, *Sein und Zeit,* 221.
21. "To care belongs not only being-in-the-world, but being together with innerworldly beings. The being of Da-sein and its disclosedness belong equiprimordially to the discoveredness of innerworldly beings," Martin Heidegger, *Sein und Zeit,* 221.
22. Martin Heidegger, *Sein und Zeit,* 243.
23. Martin Heidegger, *Sein und Zeit,* 262.
24. Martin Heidegger, *Sein und Zeit,* 264.
25. Martin Heidegger, *Sein und Zeit,* 264.
26. Heidegger's readings of Plato's *Theaetetus* in *Gesamtausgabe* 22 and 34 also explore this theme. Likewise, this is the central theme in Heidegger's reading of Plato's Allegory of the Cave in "Platons Lehre von der Wahrheit," in *Wegmarken.*

27. Martin Heidegger, GA19, *Platon: Sophistes* (Frankfurt: V. Klostermann, 1924), 303. Hereafter I will insert the page references to GA19 in brackets in the text. *Plato's Sophist,* trans. Richard Rojcewicz and Andre Schuwer (Bloomington: Indiana University Press, 1997).

28. Plato's negative view of rhetoric is especially exemplified in the *Gorgias,* as Heidegger points out in section 50 of his *Sophist* course.

29. Ironically, Heidegger's *Beiträge* also uses the word "attempt" to describe his own efforts at thinking *Ereignis* and the truth of being. GA65, *Beiträge zur Philosophie (Vom Ereignis)* (Frankfurt, V. Klostermann, 1989), 8.

30. Plato, *Theaetetus,* 149b ff.

31. Heidegger points out that Aristotle says in the *Topics* at 176 b6 that "the dialectician speaks *kata to pragma,* with regard to the matters themselves" (GA19, 216).

32. For Heidegger's more detailed analysis of Aristotle's *Rhetoric* and its connection to his *Nichomachean Ethics,* see GA 18 *Grundbegriffe der aristotelischen Philosophie.*

33. The most poignant passages condemning sophistry come in the middle of this dialogue beginning at 172c. These passages mark a transition in the dialogue. The whole dialogue appears to be organized out of these passages that include the famous story of Thales falling into the well.

34. Plato, *Theaetetus,* 173a.

35. Plato, *Phaedrus* 229e5ff.

36. For a more extended reading of this ontological understanding of *agathon* in Greek philosophy, and its connection to *hexis* and *aretē* in Aristotle's *Nichomachean Ethics,* see GA18, *Grundbegriffe der aristotelischen Philosophie,* section 10 and 17.

37. See chapter one for an earlier discussion of this connection between *sophia* and *technē* in the context of Heidegger's 1922 essay "Phänomenologische Interpretationen zu Aristoteles."

38. Martin Heidegger, Phänomenologische Interpretationen zu Aristoteles, 252.

39. In his essay "*Ousia et Grammē,*" in *Marges* (Paris: Les Éditions de Minuit, 1972), 64ff., Jacques Derrida suggests that the entire force of Aristotle's thinking hinges on the tiny word *hama.*

40. See the more extended treatment of this topic at the end of chapter three.

BIBLIOGRAPHY

Works by Heidegger

GA 9 *Wegmarken*. Frankfurt: V. Klostermann, 1967. Gesamtausgabe edition, vol. 9. Frankfurt:V. Klostermann, 1976. Trans. *Pathmarks*. Cambridge: Cambridge University Press, 1998.

GA 18 *Grundbegriffe der aristotelischen Philosophie*. Frankfurt: V. Klostermann, 2002.

GA 19 *Platon: Sophistes*. Gesamtausgabe vol. 19. Frankfurt: V. Klostermann, 1992. Trans. Richard Rojcewicz and André Schuwer. Bloomington: Indiana University Press, 1997.

GA 20 *Prologomena zur Geschichte des Zeitbegriffes*. Gesamtausgabe vol. 20. Frankfurt: V. Klostermann, 1979. Trans. Theodore Kisiel, *History of the Concept of Time*. Bloomington: Indiana University Press, 1985.

GA 21 *Logik: Die Frage nach der Wahrheit*. Gesamtausgabe vol. 21. Frankfurt: V. Klostermann, 1976.

GA 22 *Die Grundbegriffe der antiken Philosophie*. Gesamtausgabe vol. 22. Frankfurt: V. Klostermann, 1993.

GA 24 *Die Grundprobleme der Phänomenologie*. Gesamtausgabe vol. 24. Frankfurt: V. Klostermann, 1976. Trans. Albert Hofstadter, *The Basic Problems of Phenomenology*. Bloomington: Indiana University Press, 1982.

GA 26 *Metaphysische Anfangsgründe der Logik im Ausgang von Leibniz*. Gesamtausgabe vol. 26. Frankfurt: V. Klostermann, 1978. Trans. Michael Heim, *The Metaphysical Foundations of Logic*. Bloomington: Indiana University Press, 1984.

GA 33 *Aristoteles, Metaphysik Θ 1-3: Von Wesen und Wirklichkeit der Kraft*. Gesamtausgabe vol. 33. Frankfurt: V. Klostermann, 1980. Trans. W. Brogan and P. Warnek, *Aristotle's* Metaphysics *1-3: On the Essence and Actuality of Force*. Bloomington: Indiana University Press, 1995.

GA 34 *Vom Wesen der Wahrheit: Zu Platons Höhlengleichnis und Theätet*. Gesamtausgabe vol. 34. Frankfurt: V. Klostermann, 1988.

GA 61 *Phänomenologische Interpretationen zu Aristotleles. Einführung in die phänomenologische Forschung*. Gesamtausgabe vol. 61. Frankfurt: V. Klostermann, 1985.

GA 65 *Beiträge zur Philosophie (Vom Ereignis)*. Gesamtausgabe vol. 65. Frankfurt: V. Klostermann, 1989.

Basic Writings. Edited by David Farrell Krell. New York: HarperCollins, 1993.

Die Frage nach dem Ding. Tübingen: Max Niemeyer, 1975. Trans. W. B. Barton and Vera Deutsch, *What Is a Thing*. Chicago: Henry Regnery, 1967.

Early Greek Thinking. Trans. David Farrell Krell and Frank A. Capuzzi. New York: Harper & Row, 1975.

Erläuterungen zu Hölderlins Dichtung. Frankfurt: V. Klostermann, 1971.

Einführung in die Metaphysik. Tübingen: Max Niemeyer, 1953. Trans. Ralph Mannheim, *An Introduction to Metaphysics.* New Haven: Yale University Press, 1959.

Holzwege. Frankfurt: V. Klostermann, 1950.

Identity and Difference. Trans. Joan Stambaugh. New York: Harper & Row, 1969.

Nietzsche I-II. Pfullingen: Günter Neske, 1961. Trans. *Nietzsche I-IV.* New York: Harper & Row.

"Phänomenologische Interpretationen zu Aristoteles, Anzeige der hermeneutischen Situation," *Dilthey-Jahrbuch* 6, 1987.

Sein und Zeit. Tübingen: Max Niemeyer, 1972. Trans. Joan Stambaugh, *Being and Time.* Albany: State University of New York Press, 1996.

The End of Philosophy. Trans. Joan Stambaugh. New York: Harper & Row, 1973.

Vorträge und Aufsätze. Pfullingen: Günter Neske, 1954.

Was Heisst Denken? Tübingen: Max Niemeyer, 1971. Trans. J. Glenn Gray, *What Is Called Thinking.* New York: Harper & Row, 1968.

Zur Sache des Denkens. Tübingen: Max Niemeyer, 1976.

Works by Aristotle

Aristotle. *The 'Art' of Rhetoric.* With trans. by J. H. Freese. The Loeb Classical Library. Cambridge: Harvard University Press, 1926.

———. *The Categories.* With trans. by H. P. Cooke. The Loeb Classical Library. Cambridge: Harvard University Press, 1938.

———. *The Physics.* 2 vols. With trans. by P. H. Wicksteed and F. M. Cornford. The Loeb Classical Library. Cambridge: Harvard University Press, 1957.

———. *The Metaphysics I–IX.* With trans. by H. Trendennick. The Loeb Classical Library. Cambridge: Harvard University Press, 1925.

———. *The Metaphysics X–XIV.* With trans. by G. Cyril Armstrong. The Loeb Classical Library. Cambridge: Harvard University Press, 1935.

———. *The Nicomachean Ethics.* With trans. by H. Rackham. The Loeb Classical Library. Cambridge: Harvard University Press, 1990.

———. *The Nichomachean Ethics.* Trans. by Martin Ostwald. New York: Macmillan, 1987.

———. *On the Soul.* With trans. by W. S. Hett. The Loeb Classical Library. Cambridge: Harvard University Press, 1957.

———. *Posterior Analytics.* With trans. by H. Tredennick and E. S. Forster. The Loeb Classical Library. Cambridge: Harvard University Press, 1930.

———. *The Complete Works of Aristotle.* The Revised Oxford translation. Ed. Jonathan Barnes. Princeton: Princeton University Press, 1984.

Other Works

Aubenque, Pierre. *La Prudence chez Aristote*. Paris: Presses Universitaires de France, 1963.

———. *Le Problème de l'être chez Aristote*. Paris: Presses Universitaires de France, 1972.

Bernasconi, Robert. *Heidegger in Question: The Art of Existing*. Atlantic Highlands: New Jersey: Humanities Press, 1993.

———. "Heidegger's Destruction of *Phronesis*," *The Southern Journal of Philosophy 28* (1989). 127–147.

Brague, Remi. *Aristote et la Question du Monde*. Paris: Presses Universitaires de France, 1988.

Brentano, F. *Von den mannigfachen Bedeutung des Seienden nach Aristoteles*. Hildesheim: G. Olms, 1960.

Bröcker, Walter. *Aristoteles*. Frankfurt: Klostermann, 1835.

Chanter, Tina. "Heidegger's Understanding of the Aristotelian Concept of Time," in *Interrogating the Tradition: Hermeneutics and the History of Philosophy*, ed. John Sallis and Charles Scott (Albany: State University of New York Press, 2000).

Derrida, Jacques. "*Ousia and Grammē*," trans. Edward Casey, in *Phenomenology and Perspective*, ed. J. Smith. The Hague: Nijhoff, 1966.

Diels, H., and Kranz, W. *Die Fragmente der Vorsokratiker*. Berlin: Weidermannsche, 1956.

Dreyfus, Hubert. *Being-in-the-World: A Commentary on Heidegger's Being and Time, Division I*. Cambridge: MIT Press, 1991.

Ellis, John. "Heidegger, Aristotle, and Time in *Basic Problems* #19," in *Interrogating the Tradition: Hermeneutics and the History of Philosophy*, ed. John Sallis and Charles Scott (Albany: State University of New York Press, 2000).

Figal, Günter. *Martin Heidegger zur Einführung*. Hamburg: Junius Verlag, 1992.

Gadamer, H-G. *Wahrheit und Methode: Grundzüge einer philosophischen Hermeneutik. Gesammelte Werke I*. Tübingen: Mohr Siebeck, 1990.

———. "Heidegger's 'theologische Jugendschrift,'" *Dilthey-Jahrbuch* 6, 1989. 228–234.

Hanley, C. *Being and God in Aristotle and Heidegger: The Role of Method in Thinking the Infinite*. Lanham: Rowman and Littlefield, 2000.

Jaeger, Werner. *Aristoteles: Grundlegung einer Geschichte seiner Entwicklung*. Berlin: Weidermannsche, 1923.

Kisiel, Theodore. *The Genesis of Heidegger's Being and Time*. Berkeley:University of California Press, 1993.

———, and van Buren, John, eds. *Reading Heidegger from the Start: Essays in His Earliest Thought*. Albany: State University of NewYork Press, 1994.

———. "Diagrammatic Approach to Heidegger's Schematism of Existence." *Philosophy Today 28* (Fall 1984), 229–241.

———. "The Missing Link in the Early Heidegger." In *Hermeneutic Phenomenology: Lectures and Essays*, ed. J. Kockelmans. Washington, D.C.: University Press of America, 1988, 1–40.

Klein, Jacob. *Greek Mathematical Thought and the Origin of Algebra.* Trans. Eva Brann. New York: Dover, 1992.

Krell, David. *Intimations of Mortality: Time Truth, and Finitude in Heidegger's Thinking of Being.* University Park: The Pennsylvania State University Press, 1986.

Liddell, H. G., and Scott, R. *A Greek-English Lexicon.* Oxford: Clarendon Press, 1968.

Long, Christopher. *The Ethics of Ontology: Rethinking an Aristotelian Legacy.* Albany: State University of NewYork Press, 2004.

MacIntyre, Alasdair. *After Virtue: A Study in Moral Theory.* South Bend: University of Notre Dame Press, 1984.

Makkreel, Rudolf. "The Genesis of Heidegger's Phenomenological Hermeneutics and the Rediscovered 'Aristotle Introduction' of 1922," *Man and World* 23 (1990), 305–320.

Marx, Werner. *Heidegger and the Tradition.* Trans. T. Kisiel and M. Greene. Evanston: Northwestern University Press, 1971.

———. *The Meaning of Aristotle's 'Ontology.'* The Hague: Nijhoff, 1954.

McNeill, William. *The Glance of the Eye: Heidegger, Aristotle, and the Ends of Theory.* Albany: State University of NewYork Press, 1999.

Owens, Joseph. *The Doctrine of Being in the Aristotelian Metaphysics.* Toronto: University of Toronto Press, 1951.

Paul, Hermann. *Deutsches Wörterbuch.* Tübingen: Max Niemeyer, 1968.

Plato. *The Republic,* vols. 1–2. With trans. by Paul Shorey. The Loeb Classical Library. Cambridge: Harvard University Press, 1982.

———. *The Republic of Plato.* Trans. Allan Bloom. New York: Basic Books, 1968.

———. *The Sophist.* Trans. Eva Brann, Peter Kalkavege, and Erik Salem. Newburyport: Pullins, 1996.

———. *The Theaetetus and Sophist.* With trans. by H. Fowler. The Loeb Classical Library. Cambridge: Harvard University Press, 1996.

Raffoul, F., and D. Pettigrew, eds. *Heidegger and Practical Philosophy.* Albany: State University of New York Press, 2002.

Reinhardt, Karl. *Parmenides.* Frankfurt: V. Klostermann, 1977.

Rese, Friederike. *Praxis und Logos bei Aristoteles.* Tübingen: Mohr Siebeck, 2003.

Richardson, William. *Through Phenomenology to Thought.* The Hague: Nijhoff, 1963.

Sadler, Thomas. *Heidegger and Aristotle: The Question of Being.* London: Athlone, 1996.

Sallis, John. *Echoes: After Heidegger.* Bloomington: Indiana University Press, 1990.

———. *Being and Logos.* Bloomington: Indiana University Press, 1996.

———. *Delimitations: Phenomenology and the End of Metaphysics.* Bloomington: Indiana University Press, 1995.

Schadewaldt, Wolfgang. *Die Anfänge der Philosophie bei den Griechen.* Tübingen: Suhrkamp, 1979.

Schmidt, Dennis. *On Germans and Other Greeks: Tragedy and Ethical Life.* Bloomington: Indiana University Press, 2001.

Schürmann, Reiner. *Heidegger on Being and Acting: From Principles to Anarchy.* Bloomington: Indiana University Press, 1987.

Sheehan, Thomas. "Heidegger, Aristotle and Phenomenology," *Philosophy Today* 19 (1975), 87–94.

———. "Heidegger's Interpretation of Aristotle: *Dynamis* and *Energeia*," *Philosophy Research Archives* 4 (1978), 278–314.

———. "*Hermeneia* and *Apophansis:* The Early Heidegger on Aristotle," in *Heidegger et l'idée de la phénomenologie,* ed. F. Volpi. Dordrecht: Kluwer, 1988, 67–80.

———. "On the Way to *Ereignis:* Heidegger's Interpretation of *Physis.*" In *Continental Philosophy in America,* eds. H. Silverman, J. Sallis, and T. Seebohm. Pittsburgh: Duquesne University Press, 1983, 131–164.

Scott, Charles. *Live Things.* Bloomington: Indiana University Press, 2002.

Taminiaux, Jacques. *Heidegger and the Project of Fundamental Ontology.* Albany: State University of New York Press, 1991.

———. *The Thracian Maid and the Professional Thinker: Arendt and Heidegger.* Albany: State University of New York Press, 1997.

Tugendhat, Ernst. *Ti Kata Tinos: Eine Untersuchung zu Structur und Ursprung aristotelischer Grundbegriffe.* Freiburg: Alber, 1958.

Ulmer, Karl. *Wahrheit, Kunst, und Natur bei Aristoteles.* Tübingen: Max Niemeyer, 1953.

Vallega, Alejandro. *Heidegger and the Issue of Space: Thinking on Exilic Grounds.* University Park: The Pennsylvania State University Press, 2003.

Van Buren, John. *The Young Heidegger: Rumor of the Hidden King.* Bloomington: Indiana University Press, 1994.

Volpi, Franco. *Heidegger e Aristotele.* Padova: Daphne Editrice, 1984.

Weigelt, Charlotta. *The Logic of Life: Heidegger's Retrieval of Aristotle's Concept of* Logos. Stockholm: Almquist & Wiksell, 2002.

Weiss, Helene. *Kausalität und Zufall in der Philosophie des Aristoteles.* Basel: Haus zum Falken, 1942.

Wiplinger, Fridolin. *Physis und Logos.* Freiburg: Alber, 1971.

INDEX

ousia 42

ont diff 51, 72

epogase 54

poetic logos (your reply) 56

x ownership 154

running 141

To ask the question of the meaning of being
is to ask what persists in being

|| to Collingwood?

|||